1981

W9-AFG-358

WRITTEN LANGUAGE INSTRUCTION

Theory and Remediation

Trisha Phelps-Gunn
Diana Phelps-Terasaki

With a contribution by Barbara Foorman

AN ASPEN PUBLICATION ®
Aspen Systems Corporation
Rockville, Maryland
London
1982

Library of Congress Cataloging in Publication Data

Phelps-Gunn, Tricia.
Written language instruction.

Includes bibliographies and index.
1. English language—Composition and exercises.
2. English language—Remedial teaching. 3. Learning disabilities.
I. Phelps-Terasaki, Diana. II. Title.
LB1576.P565   808'.042'07   81-10824
ISBN: 0-89443-360-1   AACR2

Library of Congress Catalog Card Number: 81-10824
ISBN: 0-89443-360-1

Printed in the United States of America

1 2 3 4 5

The authors wish to thank *Curtis Whitesel* for his continued support, inspiration, and camaraderie; *Carolyn Phelps* for her devotion; and *Dr. Barbara Foorman* for her contributions to Chapter 6.

Table of Contents

Introduction to the Total Writing Process Model

ISSUES IN INSTRUCTION AND REMEDIATION

Writing is a useful, effective, enjoyable, and above all necessary component of the modern world. It provides the pleasure of sending a personal message to a friend. It assumes career and financial importance in the composition of a resumé or a business letter.

In recent years, great concern has been directed toward the inability of many students, from elementary to college level, to express themselves adequately in writing. This concern has reached national proportions and has been the subject of a number of media reports. For several reasons, the answer to this problem is not simple.

First is the issue of which remedial program to use. A number of approaches exist but they are very diverse. Individuals need to survey the wide range of literature and judiciously select the approach most appropriate for their professional needs.

A second issue revolves around the lack of sufficient research in written expression. Both the oral language system and the written receptive (reading) mode have been studied in detail by a wide array of professionals. The written expressive mode, however, has been virtually neglected. According to Myklebust (1973), "Evaluation of the visual language system has not been approached in terms of receptive and expressive functions. Study of reading has gone forth essentially without concern for the relevance of output" (p. 161). But research into writing remediation has increased significantly in recent years. This already has yielded important data, and should continue to do so as the work proceeds. However, it has not yielded a systemized schemata that relates writing and all its components to student production with all its demands and requirements.

Not until comparatively recently have professionals who work with language and learning disabled children realized their needs in this area and

1

how little diagnostic and remedial material existed. It also has been only recently that regular education teachers have discerned that something needs to be done for disabled writers in their classrooms. This trend for professionals in education to take an active interest in writing remediation may be a result of several recent events: (1) mainstreaming, (2) widespread media coverage of writing disability, and (3) the inclusion of disorders of written expressive language as a handicapping condition in Public Law 94-142, the Education for All Handicapped Children Act of 1975. However, some professionals always have been concerned with their students' written language needs and simply have developed their own programs or used the few available commercially.

A third issue that makes remediation of written expressive language difficult is the extremely broad array of students' needs, ages, and abilities. A resource teacher's professional needs may focus on children at the elementary school level who have severe writing problems. One high school English teacher may need a program to correct run-on sentences; another may focus on the appropriate organization of thoughts in a paragraph. These two professionals reflect different needs, and not many remedial programs encompass students from second grade to college level. In addition, the problems of the students themselves vary widely, from the child with a hearing impairment, mental retardation, or socioemotional disorder to the high school mathematics whiz who simply doesn't write well. All kinds of categories of students evidence difficulty in written expression.

A steadily growing number of writing remediation programs are now available; however, many of them do not derive from an organized schemata of writing, covering all of its demands. As a result, the overall remediation effort at best is incomplete. The aim of this book is to present a framework within which to view the writing process holistically. This framework is used as a base from which to evaluate current remediation programs, relating them to the framework determining which area of the entire writing process they address. This book applies to the following:

1. regular education students who exhibit difficulty or dysfluency in writing
2. advanced regular education students who show a variety of strengths and weaknesses in writing
3. students who are language disordered
4. students who are learning disabled
5. students who are hearing impaired
6. students who are socially and emotionally disturbed

Perhaps the most critical objective here is to offer a workable holistic frame that accounts for the writing process from inception to end product, and then to critique the completeness and depth of current writing programs in reference to this frame. Many theories and models abound; however, they do not address the entire process nor do they integrate the remediation program into the entire schema and scope of the writing process. Rather than focusing on the gestalt of writing, these approaches look only at narrow aspects of the whole.

Thus, this book provides professionals with enough information on the various writing remediation programs and approaches so they will be able to make educated and judicious decisions as to which techniques or parts of techniques may best fit their instructional philosophy and their professional needs. Professionals then can study the original programs and incorporate any or all of the material into their own instructional systems. The book also presents a series of evaluative instruments that are representative of the types of writing tests now available. Here again professionals can become acquainted with the kinds of test instruments so they can select the type that best suits their teaching needs.

Before surveying methods of evaluation and remediation, the discussion focuses on the nature of written expression and the presentation of the proposed framework or system for approaching the total process.

THE NATURE OF WRITTEN LANGUAGE

In normal developing children, writing is the last language mode to develop and requires a complex series of prerequisites and abilities:

1. Efficiency in the written expressive mode implies development in the underlying language modes. As the highest form of language ability, writing requires prior adequate development in modes that are lower hierarchically.
2. Written expression requires that auditory, visual, motor, and visual-motor integration skills be adequate. The act of writing requires that a variety of visual abilities be smoothly integrated and coordinated with fine motor skills. Both the visual and motor systems must have integrity individually; they also must combine and integrate efficiently.
3. Writing requires a sense of audience and an ability to produce an appropriate amount and degree of information needed by an absent receptor.

In talking, the speaker can monitor the listeners constantly and assess how much they already know and how much will be new. The speaker gauges listeners' understanding of the conversation and can alter the material when necessary. In writing, no audience monitoring is possible. The writer must direct the communication to an absent reader. The writing can be targeted to the intended audience but still must include enough information for all readers to be able to comprehend and derive meaning from the communication. These three factors are essential to writing efficiency. Each factor is discussed separately.

WRITTEN LANGUAGE VARIABLES

Efficiency in written expression is built on a foundation of adequacy in receptive and expressive oral and receptive written language. The following behaviors correspond to the language mode descriptions:

- receptive oral language corresponds to listening comprehension
- expressive oral language corresponds to speaking
- receptive written language corresponds to reading
- expressive written language corresponds to writing

Writing ability is developmentally dependent on proficiency in listening comprehension, speaking, and reading. Exhibit 1 represents a horizontal flow diagram of the three basic components of the language system.

The diagram begins with the experiential base and inner language system, leading in order to receptive and expressive oral language, and then to receptive and expressive written language.

This developmental relationship of the language modes has been organized hierarchically by Myklebust (1960). His diagram has been cited often and has been widely used as the framework for designing language analysis and remedial work. The hierarchy originates with early experiences in infancy and culminates in written expression ability. In this prioritizing network, the

Exhibit 1   The Developmental Progression of Language

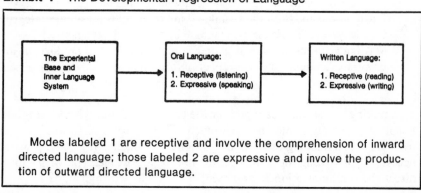

Modes labeled 1 are receptive and involve the comprehension of inward directed language; those labeled 2 are expressive and involve the production of outward directed language.

oral mode precedes the written and receptive proficiency precedes expressive ability. The uniqueness of each of the oral and written modes is stressed, since each actually has significant differences built on the linguistic core.

The base of the language hierarchy is experience—the infants' sensory relations with the world. From earliest infancy onward, children act on their world: touching, holding, dropping, tasting, and other object manipulations and sensory experiences. They learn, for example, about the properties of roundness by watching a ball bounce as they drop it, rolling it, or feeling its smooth roundness. In like manner, they build up information about other features of their world by acting on them.

By assimilating and accommodating information from these experiences, children build up a personalized mental schemata of their world. In time, they develop an inner language system that corresponds to their experiential base. According to Bates (1976), these mental symbols are an internal representation of the actions that originally were linked to the world experience. That is, inner language derives from an "action blueprint" (p. 11). Since children's action blueprints are extremely personal, the total spectrum of meaning associated with a symbol will be individualized as well.

For example, one child's experience with rocks may include a range of typical experiences, plus observing the father laying gravel on the patio. The child may then walk on, sit on, and touch the patio. The inner language experience base and schema of the world will include all these experiences under the "rock" label. Another child, however, may have a range of typical experiences plus being hit on the head by a rock thrown by a brother. This child's inner language will shade the word rock with a slightly different overall meaning. Although both children will own the basic meaning of the word rock, both also will have finer shades corresponding to their personal experiences. Thus, children build an ever-increasing inner language network composed of mental symbols that represent the original world experiences.

However, the symbols also will encompass the basic meaning of the language community, since language ultimately will be used for communicative purposes. Johnson and Myklebust (1967) describe inner language as the language of thought. It is the mental manipulation of the symbols representing experience that constitutes the thinking process. All other language modes are associated intimately with inner language—the internal symbolic system ordering and organizing data in and for the other modes. The ability to so represent things symbolically forms a basis from which listening comprehension can develop.

Listening Comprehension

The receptive oral language system (listening comprehension) derives from the inner language system. It is characterized by children's uniting auditory language with their inner language system. This interface probably occurs very soon after the inner language system is functioning. Inner language focuses on the intent of the language process. As such, it organizes and orders the shape of the language context. Receptive oral language competency requires that the coded information heard auditorily be matched or conformed to the inner language. Listening directs the individual back into inner language, where the external symbol is matched to the internal version. If the two match well, the communication is successful. If not, the mismatch creates a communicative breakdown. The inner language symbol is a personalized and individualized refinement of children's outer language experiences.

Receptive oral language and inner language are mutually beneficial. Listening adds new language data and experience to the inner language base; inner language analyzes, orders, and integrates the new information with the old, building a more in-depth base from which to interpret future experiences. There must be enough shared meaning between what is heard and what is stored in inner language meaning to achieve efficient communication, while accounting for the individual experiences that shade and create a unique dimension to each person's meaning base.

Listening comprehension also builds a base from which speech can develop. Speech, then, derives from listening comprehension and also refines inner language to some degree. Expressive oral language (speaking) emerges from the inner language base outward to potential listeners. Unlike listening, which is inner directed, speaking is outer directed. Whereas listening matches auditory symbols to inner symbols, speech matches auditory symbols to audience response. When the intended audience responds appropriately, the speech act is successful. When the audience expresses confusion, the speaker knows to reform and reshape the speech act.

According to Vygotsky (1962), throughout the preschool years inner language and oral expression seem to be coded very similarly. That is, language for self and language for others are not differentiated. As children develop, however, they begin to discern the difference between the two; this recognition is evidenced in an abbreviation of inner language while complexity increases in oral expression. This means that the children recognize the social need to provide adequate linguistic complexity and content to others and that they have discerned that private speech for self is different in form and purpose from social speech for others.

While inner language becomes abbreviated into a mental shorthand of meaning units, oral expression increases in complexity. Thus, the oral expression process eventually requires an extra step—that of recoding the mental shorthand into complex sentences for an audience. The relationship between inner language and externally directed language, however, remains very close.

The Two Controllers

The success of speaking is under the control of the audience, while listening is under the control of the listeners' decoding and inner language matching. Oral expression encodes inner language intent into the phonological sound system, identifies speaker intent, and derives meaning by interfacing with the inner language system. Thus, both the receptive and the expressive modes contribute to inner language refinement, but the expressive mode—speech— develops from competence in the listening comprehension mode.

Reading and writing follow the same progression as listening and speaking, according to Myklebust (1960). Reading derives from successful oral expression and further refines inner language. It represents a recoding of auditory language symbols into visual language symbols. This is similar to Mattingly's (1972) model of the primary and secondary language loops. He describes the primary loop as composed of the oral language modes of listening comprehension and speaking. Built on and around this primary loop is the secondary language loop, composed of reading and writing. The latter is contingent on adequate development in the primary loop.

Myklebust defines reading and writing competence as deriving from oral competence, both receptively and expressively. Reading and writing skills build the visual component onto the auditory component developed earlier. Reading, then, is three times removed from inner language. This means that reading requires competence in oral receptive language, which is once removed, and oral expressive language, which is twice removed.

Writing is the most complex language mode, being four times removed from inner language, and adds the component of written expression to the earlier abilities. To Myklebust (1960), writing is composed of successful development in three other language modes, deriving its focus from aural, oral, and visual receptive components. For the most part, Myklebust assumes that competency in writing will stem from abilities in the other three modes. He also assumes that in normal developing children, writing will follow naturally from reading competency, which will follow naturally from oral language competency.

Before any language capacities can be developed, children must have certain intellectual and psychological abilities. A person cannot produce the individual sounds of language without the prerequisite perceptual, discriminatory, and categorical abilities to respond to sound stimuli. Students also must be able to formulate and execute the articulatory program that comes from an inner language directive.

Necessary to effective language is the cognitive strategy that allows individuals to code experiences correctly. Language implies linguistic, cognitive, and perceptual components. Because language can be used to code verbal and nonverbal reality, it contains a considerable abstract and symbolic dimension. Oral language acts to code and structure experience into auditory signals; written language codes experience into orthographic signals.

When the individual listens or reads, only one task is required to decode the incoming auditory or written message. However, expressive language (writing or speaking) is more demanding because the symbolic codes must be transformed into their auditory or visual counterparts. Speech involves the production of temporal linear units and writing the production of spatial linear units.

PERCEPTUAL AND MOTOR REQUIREMENTS

Referring back to Exhibit 1, the two forms of expressive language are indicated by the numeral 2 in the oral and written system components. These modes represent outer directed language, both auditory and visual. In oral expression, the speaker must interface intent with the appropriate language structure (recode mental shorthand), then execute a corresponding articulatory program that transforms the message into its auditory form. This articulatory program requires proficiency in auditory perception and fine motor integration. In speech, the key element is the auditory message.

In writing, the expressive message is built on the previously refined auditory expressive base. Written expression visually recodes experience that previously was auditorily coded. The visual symbols used in writing represent the auditory symbols used in speaking. Thus, writing requires a double recoding task: (1) from mental shorthand to auditory language and (2) from auditory language to visual language. Efficient writing requires learning the visual recoding system, which is abstract and arbitrary but in English is anything but consistent and systematic. Auditory perceptual abilities must be integrated with visual ones in order to learn and stabilize the written code. An unsystematic graphic "system" must be mastered by rule learning, memorization, and generalization of learning.

While speaking requires well-executed fine motor movements in the oral cavity, writing requires proficiency in the motor requirements of handwriting. Thus, not only must the auditory and visual systems be integrated, the visual and motor systems also must be coordinated and must work together smoothly. Writing requires a high degree of competency in integrating perceptual and motor processes. It must represent auditory information in visual form and integrate this form with the motor movements required in handwriting.

This level of writing represents the initial learning process. Handwriting, letter formation, and initial spelling competency can be considered prerequisites to true writing. Until this basic prewriting fluency is achieved, the communicative aspect of writing is decreased significantly; however, once children have learned to write letters and spell basic words, they begin to generate written communication in the true sense of the word.

This initial teaching of the writing act is the one aspect of the total process that has been studied extensively and for which numerous programs exist. As such, this aspect of writing is not addressed directly in this text. Of greatest concern to educators today is the limited array of remedial programs designed to instruct students in the other components of writing. An additional problem is the lack of a model or framework for approaching the writing process as an integrated whole. This text addresses the issues of a holistic writing process model and a survey of existing remedial approaches as they correspond to the proposed model.

THE AUDIENCE AND MODE OF DISCOURSE

The ability to attend to audience and mode is critical in writing and is significantly different from the audience attention in speech. The speaker is allowed four distinct advantages in tailoring communications to an audience:

1. The audience is present and known and the form of the communication (particular speech act, degree of politeness, etc.) can be suited to the specific group or individual.
2. The knowledge of audience allows the balance of given-new (known and unknown) (Clark & Clark, 1977) information to be gauged more reliably.
3. The presence of the audience allows the speaker to monitor comprehension constantly, adding information if the individual has assumed erroneously that the audience "knows too much" or deleting material if some of the communicative content is known already.
4. These three factors permit the form of communication to be more time efficient; that is, the structure of speech often is in phrases or fragments, which in the context of an audience is appropriate and effective.

Writing, on the contrary, does not have a present audience; in fact, the specific audience may not even be known. It is difficult to gauge the absent audience's given and new information base and impossible to monitor comprehension and then add or delete material as necessary.

The writer must include the entire scope of information and provide the premises and content clearly so that a broad audience will be able to read and understand the message. Sentence fragments must be avoided because they illustrate incomplete communication. Rather, syntactic complexity is required to elaborate the content completely and cohesively. Thus, writing requires a more abstract decentration. This refers to the individual's ability to not center or direct information to himself but rather to objectify content and adjust it to the needs of a particular audience.

As mentioned, writing requires a double recoding of inner language, as illustrated in Exhibit 2. The form of inner language is said by Vygotsky (1962) to be in compact units, a kind of mental shorthand. When a communicative intent exists, oral expression must recode it into a more complex form. Speech often takes the form of sentence fragments and phrases, a structure not used in writing. On the contrary, writing is more elaborate, formal, and complex than speech and recodes the auditory form of language. The visual language modes are based on the auditory and both stem from inner language. Thus, writing requires a double recoding of intent.

Writing also requires an awareness of the appropriate mode to be used in a given situation and the methods of successfully using that mode. Four modes exist: narration, description, exposition, and argumentation.

Thus, writing is an abstract and difficult language process, requiring a highly developed sense of audience and mode and a double recoding of inner language.

WRITING AS A DYNAMIC, MULTIMODAL PROCESS

Rather than viewing writing as a hierarchical system of development, the authors prefer to view it as encompassing multiskills in a constant but dynamic framework. Writing is not perceived as an outgrowth of developing skill success in various other language modes, but rather as containing all modes in various levels of competency at all times. For example, writing involves attending to the composition as it is being produced in order to detect the success in communicating the intent of the inner language. Although this skill may be successful for oral listening comprehension, it may not be so for written. Essentially, the skill is the same but in a different context. To assume that writing develops from successful listening comprehension is to ignore the interfacing of those two elements. Written expression, then, encompasses its own unique version of receptive auditory language.

In the same way, writing uses its own version of speaking and reading ability. Effective speech and written communication both require attention to an audience. However, success in the former does not assure it in the latter. It is inappropriate to assume that a writer is competent in audience awareness simply because speech production requires that awareness. Again, the skill—attention to audience—is similar but because of the context cannot be assumed to be a given.

Exhibit 2   Flow Chart of Double Recoding in Written Language

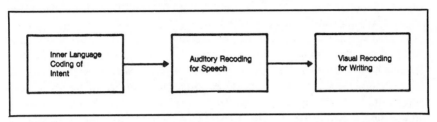

Writing also makes use of a receptive written language (reading) ability. When proofreading and editing a composition, the writer calls upon the aspects of the reading process that guide the use of appropriate structures and eliminate incorrect language forms.

Writing, though deriving from the other language modes, develops differently and depends upon variations of the earlier developed modes.

Unlike the progression in Exhibit 1 and Myklebust's (1960) position that writing represents a prerequisite development in the three other language modes, writing instead is a redefinition of the earlier abilities, requiring their integration into a different communicative task. These earlier language modes need to be developed adequately in their original forms; however, the change in form required for efficient writing demands a relearning and reintegrating of these other modes. Writing thus is a dynamic process that at its optimum derives from competence in all language modes but in reality often occurs in the face of a specific language modal incompetence. Revision in writing requires receptive auditory skills; however, children may be fluent auditorily in those skills but deficient in writing.

THE TOTAL WRITING PROCESS MODEL

Component 1

Exhibit 3 illustrates the reshaping and redefinition of the language modes into the three components involved in effective written expression. At the top of the Total Writing Process Model, developed by the authors of this book, is effective written language expression, which in its optimum level of efficiency contains three components. The first component is similar to receptive oral language. In listening comprehension, individuals match communication heard auditorily with the inner language coding system. Hence, meaning is achieved. Likewise, in comprehension of writing (Component 1), individuals in the process of writing "listen" to the production and check for a match between intent and output. It is at this point that the double recoding, mentioned earlier, takes place. This monitoring occurs during the writing task and is virtually unconscious.

Just as the listener is not consciously aware of the mechanics involved in comprehension—the person just understands—so is the writer not aware of the mechanics of generation. For example, speakers may not be overtly aware of an articulatory error until one or two sentences further along in the conversation. The auditory feedback mechanism alerts speakers to an error to which they suddenly attend. However, speakers do not consciously direct this speech monitoring; rather, an intuitive sense for languaging coupled with the auditory feedback mechanism provides the necessary information to "sense" a mismatch.

The same mechanism applies to writing as well. A writer expressing a communicative intent often is alerted by a similar mechanism to add, delete, or rearrange a statement. A redefinition of the listening comprehension act is involved. Without consciously being aware of a problem, the writer senses the need to correct. This is *not* the same as the second component of Exhibit 3, in which the writer consciously addresses rhetorical and compositional demands. Both speaker and writer unconsciously are alerted to their respective oral and written errors.

Component 2

Component 2 is similar to oral expressive language. In speech production, the speaker addresses the needs of the audience, relying on feedback to monitor the success of this communicative intent. Likewise, "Attention to Audience and Mode" requires the writer's recognition of the needs and demands necessary to effect a purpose. Just as the speaker relies on audience feedback, the writer relies on cognitive abilities to predetermine or hypothesize the needs of the audience and the requirements of the mode.

The effective writer knows when and how to gear communication to an audience, recognizing its varying needs. For example, there is a significant difference between addressing composition to a child, to a minister, and to a boss. Mode requires the same cognitive awareness. The writer must meet the demands of argument if that mode is to be successful, or fulfill the requirements of narration, description, and exposition where appropriate. This attention to the various demands of audience and mode is pragmatic, overt, conscious, and writer directed. The writer attempts to fit previously generated language into an arbitrarily designed structure that, through cognitive and pragmatic analysis, is deemed appropriate. The writer's abilities to address the audience and mode requirements of the composition successfully are examples of the person's conscious manipulation of the language intent. Component 1 is automatic, whereas Component 2 is a conscious effort to evaluate whether the writing product matches the desired intent.

Component 3

Component 3 is similar to receptive written language. Reading requires students to decode visual symbols and derive meaning. Proofreading similarly requires them to decode the symbols of the written composition to ascertain whether meaning is accessible to the reader by following the conventional systems of grammar, mechanics, capitalization, and punctuation. Proofreading is under the students' conscious control, requiring recognition of acceptable language patterns as well as the ability to shape the generated language to match this conventional model. Proofreading is under the control of the writer, who has to shape the writing to match conventional standards; however, it is not under the individual's control to determine what is or is not conventional.

In effective writing, each component follows the successful resolution of the demands of its precursor. Proofreading is more effective as a final than as an initial component. However, as Exhibit 3 demonstrates, not all components are in evidence in writing. For example, a person may possess Components 1 and 2 and be able to write but not as effectively as if competent in all three areas. Similarly, a writer may be very strong in appreciation of audience and appropriate mode but be unable to generate the syntax necessary to convey the analysis. A student may demonstrate the ability to generate written communication but be unable to tailor it to the audience and mode, thereby losing communicative effectiveness.

The Total Writing Process Model accounts for the process and nature of writing. This model also gives a framework within which to analyze writing disability; however, unlike many other models, it adequately represents the process of writing from inception to completion, focusing on all the necessary components involved. The model accounts for problems in language generation, syntax, audience, mode, and error recognition, which in combination or individually can decrease writing effectiveness significantly.

The authors postulate that for any remediation program to be successful it must analyze the writing problem within a framework that accounts for the entire process. As a result, the authors have researched and reviewed current theories, approaches, and programs of writing remediation within that framework as illustrated in Exhibit 3. Interestingly enough, at this time no writing programs address all three components; instead, they cover specific elements without interfacing or relating to the process as a whole.

Following is an overview of the different approaches to writing. These are presented as they correspond to the Total Writing Process Model.

Exhibit 3   The Total Writing Process Model

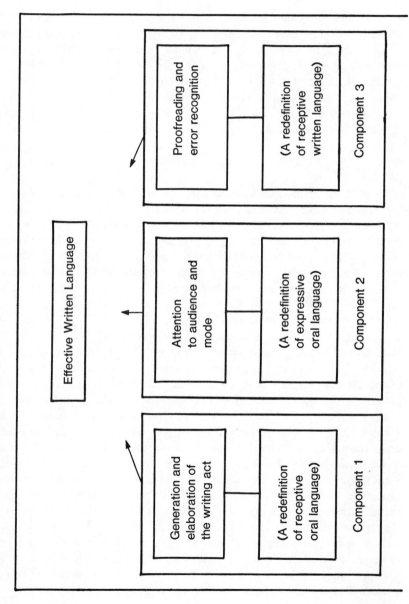

Effective Written Language

Component 1

Generation and elaboration of the writing act

(A redefinition of receptive oral language)

Component 2

Attention to audience and mode

(A redefinition of expressive oral language)

Component 3

Proofreading and error recognition

(A redefinition of receptive written language)

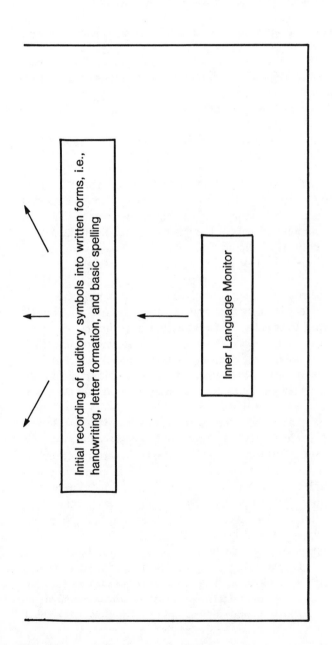

COMPONENTS OF THE MODEL

Component 1: Generation and Elaboration of the Writing Act

For a remediation unit to be successful, it must account for the following factors:

1. It must propose a method by which students generate language in acceptable patterns.
2. It must enable students to elaborate those newly generated language patterns.
3. It must enable students to hone their intuitive skills for matching language output with inner language intent.

As a result, any remediation program in this area should have a strong linguistic basis. Unit I of this text reviews five programs or approaches that remediate writing disability from a primarily linguistic perspective. Some of these approaches do contain elements of the other components in the model; however, their major emphasis is linguistic.

The first is the writing aspect of the Fitzgerald Key program, used for many years but published in 1966. This approach was designed originally for use with hearing impaired children; however, since that time it has been adapted and widely used with language and learning disabled children. It uses a visual framework to teach sentence structure, focusing on all grammatical sentence components. The Key's success with the hearing impaired, its effectiveness with language and learning disabled populations, and its occasional use in adapted form with regular education children make it an important program to review in the context of reviewing major writing programs in use today.

The second is the Sentences and Other Systems program (Blackwell, Engen, Fischgrund, & Zarcadoolas, 1978), also originally designed for use with hearing impaired children. This uses a transformational-generative grammar base to teach five basic kernel sentences, then the combination of those sentences into more complex structures. As with the Fitzgerald Key program, the Sentences and Other Systems program has been adapted to other non-hearing impaired populations. However, this program is considerably newer and so has not been adapted as widely as the Fitzgerald Key.

The third is the approach developed by Johnson and Myklebust (1967). More a philosophy and perspective than a program, this approach hypothesizes a language mode hierarchy, the range of disorders that can be associated with a writing difficulty, an in-depth description of the components of a differential diagnosis, and remedial suggestions. In addition, Myklebust

(1965) has developed a test of written expression that evaluates quantitative and qualitative aspects of writing.

The fourth is the Phelps Sentence Guide program (Phelps-Terasaki & Phelps, 1980), a system that uses a visual frame for teaching writing from the initial level of simple sentences to the complex arrangement of paragraphs. It encompasses a cognitive base expressed within a linguistic frame.

The fifth is sentence combining, an approach in use for a number of years. Sentence combining derives from a transformational-generative grammar base, teaching complex sentences by practicing the combining of simple kernel sentences.

Little research has concerned the generation and elaboration of the writing act. Rather, most of it has focused on error recognition and audience awareness. Yet this first component of the Total Writing Process Model is critical and essentially is the base of effective sentence development in writing. The five approaches just described compose the first unit of this text.

Component 2: Attention to Audience and Mode

Unit II of this book concerns the writer's attention to audience and mode of discourse. This unit focuses on the cognitive processes and development necessary for the writer to express adequately the external demands of audience and mode of discourse. Unit II is composed of two chapters, one on audience needs and the other on mode of discourse requirements.

Component 3: Proofreading and Error Recognition

Unit III surveys programs designed to teach error recognition. The focus is on the writers' ability to read their own discourse, correcting errors that are recognized as not matching the acquired model of language usage. Traditional grammar instruction and a behavioral approach are discussed in reference to giving students a model upon which to base error recognition of mechanics, grammar, capitalization, and punctuation.

Additional Writing Perspectives

Unit IV analyzes programs designed to remediate writing through emphasis on motivation. Such programs do not fit into the Total Writing Process Model. Instead, they substitute motivation for skill development, defining writing disability as a conscious act of the student rather than a deficiency. This area has received the most general discussion in journals and magazines but has yielded the least research or experimental evidence. This may be accounted for by the fact that motivation cannot be measured or systematized into an appropriate research design.

ORAL AND WRITTEN EXPRESSIVE LANGUAGE

Many educators have stressed that the greater the number and variety of oral language experiences, the greater the competency developed in writing. These educators assume that speaking competence can improve and direct skills in writing. Such a position ignores the critical differences between writing and speaking. Although both derive from an essential inner language experience base, transforming that base into spoken language requires far different cognitive skills than into written form. Both modes code experience expressively but demand different abilities to so express the language. An analysis of the major differences between oral and written language, in terms of linguistic, cognitive, and situational demands, demonstrates the essential nature and uniqueness of written expression.

Oral Dictation, Pretask Planning, and Writing

Children do not write as they speak, and they do not appear to dictate to themselves orally as they write. Oral language does not serve as a guide for written language; that is, writing is not talk written down. In one study, Graves (1975) describes the writing of 7-year-old reflective and reactive writers. Reactive children used their oral language in composing and writing, rehearsed both their writing and their orally practiced sentences, rarely proofread their work, were erratic in logical expression, and lacked an ability to tailor their material to an audience. Reflective writers used little overt oral language, little rehearsal, were better able to tailor their material to an audience, used more logical development, and were able to make more reasonable evaluations of their finished products. The reflective children also wrote longer and more organized compositions and used more pretask planning.

In the Graves study, oral dictation did not appear to contribute to better writing. Oral guidance differs from pretask planning. The latter involves the organization and understanding of the content of a written passage, followed by the expression of this material in linguistic units. Oral guidance involves attempting to equate ideas expressed orally with the same structure in writing. The difference in the two language modes is ignored by some researchers and professionals. Sawkins (1971) reports a study in which students who had been involved in an oral discussion of a topic prior to a writing assignment did not write better than other students who had not participated in such a conversation. That is, pretask planning may in fact prepare students to write but does not alter the syntax used in the end product.

Structural Differences between Speech and Writing

Not only is writing not aided by oral dictation, it also has a different base in linguistic and structural elaboration. Elaboration refers to complexity of sentence structure, verb choice, and diction. By the middle grades, children's writing is more fluent and complex and of higher syntactic quality than their oral language (Bavery, 1968; McLean, 1964; Martellock, 1972; Lemon & Buswell, 1943). The writing process is under more control than speech since the writer can fashion and refashion a sentence to suit the intent.

Oral and written language have separate and distinct linguistic functions and structures. In a study by Lewis and Lewis (1965), monolingual and bilingual students by the middle grades evidence no significant differences in "verbal output, vocabulary, quality of sentence structure, and effectiveness of expression" (p. 184). However, their oral language shows a significant difference in fluency, demonstrating that the students not only do not speak as they write but also use different linguistic skills and structures in their writing. These written structures are not apparent in their speech.

In DeStefano's (1972) study, fifth grade black students who spoke non-standard English made more errors in oral than in written language. Non-standard English was present in 25 percent of their oral sentences as compared to 4 percent of the written sentences. Thus, the students did not write as they spoke, possibly modifying their syntax in writing to a more acceptable standard. Specific semantic black English items may remain in writing and speech, perhaps because there are no replacements for those terms in the students' vocabulary, but the written syntax differed. It may be that instruction in oral language develops verbal skills but has little effect on writing since the students use a different syntax then.

Speech involves finite, temporal units that, once produced, are finished and unchangeable in their initial form. Writing, however, involves spatial units that can be manipulated and refashioned to suit the author's intent. For children who process ideas slowly, writing allows them the time to fully own and execute a communicative task, whereas speech, because of its immediacy, entails rapid delivery. Nonetheless, although speech generally is easier, the spatial quality of writing requires children to display their linguistic resources to the fullest.

University freshmen were compared by Poole and Field (1976) on the basis of the structural intricacy, language elaboration, verb complexity, and personal referents used in a written and oral situation. Analysis of the writing on the basis of the complexity of sentence structure, verb choice, and diction indicated that the product was more advanced in structure, in verb usage, and in language choice. Writing also used fewer personal referents. Speech was described as "looser, more flexible, more redundant, more repetitive" (p. 309) and writing as more complex, concise, and specific. These results indicate again that writing is not dependent linguistically upon oral speech for formulation and is much more complex structurally.

Decentration Differences between Speech and Writing

Development in written expression may mirror the pattern of cognitive development. In particular, writers must be able to assume a nonegocentric stance. Egocentrism is defined as an inability to take the role of another person; that is, to step out of self and take another's perspective.

Most children progress from a level of egocentric presocial speech to a social stage characterized by increasing decentration. An example of egocentric speech is children who cannot give clear directions because they cannot assume what the listener does or does not know. The inability to give appropriate oral directions may be comparable to the difficulty in writing clearly because of egocentrism in audience perception. Thus, children need to develop an ability to decenter and consider audience both in speech and in writing; however, the decentration required in writing is more abstract.

According to Vygotsky (1962), writing requires "a deliberate analytical action on the part of the child" (p. 99). The decentration in speech and reading is less abstract and requires less deliberation. Cazden (1972) has described written expression as "the final point on the developmental dimension toward independence from nonlinguistic context" (p. 190).

Written language requires individuals to create a situation, represent it to themselves, and communicate it through symbols to someone else. Writing clearly is more demanding cognitively than is oral expression. The use of primarily egocentric language may indicate less abstract thinking abilities. Effective communication skill will be reduced, of course. The egocentric child's writing also would be inefficient because its abstract nature would place it beyond the individual's cognitive competence.

It should be noted that cognitive egocentrism differs from what the authors term "affective" egocentrism. Affective egocentrism implies not a general thinking problem but a specific linguistic disability in encoding ideas in written form. Such a person may exhibit adequate or superior oral expressive language skills but be deficient in linguistic operations required for expression in the written mode. In both cognitive and affective egocentrism, written expression is inefficient.

The demands of writing may encompass a situation in which cognitive growth results. Bruner (1973) states that "written language . . . makes possible cognitive growth because in writing the referent is not present" (p. 49). Without a concrete referent (the audience) the writer must abstractly code ideas, utilize logic, and create relationships and connections. In such a referent independent situation as the writing task entails, Bruner feels the "stage is set for symbolic processes to run ahead of concrete fact, for thought to be in terms of possibility rather than actuality. At this point, symbolic representation can go beyond the capacities of the iconic system [visual-imagery] and the way is open for Piaget's (1953) stage of formal operations, where the real becomes but a subset of the possible" (p. 49).

The Dynamics of Oral Language

Oral expression takes place in a dynamic situation and is contingent upon immediate feedback, not consciously directed (Weiner, 1975). Oral communication relies on many nonverbal and other clues, such as phonetic features, pitch, stress, and intonation, often referred to as suprasegmental clues, and can be modified easily should the necessity arise. Written language, however, is independent of context, permanent, and not immediately modifiable. Written language allows time for reflection, revision, and editing. Oral speech is temporal and modified after the fact; writing is spatial and can be modified at any point before completion. Oral communication revolves around intonations, pauses, facial expressions, and gestures, all of which are cued to a physically present and visibly responsive audience. The understanding of the audience can be monitored constantly, and additional information can be added if necessary. Meanings are "negotiated in terms of social relations, the context, and prior world knowledge of the participants" (Olson, 1977, p. 10). Writing, however, must transmit meaning without audience negotiation; the meaning occurs independent of context.

Thus, the oral and written expressive modes require different kinds of planning that do not overlap (Cazden, 1972). Speech requires modification and additions based upon immediate audience response; writing involves a prediction of the audience's probable response.

Olson describes meanings found in negotiation or context (oral expression) as utterances that map scientific reality. Oral expression is active, practical, and concerned with the listener, while written expression is reflective, conceptual, and concerned with logical or truth values. Oral expression does not require logical, scientific skills to be developed; text does need this. Writing that qualifies as text requires logical analysis; some types of writing may not qualify as text. Speech depends upon immediate feedback and modification, and aims for time efficiency, resulting in the frequent use of fragments or phrases instead of complete sentences. Writing must rely on complete sentence units for clarity of expression and standard form.

Thus, writing differs from oral expression in that it is cognitively more abstract, is context independent, allows time for reflection and modification, uses complete sentences, and is concerned with presenting the textual information necessary for an absent audience.

EXAMPLES OF WRITING DEFICIENCIES

The Total Writing Process Model offers a framework for classifying specific writing problems within the larger context of written language. Problems that may be classified as belonging to Component 1 (Generation and Elaboration of the Writing Act) of the model are:

1. nonspecific sentences
2. nonelaborated sentences
3. discrepancy between oral intent and written product
4. reliance on simple constructions
5. fragments (not pieces of oral discourse but incomplete idea formulations despite oral "explaining")

Problems that may be classified as belonging to Component 2 (Attention to Audience and Mode) are:

1. lack of organization
2. lack of logical explanation
3. lack of clarity
4. lack of focus
5. lack of unity
6. lack of coherence
7. lack of successful communication to the intended audience
8. lack of supporting detail
9. lack of emphasis

Problems that may be classified as belonging to Component 3 (Proofreading and Error Recognition) are:

1. grammatical errors
2. punctuation errors
3. mechanical errors
4. capitalization errors
5. sentence structure errors

In addition, syntax errors can evidence a problem in any of the three components; for example, a syntax problem could evolve from faulty internalization of grammatical rules or from inadequate recognition of the demands of the audience or mode of discourse. A diction error could evidence a problem in any of the three components.

A final issue concerns the students' inner language monitor. If they lack inner language experience, the base from which they generate communication is faulty, thereby affecting every mode—listening, speaking, reading, and writing. However, in most cases the difficulty lies not in a lack of experience but rather in an inability to anchor new information or demands to what the students know. They have enough experience to encounter the new demands; their problem is a dysfluency in the written language mode that would allow them to interface the writing task adequately with the new subject.

SAMPLES OF WRITING SKILL DEFICIENCIES

The following ten samples illustrate some of the most common errors and disabilities that teachers and clinicians encounter in student writing. These represent actual compositions by students in a public school or clinical setting. The age and sex of each student is provided, as well as the writing topic. The compositions are categorized according to the deficiency they illustrate and in relation to the authors' Total Writing Process Model.

Difficulties in Writing Generation and Elaboration

Sample 1

Student: 11-year-old female
Assignment: to write a story about the events in a colorful action picture.

The man fell down the stairs. He got hurt and cried. He was sad.

Sample 2

Student: 13-year-old male
Assignment: to write an essay on the effects of voter apathy.

Nobody cares when they don't vote. They just stay at home and then they complain about things. Then next time they don't go again. Then they complain some more.

Sample 3

Student: 17-year-old male
Assignment: to write a composition on what courage meant to the old man in Hemingway's *The Old Man and the Sea.*

The old man wanted to catch the fish a whole lot. He really worked hard at it and struggled. The fish meant that he could still do things even though he was old. But the sharks got the fish. The old man had nothing left. But he tried.

All three of these compositions illustrate difficulty in the use of written language structure at the Component 1 level. These writers demonstrated an inability to generate descriptive sentences to communicate a greater depth of meaning. None of them exhibited oral language or reading problems; the disability was in the written expressive mode. As would be expected based on the Total Writing Process Model, if Component 1 is deficient, performance in terms of Components 2 and 3 also will be reduced significantly.

It should be noted that the voter apathy topic and the novel had been discussed in detail in several class sessions before the assignment was given. The subjects therefore were not unfamiliar to the students.

Difficulties in Attending to Audience and Mode

Sample 1

Student: 10-year-old male
Assignment: to write a story describing a secret picture. A friend then was to read the story as a basis for selecting which of four pictures it described.

The horses kind of go up and down in a circle. The people stand in line and buy tickets and then they ride on it. And there's cotton candy. If your good maybe your mom will buy you some.

Sample 2

Student: 14-year-old female
Assignment: to write an essay to prove that women should be drafted.

Everybody should have to serve their country. Women are part of this country too and so they should fight just like men. Its not fair to make men do all of it.

Sample 3

Student: 17-year-old male
Assignment: to write an essay to convince the principal that smoking should be permitted in the halls between classes.

Its not fair to outlaw smoking. Teachers get to smoke so why not us? Its a free country. If smokers keep the place clean then its O.K. That's what I think and I don't even smoke!!!

These three compositions demonstrate a markedly poor sense of audience and effective use of mode. In the first, the assignment was designed specifically to elicit a report directed toward and helpful to a particular audience. The student's written description did not provide enough information for the audience to use in selecting the target picture.

The second and third compositions show faulty use of both audience and mode. In both, the information is poor and not tailored to suit an uninformed reader. The argument mode is haphazard, illogical, poorly ordered, and incoherent. As in the previous section, these topics had been discussed in depth before being assigned.

In reference to the Total Writing Process Model, if performance is deficient in Component 2 abilities, work in Component 3 also can be expected to be impaired or reduced.

Difficulties in Error Recognition

Sample 1

Student: 10-year-old male
Assignment: to write an essay describing his Christmas vacation. (The errors are labeled in parentheses.)

My christmas (no capital letter) was good this year. I got lots of toys and stuff and (run-on sentence) Mommy was happy. The best toy is (verb shift) a Star Wars fighter. Pretty lights was (subject-verb agreement) all over the tree. I liked the blue ones best.

Sample 2

Student: 13-year-old male
Assignment: to write an essay describing his summer vacation. (Errors are labeled in parentheses.)

What I would like to do is go to Diseyland (spelling) and get to do it (nonreferent "it") all because it (nonreferent "it") is fun and my dad (run-on sentence) says maybe we can. My dads (no apostrophe) car runs good (adverb problem) and each of us get (subject-verb agreement) their (pronoun reference) own suitcase. Even me (pronoun usage) and Bobby (fragment).

Sample 3

Student: 17-year-old female
Assignment: to write a composition describing "where I would like to be ten years from now." (Errors are labeled in parentheses.)

> Me (pronoun reference) and my brother like the ocean and sailing. We want to buy a boat and he (run-on sentence) knows how to sail it. When we get the money. (fragment) I once went to Florida and these guys sail boats real good. (adverb problem) These guys (no apostrophe) boats are (verb shift) fast. One saw a shark but that didn't bother me cuz (word error) I never believed the movie anyway.

These three compositions illustrate difficulties in the proofreading and editing of written work. These students demonstrated significant problems in final polishing of written work.

Disorder of the Inner Language Monitor

Sample 1

Student: 15-year-old male
Assignment: to write an essay describing Puritanism.

> These guys wore black and burned people like women and never smiled. Thats all I know about them.

SUMMARY

The following chapters elaborate on the remediation programs available that correspond to the components of the Total Writing Process Model. The dimensions of each component are discussed, the remediation program explained, and its appropriateness in addressing the needs of the writing process evaluated.

BIBLIOGRAPHY

Bates, E. *Language and context: The acquisition of pragmatics.* New York: Academic Press, 1976.
Bavery, E.A. A study of selected aspects of oral and written language of fifth grade pupils. *Dissertation Abstracts,* 1968, *29,* 397A-398A.

Blackwell, P.M., Engen, E., Fischgrund, J.E., & Zarcadoolas, C. *Sentences and other systems: A language and learning curriculum for hearing impaired children.* Washington, D.C.: The Alexander Graham Bell Association for the Deaf, Inc., 1978.

Bruner, J. *The relevance of education.* New York: W.W. Norton & Co., Inc., 1973.

Cazden, C. *Child language and education.* New York: Holt Rinehart Winston Inc., 1972.

Clark, H., & Clark, E. *Psychology and language: An introduction to psycholinguistics.* New York: Harcourt Brace Jovanovich, Inc., 1977.

DeStefano, J.S. Productive language differences in fifth grade students' syntactic forms. *Elementary English,* 1972, *49,* 552-558.

Fitzgerald, E. *Straight language for the deaf.* Washington, D.C.: The Volta Bureau, 1966.

Graves, D.H. An examination of the writing processes of seven-year-old children. *Research in Teaching English,* 1975, Winter, 227-241.

Johnson, D., & Myklebust, H.R. *Learning disabilities: Educational principles and practices.* New York: Grune & Stratton, Inc., 1967.

Lemon, B.K., & Buswell, G.T. Oral and written expression in grade IX. *School Review,* 1943, *51,* 544-549.

Lewis, H.P., & Lewis, E.R. Written language performance of sixth-grade children of low socioeconomic status from bilingual and monolingual backgrounds. *The Journal of Experimental Education,* 1965, Spring, 237-242.

Martellock, H.A. A psycholinguistic description of the oral and written language of a selected group of middle school children. *Dissertation Abstracts International,* 1972, *30,* 16107A-16108A.

Mattingly, I.G. Reading, the linguistic process, and linguistic awareness. In J.F. Kavanagh & I.G. Mattingly (Eds.), *Language by ear and eye: The relationships between speech and reading.* Cambridge, Mass.: MIT Press, 1972.

McLean, H.W. A comparison of selected aspects of the oral and written language of fourth, fifth, and sixth grade students. *Dissertation Abstracts,* 1964, *25,* 943.

Myklebust, H.R. *The psychology of deafness.* New York: Grune & Stratton, Inc., 1960.

_____. *Development and disorders of written language, Vol. II: Studies of normal and exceptional children.* New York: Grune & Stratton, Inc., 1973.

Olson, D. Oral and written language and the cognitive processes of children. *Journal of Communication,* Summer 1977, pp. 10-26.

Phelps, D. *An investigation of the relationship between receptive and expressive grammatical competence and reading readiness.* Unpublished doctoral dissertation. University of Houston, 1979.

Phelps-Terasaki, D., & Phelps, T. *Teaching written expression: The Phelps sentence guide program.* Novato, Calif.: Academic Therapy Publications, 1980.

Piaget, J. *The origins of intelligence in the child.* London: Routledge and Kegan Paul, 1953.

Poole, E., & Field, T.W. A comparison of oral and written code elaboration. *Language and Speech,* 1976, *10,* 305-311.

Public Law 94-142, *The Education for All Handicapped Children Act of 1975.*

Sawkins, M.W. The oral responses of selected fifth grade children to questions concerning their written expression. *Dissertation Abstracts International,* 1971, *31,* 6287A-6288A.

Weiner, E.S. Improvement in reading through writing. *Academic Therapy,* 1975, *14*(5), 589-594.

Vygotsky, L.S. *Thought and language.* Cambridge, Mass.: MIT Press, 1962.

The Total Writing Process: Generation and Elaboration of the Writing Act

UNIT INTRODUCTION

Component 1 of the Total Writing Process Model encompasses the language abilities necessary for students to generate their writing. The students must be able to match their developing composition to their inner language intent. They need to be able to fully express and elaborate their intent in the form of written expression. They also must be able to recognize intuitively when their emerging language deviates significantly from their inner language program.

In the introduction to this book, this aspect of the writing act was compared to receptive oral language in that writers "listen" and attend to the writing as it is being produced. That is, they "listen to themselves write" and match the resulting product to their inner language and knowledge of structure and acceptability. This process is automatic and intuitive and relies on a solid base of development in oral language.

If a disability exists at this level in the Total Writing Process, remediation will focus on the content, structure, and form of language itself. Simultaneous or prior instruction may be necessary (according to whose program is addressed) in the oral or receptive written language modes, but the writing goal is focused on the nature of language and strives to make automatic the encoding of appropriate structures.

This unit focuses on five programs that address students' linguistic needs in writing:

1. the writing aspect of the Fitzgerald Key program and adaptations of the basic method

2. the writing aspect of the Sentences and Other Systems program and adaptations of the basic method
3. the approach developed by Helmer Myklebust
4. the Phelps Sentence Guide program
5. the sentence combining approach

The first two chapters focus on the writing aspects of two curricula for the hearing impaired. These programs have provided a successful approach for the hearing impaired as well as the raw material for adaptations with language and learning disabled populations. Both the writing aspects of the original programs and the adaptations are described. Chapter 3 discusses Myklebust's approach, one of the most widely applied perspectives with the language and learning disabled. His method has affected almost every professional concerned with writing disability in some way.

Chapter 4 focuses on a new method, the Phelps Sentence Guide program. Designed by the authors of this book, this represents the only complete writing remedial program for language and learning disabled and regular education students. Complete means that this program teaches writing from the sentence level to paragraph and to story in nine hierarchical stages. This new method is composed of a combination of original procedures and adaptations of other linguistic and cognitive approaches. Chapter 5 describes the sentence combining approach to writing remediation. This is used by a number of professionals in work with students from upper elementary to college level.

In summary, this unit concerns the initial linguistic and language demands that lead to generation in a written mode of students' underlying inner language program. This component underlies and supports the entire process of written expression. A disability in the performance corresponding to this element will have an inhibitory effect on students' progress in the other components of the Total Writing Process Model.

Chapter 1
The Fitzgerald Key

One of the most widely used written expressive language remedial approaches is borrowed from the area of instruction for the hearing impaired. Learning disability teachers and speech-language pathologists for many years have modified and analyzed the Fitzgerald Key Program (1966) for use with children who have language delay, language disorder, or learning disabilities. The amazing versatility of the Fitzgerald Key is apparent when viewed from the standpoint of its successful use for therapy in receptive and expressive oral and written language.

In other words, the Fitzgerald Key in some form or another can be and has been used for remediation in every aspect of language. The widespread use of the Key in the United States and Canada was studied by Nelson (1949), prior to its general publication in 1966. It was found that in almost half of the schools and programs surveyed, the Key was used exclusively, while in two-thirds of the schools and programs it was used in conjunction with other methods. Moores (1978) states that "the Key continues to be by far the most widely used analytical approach" (p. 219) used to teach language to the hearing impaired.

It has been so successful, in fact, that Fokes (1976) compiled a picture categorization system that assembled the Fitzgerald Key in packaged form, something that clinicians previously had had to put together on their own by searching painstakingly through magazines and other media to find appropriate pictures and illustrations. Because of the enormous success and adaptability of the Fitzgerald Key, it is only appropriate that it should be included in the unit on linguistic approaches to writing instruction and remediation.

A thorough description of the Fitzgerald Key must include a review of the program as originally conceived, coupled with a description of the ways in which professionals have adapted all or part of it. However, it would be virtually impossible to describe all the many adaptations of the Key since modifications result from the particular needs of individual children. Instead, the Key is presented in its original form, followed by the Fokes Sentence Builder adaptation and another general modification for children with language and learning problems.

OVERVIEW OF THE FITZGERALD KEY

The Fitzgerald Key was designed by Edith Fitzgerald, used for many years, and published in 1966. It is a method of teaching written language to hearing impaired children. In English, word order is critical to the meaning of a sentence and the Key is devised in a manner that illustrates that point and allows children to learn efficient communication and correct grammar in an indirect, almost natural way. Rather than teach word classes by names, the system relies on the communicative use of a word class according to the questions it might answer or the role it plays in a sentence. For example, nouns are listed under a Who or What heading.

The Fitzgerald Key is a frame or skeleton composed of categories related to the word classes in a sentence. A sentence can be written left to right in the Key, with each word in the appropriate column. Each column has a heading that relates to the word's or words' function in the sentence. This function is related closely to the meaning and intent of the sentence. By using the column headings as cues, children can follow the Fitzgerald Key in ordering written sentences.

Since hearing impaired children cannot rely on their hearing mechanism to provide the auditory cues necessary to discern language structure, the Fitzgerald Key provides a visual system. Normal hearing children can use hearing to monitor language and to allow for the recognition of its ordering. With the Key, hearing impaired children can use their intact visual system to analyze language and generalize correct structure.

Fitzgerald's goal in devising the Key was to develop a basic system for guiding children's acquisition of reading and writing, with an emphasis on correct grammatic use. This system also can be used to expand children's lexicons and knowledge in a wide range of subjects. That is, given the sentence structuring of the Key, content can vary from history to science to health. Built into the system is the assumption that once the child assimilates the structure of written communication, correct use of language in all modes will follow. That is, the accurate internalized representation of the structure can provide for learning and facility in all language reception and expressive modes.

The Basis: Left-to-Right Categories

The Fitzgerald Key can be described best as a left-to-right series of categories organized according to standard sentence structure. The columns on the far left of the Key page relate to the subject: Whose, Who, and What. Next comes the geometric symbol representing the verb, followed in order by the categories What/Whom, Whose, Whom/What, Where, For/With/How/Why/How Far/How Often/How Long/How Much, and to the far right of the page, the When category. These categories are arranged as headings across the page and sentences are written in the appropriate columns.

The other geometric symbols are used, when needed, to signify their particular grammatic meanings. Thus, if components of a sentence are written under the appropriate headings, correct sentence structure will result. In this way, the Key provides a visual representation of correct sentence structure and the correct ordering of components in linear form.

The core of the program is fluency and practice in the structuring and ordering of sentences. Fitzgerald even suggests that the internalization of correct language patterns will result in more logical, ordered thought; that is, that precise language will order and have an intimate relationship with precise thought. She clearly perceives language and thought to be in a close, mutually beneficial relationship. Thus, the Key program is one that provides for language growth in the written modes, language generalization in the oral modes, and mental reliance on language to categorize, order, and make sense of the world.

Fitzgerald (1966) stresses that practice and repetition are absolutely necessary to root the learning of language firmly into children's networks of abilities. The old adage about practice making perfection most definitely applies to the Key program. However, repetition, as used in the program, avoids a mechanical, robot-like drill in which structures are memorized but not owned. Rather, she advocates that teachers compose drills which involve lively, inspired, and meaningful practice and allow for children's interests to be maintained as they work on a particular structure. Careful planning by the teacher is required so that spontaneity and creativity are maintained as opposed to rote drill.

Thus, the program is composed of a system in which a frame is used to provide a visual representation of sentence order. Into this frame, the teacher or child can write a sentence, using the Fitzgerald Key as a cue to what comes next or where to put parts of a sentence. Rather than rely on a typical traditional grammar approach, the Key program focuses on word classes in terms of use. However, seven geometric symbols are used to indicate special or distinct parts of speech—conjunctives, adjectives, predicate nouns, predicate pronouns, verbs, infinitives, and present participles.

Beginning with words, proceeding to simple sentences, and finally continuing to more and more complex sentences, the children slowly build their competency in reading and writing (receptive and expressive written language). The goal is to have the children communicate fluently in writing or obtain information from it. By stressing the grammatical structure of language, the meaning of a sentence can be made clear. Meaning in a sentence is derived in large part from the word order, making meaning and word order closely related.

In the Fitzgerald Key program, facility with the written word is perceived to generalize to the spoken word; at the same time, thought and mental processing are felt to be ordered and streamlined by the new language competency. Obviously, with such a focus on the interrelationship of thought and language, this program is a major component of the curriculum for the hearing impaired.

Interestingly enough, what Fitzgerald suggests as one of the underlying assumptions of her program is that for children whose oral language cannot guide, or has not helped, written language development, the reverse is true: written language guides oral language development. This possibility has been suggested elsewhere in relation to learning disabled children (Myklebust, 1973). Such a reversal of the accepted hierarchy and acquisition of language modes is intriguing and frequently, if not almost consistently, is ignored by professionals. More research in terms of the power of written language to effect growth and change in oral language is needed and could have a significant impact on remedial methodology for learning disabled and language disordered children.

One of the stong features of the Key program is that it is used from the very beginning of formal schooling and throughout the grades, making grammar analysis a constant part of the curriculum and not merely an element of later schooling. When not learned until upper grades, the study of grammar is more complex. It is a difficult area for the hearing impaired and if it has not been an everyday part of the curriculum, it may be dreaded and feared when encountered in the upper grades.

Basic Suggestions and Guidelines

A number of suggestions and guidelines are basic to the efficient and appropriate use of the program and are discussed here before the methodology is described.

1. The teacher never should orally correct errors made by the children. The pupils then must rely on auditory memory to remember a correction instead of understanding the reason behind it. By putting an error into the Fitzgerald Key, children can see clearly why a certain structure is wrong, thereby developing a conceptual understanding and recognition

that will be more permanent than auditory memory because it involves the concept underlying the mistake.

2. The teacher should be aware that teaching deaf children is not the same as teaching English as a second language. The latter persons have a linguistic system on which to build and compare the new language; they already own an organized, linguistic perception of the world. Their mental schemata of experience already are cued to language. Hearing impaired children, however, must organize thought on a linguistic dimension, building the mental images of a first language system. Thus, the teacher has to work to fit instruction into the children's mental schemata while trying to broaden and organize development.

3. The teacher must be ready to meet the children's interests and needs on an individual basis since some of them will be ready for material that may be above grade level.

4. The teacher should always be careful to analyze errors, which indicate the way in which children are understanding certain curriculum components. These errors indicate what instruction still needs to be provided and what modifications the students may need in understanding classroom materials.

5. The teacher should not abbreviate words when writing in the Key, no matter what the reason. Children need to see the complete form visually in order to get the whole word in memory and allow for revisualization.

6. The teacher should allow the students to see that there is no single way to say something in writing. Although syntax defines what is and is not appropriate, written expression is characterized by wide flexibility in sentence formulation. Content can be written in a number of ways within a frame of correct syntax.

7. The teacher should insist on correct writing mechanics such as posture, pencil grip, and handwriting from the very beginning of work. Habits appropriate to efficient writing are thereby reinforced.

8. The teacher should use the vocabulary that the children learn in many other contexts as well. During the school day, the teacher can arrange for any number of activities that will use and reinforce vocabulary learned. During these activities the teacher can present the words but also should prompt the students to try to use some of them. The children must get to the point at which they spontaneously use more and more of the newer items in their lexicon.

METHODOLOGY OF THE FITZGERALD KEY

The Fitzgerald Key (1966) is kept on a chalkboard in a prominent part of the classroom. The children write on it and on paper Keys that are on their desks and in their notebooks.

The Key is designed to act as a "substitute for the hearing sense that guides hearing children" (p. 72). Whereas normal children can rely on their healthy auditory system to cue, structure, and reinforce the correct language they hear, hearing impaired students are without a well-functioning listening system. The Fitzgerald Key allows these children to receive cueing, structure, and order visually. It segments sentences according to classes of words and phrases. The teacher does not write in the Key for the children, but rather, they use it as a system through which they can work out sentences on their own. By doing it themselves, they learn the correct structure and how to build sentences and begin to develop an internal representation of their structure. They eventually will use this internal representation in place of the Key so they can generate and order their sentences mentally. Parts are added to the Key as quickly as each child needs them. This requires the teacher to monitor each child constantly as to individual language needs.

In her book, Fitzgerald describes two goals in the curriculum involving the Key: (1) the content of language is to be expanded and (2) the form of language is to be learned and stabilized.

The first goal, content, refers to the semantic, vocabulary, and conceptual aspects of language. It relates to such factors as concept of time and space, adjectival structures, and vocabulary items, as well as the ways these elements interface and blend. Content also relates to the children's mental encyclopedia as it is linked to the linguistic counterparts of the entries—in other words, to the mental lexicon.

The second goal involves the stabilization of correct language form: the syntactic, morphological, and phonemic elements. The Key does not address phonemic factors directly, but does emphasize syntax and morphology. By its very structure, the Key builds correct word order into a sentence and the morphological elements can be blended in effectively by a perceptive teacher. Thus, such elements as subject-verb-object ordering or subject-verb agreement can be a part of the instructional focus.

The Primary Key

The Fitzgerald Key begins with vocabulary and concept work. A distinction is made between the word Who and the word What (the first column of the Key), one related to animate objects, the other to inanimate ones. Initially, this is done in a very concrete manner by the teacher's naming a series of things and categorizing them according to their being a Who or a What. These nouns then are listed in vertical columns under the appropriate heading. Later, adjectives can be taught, since they pair naturally with nouns. These adjectives correspond to the columns with labels such as How Many, What Kind of, and What Color.

Adjectives present a special instructional problem because children must learn their correct order in a descriptive noun clause. In the English language, adjectives are strung together in a particular way. The teacher's job is to find a way to stabilize their correct ordering in the children's written sentences. Hearing impaired students often have difficulty grasping the order of adjectives in a descriptive subject. Without ever paying much attention, normal children simply adapt to the rules of adjective order and produce correct utterances. Hearing impaired, and for that matter language and learning disordered, pupils often do not internalize this rule system and so produce a string of adjectives in a bizarre sounding and erroneous manner.

Fitzgerald's system teaches students to order the descriptive subject as follows:

quantity + noun
quantity + color + noun
quantity + attribute + color + noun

Initially, work on adjectives should be at a concrete level. For example, three green blocks are placed on the table in front of the children, who practice writing number, color, and then noun. Objects are changed and manipulated to allow for numerous drills. The pupils, through written practice, learn that number is followed by color, and it is hoped will internalize the rules for stringing adjectives together.

The articles "a," "an," and "the" are used in drills on adjective order. These drills are very concrete at first, involving objects and pictures to stimulate the sentence written in the Key.

The Primary Fitzgerald Key also includes columns for the Verb, Whose, Whom or What (direct object), Where, Why, and When. The hearing impaired child may advance in work with the Key without utilizing the oral expressive language mode. The oral mode will develop in time and be rooted in the structure that has been stabilized in the written mode.

The seven geometric symbols used for special words—conjunctions, adjectives, predicate nouns, predicate pronouns, verbs, infinitives, and present participles—provide cues to the children as to certain subgroups of word classes. These subgroups correspond to particular meanings or have a special semantic value by virtue of their being included in a sentence. The symbols cue the students to recognize that a particular meaning is being encoded in the sentence and they must be alert to it. Fitzgerald suggests that in a relatively short time, the children learn to recognize the symbols and react appropriately.

Fitzgerald defends the use of such symbols. She recognizes that many professionals hold that language is a symbolic code and that super-imposing a second geometric symbol code on top of the first—in which children already have demonstrated a lag—makes no sense. These professionals contend that language problems are compounded by the increase in the complexity required in learning two symbolic systems. Fitzgerald maintains that the seven symbols, as she uses them with the hearing impaired, are very successful and not too complex. She reports that in her research she finds "that the children sense the difference between parts of speech more easily when the symbols are used than when verb, adjective, etc., are introduced in conjunction with the key-words, which key-words present definite *thoughts*" (1966, p. 25).

This argument is incomplete. The statement revolves around the notion that a geometric symbol system *with* naming of grammatical parts of speech is superior to a teaching strategy of naming only the grammatical parts. There is cause to wonder why instruction must be so dichotomized. Why use geometric symbols *or* the naming of parts of speech? One of the major criticisms of the Fitzgerald program is that it is so analytical as to reduce the naturalness of language learning (Moores, 1978). Perhaps labeling parts of speech is too analytical a demand and should be replaced with instruction that highlights the function and force of grammatical elements.

Fitzgerald feels that children have an internal awareness of what meaning the parts of speech encode. By marking them with corresponding symbols and having the teacher say their grammatic name, she finds children are led to note these particular structures and their use and place in the communication of meaning. An alternative is to demonstrate the communicative value and use of parts of speech, rather than to require actual labeling.

The Key can be used to teach word order or to analyze error structures. Hearing impaired children often have great difficulty with word order. In many cases, such errors can be corrected without the teacher's even using an elaborate oral explanation. For example, an error such as "He gave me them" can be put into the Fitzgerald Key in appropriate form. This will yield "He gave them to me," since "He gave me them" will not fit into the Key.

Since the Key has been accepted as the frame for learning correct grammar, by inserting the error sentence and observing the mismatch, the children see the error. They then can be shown the correct way to produce the sentence. Further practice with similar sentences should follow to stabilize the concept through the use of drill.

Receptive, Then Expressive

In learning to write and read the items in the various columns, the children's receptive understanding of a category must precede their expressive use of that category. Thus, concrete experiences with nouns or verbs are followed by listing them. By focusing initially on the individual word classes, students also can work within the classes themselves. For example, when working on the Who and What category, pluralization can be introduced.

In developing competency in using the Fitzgerald Key, the teacher engages the children in a variety of activities. First, the teacher dictates a phrase or sentence, then for each part of the sentence asks the children where that element should be written in the Key. The classification work up to this point has prepared the children to analyze sentence components, so the pupils should be able to write the elements in the correct columns. In this way, the sentence "I see a ball" would be dictated by the teacher and written by the children in the Fitzgerald Key as follows:

Who:	What:	Whom:
Whose:		Whose:
What: (Verb)	Whom:	What:

I |see|→| a ball.

Phrases that go together naturally should be classified as a unit by the children. If a teacher says, "Susan went to the schoolyard," then asks for the Key word that indicates under which column "to the schoolyard" should be written, the answer should be the Where column. The point is that the "to the schoolyard" phrase is a unit of meaning and should remain so.

Older children keep notebooks in which they list the vocabulary that corresponds to the variety of word classes they learned with the Key.

Before describing some of the main issues in expanding children's fluency and the complexity of written expression in the Key, some of the content-related aspects of instruction are summarized.

With the hearing impaired, the focus of language content after beginning Fitzgerald Key sentence work is on such topics as the weather, the four seasons, the calendar, or basic time, as well as understanding and using polite forms of address and listening and following oral and written directions. The mental development of hearing impaired students is a constant part of the curriculum. At all times, their reasoning and problem-solving skills should be expanded, because from this conceptual base comes the content and meaning they will use in communicative interactions and in functioning smoothly in day-to-day living. In communication, to understand another's intent and to generate meaningful compositions requires a high degree of cognitive ability. Children who reason, categorize experience, interrelate experience, and solve problems build up their mental storehouses of information. Teachers will need to refer to this storehouse again and again in reference to children's understanding and expressing self in language.

Fitzgerald's book also presents an overview of some of the main issues of form in the program, those that center on particular parts of speech. These issues are discussed next to provide insight into the detail and organization of the program.

Pronouns

One of the unusual features of the Fitzgerald Key program is the way it teaches pronominalization. The rationale is that for students to relate a pronoun to its antecedent, the two should be linked together in the sentence. That is, for the children to learn that a pronoun reflects a direct correspondence to a person or object, they must appreciate the person or object to which it refers. When teaching pronominalization and writing sentences in the Key, the instructor uses elliptical sentences and allows the children to visually appreciate the role the pronoun plays.

A slow instruction in pronominalization coupled with this use of elliptical sentences to stress the antecedent of each pronoun is thought to result in more success in this area. Later in the program, the antecedent can be dropped. Examples of such elliptical sentences are:

He, Bob, went to the store.
She, Alice, has on a blue dress.
They, Susan and Jane, saw a bird.

In this way, pronouns can be introduced carefully, the antecedent is clear and direct, and the pupils have a less complex system to learn in the beginning. The only problem with such a system is that the elliptical sentences are stilted and unnatural in actual communication; however, the benefits to the instruction process of a clear antecedent may outweigh this concern.

The progression of pronouns to be taught depends on the individual child's oral use or cognitive awareness of a word that is needed but is not in the immediate repertoire. In time, all the pronouns will evidence a need to be focused on or will be taught. Pronoun lists and wall charts can be sources of practice and drill materials.

Inasmuch as pronoun use and agreement are one of the typical difficulties of children with hearing impairment, this system is perhaps an easier way to teach pronominalization. On the other hand, as mentioned earlier, the sentences written with the antecedents certainly are not natural, and when the children read them back they experience language that is stilted in form. It would seem that the natural use of pronouns would be the best way to approach this area of study; however, Fitzgerald claims her program's method is successful with this population.

Adjectives

The Key program teaches adjectives to children whenever they evidence a need for a descriptive word in order to communicate. That is, when students are cognitively aware of the need for a descriptor that is not in their lexicon, the teacher can focus a lesson on that word. Meaning in its various forms must be emphasized and the word must be used in a variety of contexts. Fitzgerald does not advocate the use of word-opposite drills in teaching adjective use. She does not utilize the teaching of adjectives in pairs: hot/cold, empty/full, big little. Rather, she believes that teaching the needed adjective in its natural context within the sentence should be sufficient. If pupils need a word to modify a noun, they are given that word, and no opposite drill is needed or provided. Word-opposite drills are one of a number of paradigmatic language manipulations used extensively and successfully in remediation. Why Fitzgerald does not advocate this procedure is unknown to these authors.

As adjectives are learned and added to the repertoire, sentences are constructed that have more than one adjective. As these sentences are written in the Fitzgerald Key, the order of adjectives is taught systematically as described earlier.

Fitzgerald divides comparatives and superlatives into groups:

1. Those that have to have an "er" added to indicate a comparison, including words that must have the final consonant doubled before the "er"is added, for example, the word "sadder;"
2. those that are prefaced with the word "more" instead of adding a suffix, such as "more special;"
3. those that are irregular, for example, "bad."

These words are taught in this order, and lists of each type are put on charts and mounted on the wall.

Conjunction

Connectives are taught as children experience the need to combine thoughts or when the teacher notes they are using many simple sentences repetitiously in preference to a single complex sentence. For example, the following two sentences are redundant:

The girl is pretty.
The girl is nice.

These could be combined by the teaching of the conjunction "and":

The girl is pretty and nice.

In this way, the children's reservoir of connective words is built up steadily. Fitzgerald cautions against children's use of too many "ands" in a sentence. A run-on sentence of this type can be equally as cumbersome as the use of a string of simple sentences; however, when sentences with too many "and" connectors are written in the Key, the misuse of this conjunction is perceived easily.

Verbs

Of particular interest in the Key program is the manner in which written competency in the use of verbs is built. Several cautions are suggested for verb instruction:

1. Verbs should not be conjugated. This is an artificial manipulation of language and leads only to rote drill. When children are introduced to the conceptual basis of time that underlies different verb forms, they soon will come to own the different verb structures they must use in expressing an idea.
2. Infinitives should not be used as the way to introduce a verb, since children may not need this form until later. Present tense verb use is acquired before future tense use.
3. The negative should not be introduced until much later in the program. Until this construct is really needed, work on negation will be unnecessarily complex. After fluency and competency have been demonstrated in the affirmative, the negative can be introduced. In any case, Fitzgerald points out that in many cases by using an affirmative sentence, the negative actually is implied. That is, "the boy is happy" also implies that the boy isn't unhappy.
4. The time concept underlying each verb tense should be stressed so that the children are aware of the full meaning and implication of the particular one used in a sentence. For example, the teacher writes on the board future tense sentences that relate to events that actually will take place in the context of the classroom. As each event described by a sentence is completed, the sentence is erased. Thus, the sentences on the board relate only to what will be, not what is or has been.

Verbs are divided into two classes: drill verbs and nondrill verbs. Drill verbs normally do not have a present progressive tense: "see," "have," "has on, "or like." Nondrill verbs commonly do use the present progressive tense: "cry," "work," or "sing." Drill verbs are taught first and easily interface with subject-verb-object sentence lessons. For example, drills can require the children to write what they see, with a variety of things and people around the room being targeted.

I see a desk.
I see a red apple.
I see an orange pencil.

The past tense of "see" is introduced easily at this point. Drills emphasize the time factor underlying the verbs. For example, the teacher places a ball on the desk and asks the children to write what they see in the Fitzgerald Key. The response should be something like

I see a red ball.

The teacher then takes the ball away and asks for the corresponding sentence, which should be:

I saw a red ball.

Drills then can be designed that interplay the "see" and "saw" verbs in relation to objects and pictures.

Other drill words can be taught in the same context. "Has" and "have" can be taught by noting what a child has in hand and asking the pupil to write the corresponding sentence, for example:

I have a book.

Sentences such as the following also can be written:

I have one nose.
I have black hair.
I have two eyes and one chin.

The method to teach "has" can be introduced easily by asking one child to write a sentence corresponding to what another child has.

Bill has brown hair.
Susan has a red skirt.
Matt and Jerry have green shoes.

In this way the "has/have" distinction is introduced and reinforced in a natural way. Further drill will stabilize the use of these words.

Other drill words can be introduced in a number of creative and innovative ways. The order of drill verb instruction is: present tense, past tense, and future tense. Thus, each tense is steadily worked through for each verb, reinforced by drill work and charts on the wall.

Nondrill words proceed in this progression: past tense, present progressive tense, and future tense. Later, the past progressive and simple present are added. In this way, words such as "fell," "found," and "played" are introduced, followed by their representations in the other tenses. Eventually, charts can be placed on the wall that differentiate drill and nondrill words and provide lists of each in the various tenses.

The verb "is" begins after work is progressing in drill and nondrill words. This can be divided into three units: its use with the predicate adjective ("I am happy"), with where ("The ball is on the table"), and with the predicate noun ("Matt is a man"). When errors are made here or elsewhere in the program, the teacher does not correct the mistakes. Rather, the children are asked to use the Key and correct themselves. Again, the Fitzgerald Key is a system of visually cueing and guiding these hearing impaired children in a way that their hearing sense cannot. Children write the sentence in the Key and can see clearly where and how mistakes were made.

The Fitzgerald Key program relies heavily on learning rules of grammar. For example, rules are used to aid the children in differentiating between the past and present perfect tenses. They must learn that one is used when the time of an action is known ("I played baseball at the park last week"), and the other when an event of unknown time is described ("I have played baseball at the park"). Other rules that are learned involve the present perfect and past perfect tenses, double verbs (looked up, cut out, tried on), infinitives, participles, gerunds, and the passive voice. These rules are recorded in the notebook and Fitzgerald Key drills accompany work with each construct.

Advanced Fitzgerald Key Work

As the hearing impaired children get further along in the program, the categories on the Key itself change in name. The Who heading becomes "Subject," the = (verb) symbol is changed to the word "Verb," and the Whom heading becomes "Direct Object." Sentences still are written in the Key, as before, but the grammatical classes are called by their proper names.

Writing Activities

Numerous writing activities are used in advanced work. For example, children write news in a part of the chalkboard reserved for current events. These children will need to have gained some proficiency in writing sentences in the Fitzgerald Key. This news corner can become an important component of the day's work. Children with news take turns writing sentences on the board, then the rest of the class reads their reports. As more writing proficiency develops, the content and structure of the news sentences can be increased. Weather reports can be written in the same manner. These activities serve to highlight the informative nature of communication.

Other writing that is worked into the classroom situation gradually includes personal experiences, minutes of meetings, telegrams (both writing them and reading them), or advertisements about all kinds of events and objects.

Letter writing is a critical component of the instruction in written expressive language. At first, the teacher will have to write the letter but the children soon can add a line or two at the beginning or end. Gradually, the pupils take over more and more of the task until they are writing complete letters by themselves. Letters to parents should become a regular part of the course.

The teacher corrects the punctuation and form of all writing from the very beginning. In this way, appropriate patterns are emphasized.

Although she does not go into enough detail, Fitzgerald explains that children must be instructed in how letter and note content varies in relation to the intended audience. The content must be tailored to the intended reader. Among those that can be practiced are business letters, thank you notes, postcards, and letters to complain about or order merchandise. Their components can be contrasted with personal letters. For example, both business and personal letters have headings, dates, addresses, and closings; however, business letters have a different kind of greeting and closing—they do not close with the word "love" or other endearments.

Another writing activity suggested is the "My Day" exercise. The students describe the events of their day, from morning to evening. The teacher may block the time off into chunks—for example, what happened before school, in the morning at school, after lunch until time to go home, and evening at home. The children present these activities orally at first, but soon are required to write them. This provides practice in ordering events, sequencing actions in a time frame, and organizing thought. Children also can read each other's stories and observe other styles of writing. Fitzgerald suggests that the "My Day" exercise begin at the second grade level and continue at all the other grade levels. Thus, a variety of writing tasks is emphasized and experienced in the program at the advanced level.

ADAPTATIONS OF THE FITZGERALD KEY

Adaptations of the Fitzgerald Key have been developed for use with children who have language and learning problems of a variety of types. In these cases, many elements of the curriculum for the deaf can be eliminated as inappropriate but much of the core of the program remains. The Key as a visual system of illustrating and offering practice in the structure of written language is most appropriate with children whose visual mode is intact and efficient. As with the hearing impaired, errors of a variety of types can be written into the Key and the corrections become clear. Simple sentences can be built, with more and more of the word classes added to create more complex sentences.

The Key and modifications of it probably have been used more than any other approach to written expression with the language disordered and learning disabled populations. Modifications of this program vary with the individual child for whom the program is to be used. Children in the language and learning disabled populations for whom this program can be used can be divided into four types. Many other types of language disorder exist, but the ones described here relate only to those that warrant remediation in the written expressive mode.

Type I

These children have demonstrated adequate oral language, both receptive and expressive, and receptive written language (reading). Their difficulties lie in written expression. They are obvious candidates for therapy aimed at isolating their strengths and weaknesses in the written mode—and implementing a remedial program to increase and expand their abilities in writing.

Type II

These students have demonstrated mild difficulties in all of the language modes. Although they do not evidence significant difficulties in any of the modes, they still make subtle but distinct errors in language in general. Since writing may be considered the most demanding of the language modes (Myklebust, 1967), these children's output will be marked by the least communicative efficiency.

Although some professionals advocate focusing on oral modes before written language, others insist on designing and implementing a therapy program that interfaces all of the modes in a mutually beneficial way. Errors should be targeted and worked on in the different modes through a number of integrative activities. These pupils can benefit from a complete language remedial program and show progress in all modes over time. That language is highly interrelated fundamentally can be capitalized on with such students, irrespective of the fact that each mode makes special additional demands on this fundamental core.

It can be argued that if the teacher provides only oral language therapy for children with mild difficulty in all modes, and then waits for proficiency before proceeding to reading, valuable time may be lost. Providing only reading remediation without written expressive help also may delay the attainment of total language competency.

These children have a certain amount of language proficiency overall, and the building of an interrelated program of remediation may well result in gains in all the modes. Despite the language hierarchy (Myklebust, 1967), these students have a mild element of disorder that runs through all modes, and a multimodal treatment system may be the most expedient. This by no means implies that pupils with significant oral language problems and little or no written language should receive a multimodal approach. Clinical judgment must be used in determining when a problem is too involved to bypass the language hierarchy.

Type III

These pupils have demonstrated difficulty in both of the written language modes, but their problem is far worse in the written expressive component than in the written receptive. Reading is not far below grade level but writing is very poor. They need reading remediation but also can benefit from a written expressive language therapy program. It may be far wiser to initiate work in the written expressive mode rather than postpone it to a later time.

Type IV

These children have demonstrated difficulty in both of the expressive language modes. Their oral expression is below par, but only mildly to moderately so. Their written expression also is below adequate. Some of them may need only oral language remediation, simply because the written system complicates their production problem. Others, however, will benefit from work in both modes. As Myklebust (1967) has pointed out, some of these children may have memory problems to the extent that they actually benefit from communicating in writing and being allowed the time to retrieve the needed information. With this second group, written language therapy often seems to provide the order and structure that is generalized into the oral mode.

Two modifications of the Fitzgerald Key as they relate to the four types of handicapped children are presented next.

THE FOKES SENTENCE BUILDER

Joann Fokes (1976) developed a now widely used pictoral version of the Fitzgerald Key. Her approach utilizes the same categories of word classes as the Key; however, this program is designed primarily for oral language development. She notes that it can be used successfully as a component of a writing program, but she does not generate much data as to how it has been used in her experience to teach and order written expression.

Basically, the Fokes modification of the Fitzgerald Key involves a series of cardboard boxes labeled with the name of the word class they illustrate. Thus, there is a box full of pictures corresponding to Who, What, Is Doing (verbs in general), Which (adjectives), Where, How (adverbs), and Why. Sentence markers indicate whether the sentence is declarative, interrogative, or negative of different types. Words such as "am," "can," or "have" are printed on cards and can be inserted where appropriate. The technique is for the teacher to decide on a particular sentence frame—for example, subject-verb-object—then pull one picture out of each box to illustrate the sentence. Thus, sentences could be built such as these:

> The astronaut is riding a bike.
> The man is holding a shoe.

The pupils then are asked to pull pictures out of the boxes and make sentences by themselves. They then can "read" the pictures.

The Fokes differs from using an actual Fitzgerald Key in that it pictures the categories and word classes independently of the paper on which the sentences are written. The Fitzgerald requires the children to write directly on the Key paper.

The Type I Children

In terms of the Type I children, the goal is to improve the written expression mode. Some examples of therapy procedures are described next. For example, the pupils can work for a time building a number of sentences of one type such as declarative, then copy them in their notebooks. If their problem is primarily organization and ordering of thought, the students can proceed to practice other sentence types. In time, they will develop competency in writing a number of types.

What the pictures provide is a concrete manner in which to manipulate word classes, beginning with simple sentences and progressing to complex ones. The children first manipulate the pictures, then write the sentence on paper. The picture manipulation is a time for ordering thoughts—in this case concrete images—but eventually the pupils will begin to internalize this imaging process and will be able to organize their mental pictures without needing the Fokes Sentence Builder material.

If Type I children have a syntactic problem, it may be necessary to target syntactic errors and provide therapy for them. For example, if the children have difficulty in the use of irregular past tense verbs, they are asked to take pictures and arrange them into sentences in the past tense. They then write the sentences they composed with pictures. Or the teacher could choose ten irregular past tense verb pictures and have the pupils insert them one at a time into a constant picture sentence frame:

The man _____ happily.

Again, the children write each sentence after composing it with pictures.

The Type II Children

Type II children also can be guided in producing picture sentences; however, these should be practiced in all of the language modes. Initially, the work might involve only simple sentence constructions. The teacher may produce a sentence and have the students repeat it as each picture is pointed to. The pupils are asked to "read" the picture sentence in graphic form, with the teacher writing it down. Finally, the teacher asks the students to write the sentence in their notebooks. From a base of competency at the simple sentence level, more and more difficult sentences can be built. The work may have to remain at the oral language level for some time when the components become very complex, but as soon as possible the sentences should be practiced in a multimodal manner. Naturally, this program is interfaced with other therapy approaches.

Syntactically, this program also focuses on the children's particular errors, practicing correct structures and using multimodal procedures. Unlike the Type I children, these do not look at a past tense picture sentence and automatically "read" it correctly. Rather, they might concentrate on five irregular past tense verbs, with oral language practice and proficiency followed by work in the written mode. Gradually, more verbs can be added to the group of target items.

The Type III Children

Type III children require therapy only in the written mode, with reading remediation completely separate from the written expression work. The goal in reading is at a higher level than for writing. Thus, reading work can focus on basal readers at a particular level, coupled with phonetic and structural analysis and sight word and comprehension exercises. Writing is at the level of putting pictures together to form sentences, "reading" the sentences orally, then writing them in the notebooks. The sentences can vary from among the various types and from simple to complex as time passes. A number of activities with the Fokes Sentence Builder are possible.

Syntax is treated as in the Types I and II. Target structures are identified and worked on through the use of picture sentence organization work which is gradually associated with the corresponding written representation.

The Type IV Children

Type IV children present a different problem remedially. Since both their expressive systems are impaired, their language production requirements will vary according to the child. Some pupils in this group may be overwhelmed by the oral and written tasks being interfaced. They may require a program involving only the oral language system; if they improve to acceptable limits, they proceed to written language.

Some children in this population, however, can benefit from combining the oral and written modes. For those with memory deficits, the written mode may be easier since it allows more time to formulate and order the words in sentences. These students may be able to work through composing sentences, with the use of pictures, and the corresponding writing requirement can be developed in relation to the picture sentences.

In other words, after developing competency in composing picture sentences, the children are taught to write the corresponding simple sentence. At first, only a limited sentence frame is used, such as subject-verb, followed by subject-verb-object, etc. Vocabulary may be limited at first; the vocabulary words can be kept in a notebook or on cards. As work progresses, more and more words can be added to the notebook or file.

As the pupils attain some degree of competency in the written mode, the oral mode can be used more. The children read their sentences aloud, in picture form, then in written form. As work continues, the oral element can be included more frequently.

In time, the reading may generalize into the oral mode and allow for internalization of the structure of sentences to be produced. The written and picture composition work may provide an internal structure that can in fact generalize to the oral mode. The teacher may allow the children longer time to compose picture and written sentences, and eventually the pupils become more rapid and fluent in the composition process. This fluency results from an increasing internal representation of sentence structure, and this awareness can be capitalized on in working with oral language. In time, the complexity of both modes can increase steadily.

This overview of the use of picture sentences, using the Fokes Sentence Builder, illustrates one of the ways in which the Fitzgerald Key program has been adapted to those who are not hearing impaired.

ADAPTATION OF A STANDARD KEY

Another frequently used method is to modify or adapt direct writing in a notebook or chalkboard key. In contrast to the use of picture sentences, this adaptation makes use of a Fitzgerald Key on notebook paper. The key may or may not have components as in the original program. Some professionals have changed the wording slightly, for example, adding an Is Doing column in place of the = (verb) symbol.

Few professionals are using Fitzgerald's geometric symbol system with the language and learning impaired. Rarely is a traditional grammar approach ever involved for this population. The use of symbols that represent parts of speech reflects a traditional grammar approach. These children are having significant difficulty with language in its standard form. One of their prime goals is the naturalness and communicative value of language. Segmenting sentences into their word classes by naming or using a symbol is unnatural and arbitrary.

However, the Fitzgerald Key without the symbols offers a way of categorizing sentence components by making maximum use of their meaning base in a sentence. Instead of the word noun, a Who or What will serve to relate directly to the meaning of the words in the class. These word headings complement the underlying intent and the use of the sentence in communicating information. Thus, the Fitzgerald Key is used with the language disordered and learning disabled populations but almost exclusively with the word headings and not with the symbols.

The Key on paper usually is paired with pictures or other media that are being used to stimulate sentence descriptions. This modified approach involves building sentences, from simple to more complex, on the modified Key, the sentences then being written in a notebook. Incorrect structures, as in the original program, are put back into the Key to be analyzed as to the error. The pupils practice with the modified Key until they are competent with certain structures, at which time they are given more complex structures. As more complex sentences are introduced, the students revert back to the Key until they achieve fluency. They then move on to other remedial activities. Whenever an error occurs, they are asked to analyze it with the modified Key, after which more drill in the Key follows.

SAMPLE THERAPY APPROACHES

As before, sample therapy approaches are presented next on the four types of writing disability behaviors in which written expressive therapy is warranted.

Type I children can begin with simple sentences using a complete modified Key, since they have adequate oral language and may generate informative sentences. Teaching at first may focus on letting the pupils practice using the Key categories. As time passes, more and different components of sentences as well as more complex ones can be introduced and practiced. A notebook is kept of sentences written in the Key. As mentioned earlier, errors are referred back to the Key for close inspection of what went wrong and how to correct it.

Syntactic errors and problems require an initial evaluation of precisely what errors are being made, followed by remediation focused on them. For example, errors in word order can be remediated by focusing attention on the order of the Key columns and headings. The children can be asked to look at a picture, compose a sentence orally, then place it in the modified Key in the order of the columns. With practice in generating sentences and putting them in the Key, the students will internalize the correct written order of words and phrases in sentences, and writing fluency will result. Similar activities can be conducted for other syntactic errors.

Type II children probably will only use the modified Key for the writing component, and possibly the reading component of therapy as well. These pupils will receive some form of oral language therapy and may learn to use the Key only in reference to written language. At first, the teacher may prepare sentences in the Key for the children to read. This introduces the students to the modified Key and makes its structure and use familiar. In time, the children may be asked to "read" a picture sentence or repeat a sentence just used in oral language therapy and put it in the Fitzgerald Key. The first sentences will be simple, followed in time by increasing complexity. A structure worked on in oral language therapy can be put in writing in the Key. A notebook can be compiled and reread frequently. In time, the activities in the other language modes may be interfaced more often with the writing component.

If the children's thread of disability through the various modes is syntactic, all four modes can be combined more easily. In the case of irregular past tense verbs, the correct words can be used in sentences orally, then in writing. A series of past tense sentences can be read, then written from memory; a series of past tense sentences can be heard, repeated orally, then written. The syntax problem is attacked from all sides.

Type III children will spend time in reading remediation above and beyond the writing program. However, beginning with simple sentences, these pupils gradually will attain familiarity with the Fitzgerald Key, work will increase in complexity, and errors in writing will be analyzed within the structure of the Key. Syntactic errors can be addressed in reading and writing in the Key. To use the same example of irregular past tense verb use, these children can read a series of sentences in the past tense (some of the sentences being wrong) and can be asked to find the erroneous sentences. Each error sentence is written in the modified Key and corrected. The teacher also can say a past tense verb, and the children must use it in a sentence in the Key. As always, the students keep notebooks, with correct sentences of a variety of types being recorded, read, and reread at later dates.

Type IV children again will evidence different needs. Those who require only oral language therapy should receive remediation in that one mode. Those who may benefit from a dual approach can learn to write within a modified Key. Beginning with subject-verb sentences, the students look at a picture, the teacher says the sentence and writes it in the Key, and the children copy it under the instructor's model. Work continues in this way until the pupils can copy ten different sentences consistently correctly. Then the teacher's model is withdrawn and the children must write the sentences from dictation. Later still, they are expected to look at a picture and write the sentence that describes it. From this base, work continues to expand the vocabulary and sentence complexity. As in the previous discussion of Type IV children, the fluency of sentence generation in the written mode may in time transfer into the oral mode, based on an ever-expanding awareness of sentence structure and production.

Inherent in both of the modifications discussed—the picture sentence approach or the modified Fitzgerald Key on paper—is the need for handwriting and spelling work to coincide with the communicative element. Depending on the severity of the problem, this remedial work will be either small or rather extensive in scope.

This overview of some of the considerations of therapy in use of modified versions of the Fitzgerald Key has been designed not to be extensive in scope but rather to illustrate some of the general methods of adaptation of the system to language and learning disordered populations. Every child is individual, with specific needs that must be met appropriately. Because of this, guidelines for modifications must be general.

EVALUATION OF THE FITZGERALD KEY

The Fitzgerald Key program as used with the hearing impaired is a proven analytical method of written language development and expansion. The method is well organized and provides the visual cues necessary to learn the structure of sentences in the English language. Fitzgerald carefully outlines the sequence of instruction, from initial work in the Who and What columns to the order of verb use and writing activities such as letters and notes. Her approach utilizes seven symbols to indicate special word classes, and while this may not be helpful for language and learning disabled children, it is reported to be successful with the hearing impaired.

Overall, the Key system is excellent in providing a framework for the practice of correct syntactic structures in written expression. It is clear, simple, lends itself to everything from simple to complex sentences, and can be used by children independently or with guidance. It allows for analysis of error structures as well as manipulation of similar, but slightly altered, ways of communicating a certain message.

Perhaps the only element of concern to these authors is the wide range of rules that the children are required to learn and apply in the original Fitzgerald Key program. Apparently, this rule network is successful with the hearing impaired but definitely would not be appropriate with the language and learning disabled. The use of geometric symbols and the work in learning grammatic rules are two of the original Key program components that almost always have been eliminated with the language and learning disabled. Both of these aspects of the program make the language learning task unduly complex for this population. These children have demonstrated a deficit of some type or degree in language learning via the conventional route. They require alternate means of acquiring communicative competency, and second symbol systems, such as the geometric forms or rule studying, are far too complex and abstract.

Fitzgerald's suggestion in terms of practicing a variety of writing tasks— letters, notes, telegrams, reports, news bulletins—is an excellent component for hearing impaired and other handicapped populations. In fact, it is appropriate for regular education students.

Overall, the Fitzgerald Key program is of great value to the hearing impaired and has proved an excellent program from which to pull, adapt, or modify components for the language and learning impaired.

In terms of writing, both of these modifications, and others like them, represent informal techniques and approaches and not complete writing programs per se. In Chapter 4, another adaptation of the Fitzgerald Key—the Phelps Sentence Guide Program—is presented. However, that modification is a complete program and focuses exclusively on the written expressive mode.

BIBLIOGRAPHY

Fitzgerald, E. *Straight language for the deaf*. Washington, D.C.: The Volta Bureau, 1966.

Fokes, J. *Fokes sentence builder*. New York: Teaching Resources, 1976.

Johnson, D., & Myklebust, H.R. *Learning disabilities: Educational principles & practices*. New York: Grune & Stratton, Inc., 1967.

Moores, D. *Educating the deaf: Psychology, principles, and practices*. Boston: Houghton Mifflin Company, 1978.

Myklebust, H.R. *The psychology of deafness*. New York: Grune & Stratton, Inc. 1960.

_____. *Development and disorders of written language, Vol. II: Studies of normal and exceptional children*. New York: Grune & Stratton, Inc., 1973.

Nelson, M. The evolutionary process of teaching language to the deaf. *American Annals of the Deaf*. 1949, *95*, 230-294, 354-396, 491-511.

Pugh, B. *Steps in language development*. Washington, D.C.: The Volta Bureau, 1947.

Chapter 2

Sentences and Other Systems

Sentences and Other Systems (Blackwell, Engen, Fischgrund, & Zarca-doolas, 1978) is a total language curriculum for hearing impaired children from preschool through high school age. It provides language instruction in oral receptive, oral expressive, written receptive, and written expressive language modes. Sentences and Other Systems has replaced the Fitzgerald Key in many educational facilities, and its popularity and use appear to be expanding to populations other than the hearing impaired. The inclusion of Sentences and Other Systems in this text is based on two facts: (1) it encompasses a well-defined written expressive component in the total program and (2) it is increasingly "being discovered" and used with language delayed, language disordered, and learning disabled children.

The writing portion of the method has proved itself quite appropriate for use with the language and learning disabled, even without the rest of the program's being used in conjunction with the written expression instruction. Thus, Sentences and Other Systems represents a significant resource for the remediation of written language, as well as other language modes, in widely varied populations.

Since Sentences and Other Systems addresses preschool through high school age children, and since the writing portion can be "borrowed" at any point in this continuum, the entire program in terms of written expression is described here as it was designed originally. From this base, there follows a discussion and examples of ways in which it can be adapted for use with nonhearing impaired populations.

RATIONALE FOR THE PROGRAM

Sentences and Other Systems was developed as an alternative to the Fitzgerald Key, which was evaluated as not being totally effective in facilitating children's internalization of the variety of syntactic and morphological rules of the language. Based on their experience in working with the Fitzgerald Key, Blackwell et al. observed that even after achieving some success with the Key, the oral language of many of the children still was marked by syntactic errors. The argument seems to revolve around the fact that the drills with the Key produced results, but mainly in situations in which it was being used at the time; carryover was not complete, and spontaneous use of correct syntactic structures often was missing or inconsistent.

A Complete Sentence Approach

In addition to breaking away from the Fitzgerald Key, Sentences and Other Systems represents the rejection of another typical component of curriculum for the hearing impaired: the initial teaching of vocabulary in isolation according to a variety of categories. After this initial vocabulary instruction in isolated units, the words are combined and built into sentences, usually simple and direct rather than complex constructs, with indirect as well as direct meanings. A system that teaches initial vocabulary in arbitrarily discrete blocks does not provide for the necessary emphasis on word relationships or the ways in which total meanings change based on the way words are positioned in a phrase or sentence.

In addition, focusing on only simple, direct sentences provides no direction and practice in understanding implied utterances and offers no experience with complex direct utterances. Since much of oral communication relies on pragmatic linguistic awareness, a critical component of the communicative process is ignored.

Sentences and Other Systems begins the language instruction process with complete sentences, allowing syntactic and semantic aspects to be recognized, manipulated, and practiced. Thus, it shifts emphasis from teaching vocabulary independently and then in sentences, to starting with words and sentences as they relate to each other and to other sentences. This approach appears to be sound in view of the fact that the meanings of words vary according to their use in sentences and their relationship to others in the sentence. A method that revolves around complete sentences rather than single words is more reflective of language as it is used naturally.

Applying Transformational Grammar

Sentences and Other Systems uses a transformational grammar base (Chomsky, 1965) for building the complete language program. This base refers to an explanation of language ability in which the underlying intent or meaning (deep structure) is transformed according to specific rules to become the surface utterance (surface structure). Although not intended or designed to provide a basis for teaching or remediation, transformational grammar is judged by Blackwell et al. to be an appropriate and advantageous foundation for their language program. As such, Sentences and Other Systems is derived from this particular interpretation and practical application of transformational grammar theory.

The program emphasizes teaching deep structure and surface structure sentence functions in order to address the frequent observation that hearing impaired children rely heavily on surface structure in interpreting communication. Because of the complexity inherent in indirect speech, these children may not be aware of the cues—both contextual and linguistic—that must be relied on in interpreting communication accurately. Blackwell et al. reason that if attention is focused on deep structure analysis, meaning will not be lost or confused.

There are a number of serious problems with this aspect of the Sentences and Other Systems rationale:

1. As Blackwell et al. themselves note in their book, transformational grammar is not designed to lead to an instructional program of any kind. Transformational grammar is an attempt to explain language, an effort to design a system that accounts accurately for the generation of all possible good sentences and eliminates inappropriate ones. It is purely a system of describing language, not a base for an instructional program.
2. Words such as "deep structure" and "surface structure" are merely descriptors or constructs in transformational grammar; they do not have "thing" value and it is inaccurate, or at best difficult, to support the ability of an instructional program to "teach" deep structure and surface structure.
3. Blackwell et al. assume that if complex sentences are built of kernel sentences, then instruction should teach the latter directly so that children will have the tools to construct complex sentences. While there may be some truth to this assumption (or at the very least it may be as workable an approach as many others), this position is not an aspect of transformational grammar, since the theory does not prescribe instruction.

In summary, Blackwell et al. have devised their own method of attempting to apply a transformational grammar structure to a practical setting. A claim that this is a transformational grammar program is erroneous, since that method does not and is not intended to prescribe instruction. Attempts to teach constructs such as deep structure also are inappropriate. While it is an excellent goal to teach hearing impaired children to seek indirect and subtle meanings in communication, it would appear better to state this objective without reference to labels that clearly are linked to a system of theoretical constructs that are not intended for such a purpose and may be misleading.

Applying Bruner's Theories of Instruction

In addition to transformational grammar, Blackwell et al. also draw heavily from the learning theories of Jerome Bruner (1966). These theories, which serve to direct the content and structure of Sentences and Other Systems, are described briefly so that the rationale for the methodology will be clear when the actual program is discussed.

As children grow and mature they interact with their surroundings; this serves as the basis of their learning and knowledge of the world. Their interaction with the world can be represented in their mental schemata in a number of ways. Bruner proposes three systems for the representation of this range of experiences:

1. There are enactive representations, which relate to actions and direct experimentation with the world. Piagetian psychologists have provided a large body of data supporting children's actions based on accumulation of knowledge. During the sensorimotor period, for example, infants learn how to anticipate the different ways in which objects of different weight will fall to the ground when dropped. They learn this by acting directly on a variety of objects—they drop light and heavy objects and somewhere along the line make some conclusions about the speed at which they reach the ground. Thus, they use an "action template" to represent certain experiences in their mental schemata of the surrounding world.
2. There is iconic representation, which refers to the images recorded in the brain after detection by perceptual processes. For example, after children view an object or scene, their precise record of the event can take the form of a mental photograph. The entire scene is represented by an image that corresponds to the original perception.
3. There is symbolic representation, which refers to the way language serves to order, categorize, and interrelate experience. The wide range of experiences can be indexed and filed, using a variety of interrelated headings, similarities, and contrasts as cross-references. Enactive and

iconic experiences are built solidly on a perceptual base, and as such are limited to what is or has been experienced; new information can be anticipated, but on the basis of experiences with the same or similar actions or perceptions. Symbolic representation, on the other hand, allows for more efficient and wide-ranging manipulation of experience. An array of data can be classified, recalled, and generalized in a more thorough and in-depth analysis. It allows more precise generalization and investigation into the realm of experiences not directly enjoyed or into experiential probabilities.

Sentences and Other Systems is designed to tie Bruner's work to classroom instruction, making enactive representation possible by providing action-based learning, iconic representation possible by utilizing time to draw and represent an experience pictorially, and symbolic representation possible by composing oral or written descriptions.

For example, the three types of experiential representation can be applied in a classroom situation on the topic of transportation. The children actually could ride in a car, truck, and bus, and on a bicycle, wagon, and motorcycle. They then could draw pictures of their experiences. Finally, they could tell stories to their classmates, write stories or letters, or dictate a story for the teacher to write. Thus, all three representational systems could be used to root the experience of street transportation firmly into the students' mental schemata.

Participatory Learning Experience

With this instructional system, the pupils participate in the learning experience and have all their information storage systems activated. They are not merely fed a series of facts and descriptions that must be learned by rote but may or may not be meaningful. The children can analyze, store, generalize, categorize, and evaluate information according to three representational systems. The result is a teaching program that uses all avenues of input, mental ordering, evaluation of interrelationships, and assessment of accuracy of information.

Such an organization of learning experiences allows for a broad and in-depth knowledge base from which to draw when communicating. Such a system also has a clear emphasis on encoding knowledge in symbolic form and transmitting it to an audience. From the point of view of writing, the children soon become comfortable with trying to represent experience in written form and to entertain or inform an audience.

The final aspect of Bruner's learning theory utilized in Sentences and Other Systems is the notion of a spiral curriculum. Rather than building a curriculum in a series of discrete units, the range of information in all levels of the hierarchy is presented at all times. In other words, whatever is considered to be a valid component of a curriculum is taught in some form at the very beginning of the school experience. This component may be extremely simplified or rudimentary at first, but the introduction has been made and can be built on further in future years. To focus on the element of writing, the preschooler can be introduced to the use of pencil and paper to scribble, later to draw and copy letters or observe a teacher writing and rereading a message, still later to write words or short sentences, and so forth until the level of writing content and sense of audience is reached.

The manner in which language must be taught to the hearing impaired is different from that for normal hearing individuals. Children who hear normally can be assumed in most cases to begin school with the oral receptive and expressive modes operational and developed. On this well-developed oral language base, instruction can be directed toward building efficiency with the written language system. Hearing impaired children, however, may have deficits in the oral language system, which thus may not be developed well enough to serve as a basis on which to build the written language system. For normal hearing children, school revolves around further expansion of oral language and instruction and expansion in the written language mode. Hearing impaired children cannot afford to wait until their oral language system is fully operational; instead, they must have instruction in the oral and written modes simultaneously. Thus, the teacher must focus on the oral language acquisition process itself as well as on other activities appropriate to compensate for the hearing sensory deprivation.

Oral language, reading, and writing all are critical components of the total language and communicative process; hence, they must be key components of the curriculum. Blackwell et al. state that "Writing is a very special type of production that is integrally related to progress in language and reading. The writing component, in turn, has its own internal organization and parameters that are also developmental in nature" (1978, p. 25). Since all the language modes are interrelated, curriculum can integrate them and use them to support each other where appropriate.

Sentences and Other Systems is a total curriculum, with oral language and reading components that are described clearly and that occupy major positions in the program. However, the focus of this book is on writing and the various methodologies of teaching and remediating written language, so it targets only the writing component of the Blackwell et al. program. The discussion of this program here should in no way whatsoever be construed to be an adequate substitute for studying the original. This text is designed to survey only existing written language remediation programs.

Writing's Three Overlapping, Interrelated Planes

Blackwell et al. note that teachers everywhere are extremely concerned about their students' writing skills, yet have little relevant research and data to study and use to devise new plans. The approach to writing in Sentences and Other Systems is built on three interrelated, nonhierarchical, overlapping planes:

1. The linguistic plane refers to the actual mapping or plotting of structures used orally onto their corresponding written representation.
2. The compositional plane refers to children's abilities in organizing and ordering their written language in terms of cognitive and semantic complexity.
3. The functional plane refers to the actual functional differences between oral or manual language and written language. Presumably this plane would encompass developing a sense of audience in writing.

In terms of the linguistic plane, the acquisition of writing, though occurring later in time, may mirror the acquisition or oral language closely. This statement remains to be proved by future research on writing acquisition; however, Blackwell et al. suggest a developmental progression for writing. In analyzing their outline of the progression of this development, it became tempting to correspond this writing outline with what is known about oral language development. The result is as follows:

- Early scribbling may be equivalent to early infant vocalizing.

- Close approximations of letters when scribbling may be equivalent to babbling.

- An ability to copy a written model and use spontaneous writing may be equivalent to copying vocal models and using some words spontaneously.

- Spontaneous and correct or at least recognizable writing may be equivalent to oral use of words and two- and three-word sentences.

- Writing of short, simple sentences may be equivalent to oral use of simple sentences.

- The generation and writing of complex sentences may be equivalent to the oral use of complex sentence structures.

In reference to the compositional plane, the suggested progression of skills is said to move from writing one word or sentence to go with a picture, to writing two to five sentences that are related but may not be ordered, to two to five sentences that are related and ordered, and finally to writing two to five paragraphs that are related but not ordered and the same number of paragraphs that are related and ordered. As to the functional plane, Blackwell et al. give no hypothesis or observational data to describe the development of a sense of audience in children.

SENTENCES AND OTHER SYSTEMS METHODOLOGY

The Preschool and Kindergarten Level

At the preschool and kindergarten level, children are exposed to a wide range of experiences to enhance self-concept, social skills, and knowledge of the world. They also are exposed to symbolic formulation of simple sentences to describe these experiences, with an emphasis on subject-verb-object orderings and the three sentence types: declarative, interrogative, and imperative. In addition, a number of language forms are introduced, such as real events, poems, fairy tales, and rhymes, and some reading readiness work (for example, sound-symbol association practice) takes place.

The key component of instruction at this early stage is simply to build a strong and rich network of world and language experiences. The mental ordering and classifying of these experiences is increased until it can service children as they move into more complex cognitive and language areas.

For many preschoolers and kindergarteners, going to school represents the first experience they have ever had with attempting to comprehend the printed word. The function of writing as a communicative mode can be illustrated in many ways. One is the experience story approach, in which children dictate a story to the teacher. The teacher writes the story down exactly as the children tell it and they then read it together. The children can immediately see the relationship between what they just said and what the teacher wrote. Thus, they begin to appreciate the value of written communication. This is facilitated when the teacher can read the story at a later date, providing a lesson on the permanence of writing and its role as a recordkeeper.

Blackwell et al. (1978) advocate using printed material around the classroom. This can emphasize the value of writing to provide information. The teacher writes down who the morning helpers are or what the morning duties are. The function of writing as a provider of information and preserver of what actually was said is reinforced.

So far, the activities revolving around writing have focused on its role as a means of self-expression, pleasure, and of giving and recording instructions. These functions are reinforced throughout the reading system, since the reading of a fairy tale can be contrasted with the reading of an assignment. Thus, the pupils not only learn that written language serves a variety of functions but also get practice in analyzing the functions used in particular stories and paragraphs. An additional insight provided is the equivalence between the various communicative modes. There is a speaker and a listener, and the child can be either one. There is a person who writes something and a person who reads it, and again the child can play either role.

Blackwell et al. note that "preschool children start to manipulate letters, scribble, copy their names and perform other writing tasks at about the same time that they are first really beginning to acquire language in an organized way" (p. 37).

Writing as a communicative mode can be highlighted by giving each child an individual mailbox and allowing the pupils to scribble letters to each other and to copy their names or other words and "mail" the message to each other. Having a mailbox and promoting interest in scribbling and copying written models make it possible to provide a pleasant atmosphere in which to learn the communicative function of written expressive language. The children also can be encouraged to scribble a whole story and "read" it to the teacher. If time is set aside every day for the children to write their thoughts, letters, or stories, the act of writing assumes a natural and important role in their school day.

The point is that active writing, even if it is unintelligible, is encouraged since the children think they really are communicating, trying to express themselves, and being meaningful in their writing. They are attempting to order their thoughts on paper, a good practice for future intelligible writing. All in all, the instruction at this point is more a function of reinforcement for any written communication and the creation of a positive mental set toward writing.

Early Elementary School Level

The next level in the program begins after kindergarten and revolves around five basic sentence patterns to structure language at the simple sentence level. As discussed earlier, transformational grammar theory is the foundation of Sentences and Other Systems. One of the core aspects of transformational grammar is the isolation of basic, kernel sentences from which other more complex sentences can be constructed through any of a number of transformational rules. Kernel sentences do not have complex noun and verb clauses but do contain the main parts of speech; these simple sentences are conjoined with the transformational rules to produce more elaborate sentences. Examples of the five basic sentence patterns are given in Exhibit 2-1.

The patterns are taught all at once, not one at a time. They are not purposely taught as a slot-filling system, where words are just inserted mechanically into slots, but rather as a way to learn the most basic of grammatical structures and relationships. The argument is that if hearing impaired children can master these five kernel sentences, they then can be taught to

Exhibit 2-1   Examples of the Five Basic Kernel Sentences

The man jumped.
(Subject + Verb)
The man threw a football.
(Subject + Verb + Object)
The girl is sunburned.
(Subject + State of Being or Linking Verb + Adjective)
The girl was a pianist.
(Subject + State of Being or Linking Verb + Predicate Noun)
The queen is in the castle.
(Subject + State of Being or Linking Verb + Adverb)

use transformational rules to conjoin, embed, and otherwise manipulate these pattern sentences linguistically to produce more complex sentences.

The five basic patterns are a way of providing children with the means for expressing themselves, after which they can learn to communicate in more complex structures. The five kernel sentences, however, allow for efficient communication early in the language learning program. Theoretically, by practicing these five, both orally and in writing, the children learn to internalize the sentences themselves and the rules become automatic. In composing sentences, the children may write one pattern, then substitute other words to make different sentences. This may be followed by pictures drawn to illustrate how meaning has changed when the words in the sentence change. Different patterns can be written and contrasted in terms of how their meanings vary and how the words relate to each other in different ways. For example, "The girl is pretty" has an adjectival pattern, "The girl is sad" an adverbial pattern. Work continues with such activities as experience stories, retelling stories heard in class, or composing sentences to describe pictures. When children are comfortable writing basic sentences to express themselves, progress continues to a more traditional grammar approach.

Middle Elementary School Level

At around 7 years of age, children begin sentence analysis work in the Sentences and Other Systems program. This work is an effort to focus on metalinguistic development—the ability to objectify the act of communication. Normal children develop this ability orally during the preschool and early elementary years (Bates, 1976), but the hearing impaired need instruction both orally and in writing. By learning to analyze a sentence into its linguistic units, that is, by increasing metalinguistic perception, hearing impaired students can "look at language they understand conceptually from a strictly linguistic point of view" (Blackwell et al., 1978, p. 74).

To meet this goal, instruction is focused on labeling the units that make up the five basic sentences—for example, the subject, verb, predicate noun, adjective, or adverb. Sentences are presented and the children are guided in labeling the components. Practice begins with a few components, such as subject and verb, and expands to labeling more and more elements. The pupils are guided to recognize that even though sentences have different lengths, a core of basic components remains constant. By observing these, the children are led to an internal awareness of the elements of a correct, well-developed sentence as opposed to a poorly developed one. This internal awareness is called upon to provide a guide to the students' structuring and composing written sentences.

Reading and writing also are studied in terms of the writer's intent and the listener's discovering that intent so as to understand the meaning and purpose of the message. Linguistic information within a text is combined with extratextual material to reveal the writer's intent. This analysis of the written word is a precursor to the children's learning to write with a particular "slant" or purpose. They must learn to receptively analyze the various ways in which a particular perspective can be composed, after which they can learn to write according to various intents and motives.

Experience stories still are used to demonstrate and provide practice in reading and in recording events in written form. Topic-comment sentences are prepared on strips of paper for the children to read and use as a guide in writing sentences.

Late Elementary School Level

After the pupils master the five basic sentence patterns, they progress to more and more complex language, leading to increased demands on reading and writing. For example, attention is focused on:

- Relativization: "She was a woman who loved to play in tennis matches."

- Use of conjunctions: "He was laughing and singing happily."

- Use of passive voice: "The car was bumped by a truck."

- Use of adverbial movement: "Before he went to bed, he brushed his teeth," instead of "He brushed his teeth before he went to bed."

The children are guided in their practice of these complex examples both by reading drills and by composing and writing sentences.

Time is set aside at this point for chart and poster writing, "private" writing for personal expression of thoughts and ideas, dictation of letters and stories to the teacher, and letter or story writing to one particular teacher. Group discussion centers on reading paragraphs, stories, or other works and comparing and contrasting the themes.

Adolescent Level

At the adolescent level, the students are introduced to tree diagraming, with considerable practice devoted to this ability. The meaning of the sentence, not just the act of tree diagraming, is emphasized. A variety of reading passages is used to analyze idiomatic and stylized literary forms. Blackwell et al. note that hearing impaired children often limit themselves in their writing to "straightforward first or third person voiceless narration" (p. 118). For these students, "a good story or poem exists as an isolated entity, largely incapable of replication in their world and hence not truly an object of vicarious appreciation" (p. 118).

Because of this serious limitation, instruction must focus on teaching the narrative voice. Questioning is used to direct the children's attention to such factors as who is speaking, who is the speaker's intended audience, or what is the speaker's viewpoint and philosophy. Literary forms such as tongue-in-cheek humor, cynicism, propaganda, or fantasy are used for purposes of analysis through comparison and contrast.

Diary and journal writing are used to practice "relating dialogue to narrative discourse" and "speaker/hearer relationships" (p. 119). In journals and diaries, students can record important experiences, feelings, or thoughts. It takes much guidance and encouragement on the part of the teacher, and much practice on the part of the children, before they can achieve fluency in journal writing. Allowing the children to read others' well-done journal, story, or other material serves as a model of the type of writing to be achieved. The students then can use the model as a guide for their own stories. Practice in analyzing and paraphrasing what someone else has written in a journal or story can be beneficial. As the pupils paraphrase, they are forced to recognize the writer's intent, or at least their interpretation of the intent, and reword the passage according to the perceived meaning. Often the teacher will need to choose a topic for the day's journal entry and in so doing can focus more attention on a particular narrative voice.

To practice identifying another writer's intent, the children can trade stories, decide their underlying purpose, and rewrite them. The students also can be guided in reading one story and rewriting it in a different narrative voice or with a different intent, thus improving their understanding of how an author's style and intent interact. One method Blackwell et al. suggest for teaching the use of different narrative voices is to retell and rewrite a story through another character's eyes. This is built on earlier practice in role playing and in answering open-ended questions about stories, such as: "What would you do if you were X?" or "What would have happened if X had not done Y?"

By rewriting a story from a different character's perspective, the students are led to perceive how individuals interface and build from one another. They also can be taught to create a mental snapshot and describe the picture in dialogue or according to the motivation behind the action in the picture. The emphasis is not on how much is written, but rather on its quality.

Reading material and written work are used to practice use of complementization: "The girl told her mother who she was;" nominalization: "Dropping the cake on the floor completed the bad day;" and deletion: "He knew that it was hot" becomes "He knew it was hot."

Finally, at the high school level Blackwell et al. suggest that concepts, vocabulary, reading, and writing be approached and expanded through an interdisciplinary faculty team effort. Instruction in writing continues along with the earlier work on style, narrative voice, and efficient communication of intended meaning.

NONHEARING IMPAIRED POPULATIONS

It is impossible to describe every way in which Sentences and Other Systems has been or could be used with children who have language and learning problems. This impossibility exists because children who are so labeled simply cannot be lumped into a group and spoken of in unified terms. Much of the criticism of research in language and learning disorders has centered on this issue of using labeled groups of children to evaluate a variety of hypotheses. One research study after another has attempted to compare groups of normal children with those of disordered children. Such data, providing the grouping procedures were acceptable, may be useful in showing group trends but are relatively meaningless for trying to extrapolate or explain the information in terms of individual children.

Each disordered child is different from every other and exhibits an individual and distinct profile on a differential diagnosis. It follows that all language and learning disordered children will need a remedial program tailored to their own particular needs and based on their own particular strengths, weaknesses, and learning style. Any attempt to explain how Sentences and Other Systems has been used with such children of necessity must be an overview or generalization, followed by some examples.

Even with such limitations, however, the manner in which aspects of the program have been tailored to the language and learning disordered populations is interesting. In remedial work with these children, professionals time after time have elected to borrow all or part of some other regular or special education program and adapt it to their own approach to therapy. This comment by no means is meant as criticism. Rather, this borrowing and adaptation has produced some of the finest and most effective eclectic programs available. It is only natural to search for new and better ideas in helping children, so borrowing from other programs and compiling an eclectic approach is to be encouraged.

As Sentences and Other Systems is a recent program, professionals working with learning disabled, language delayed, or language disordered children only now are focusing their attention on it, borrowing and adapting its components. In reference to children with language delay or severe language disorder, professionals probably will not address the writing component at all until the oral language difficulty is greatly reduced. Since this book focuses only on writing programs, it does not discuss the adaptations of the oral language aspects of Sentences and Other Systems to more severely disabled populations. Adaptations relevant to this text involve learning disabled and language disordered children who may or may not have mild or mild-moderate oral language problems but who do have significant written language difficulties.

It is critical to discuss the issue of how far to take oral language therapy. Some professionals stress continuing therapy until the children perform within normal ranges, then progressing to written language remediation. The authors of this book do not agree with this viewpoint. Obviously a severe oral language disorder would preclude instruction in written language; however, with mild or mild-moderate oral problems, the written can be interfaced very effectively with the oral language therapy. In fact, both modes can be mutually reinforcing, and equivalent therapy goals can be emphasized in a number of communicative modes. For example, if pupils are having significant difficulty with irregular past tense verbs, work can focus on improving:

1. oral language through the use of picture sentence drills or interactive story teaching
2. written receptive language through reading a series of past tense carrier sentences with the key word changed in each: "Yesterday the boy _____."
3. written expressive language through copying carrier sentences and choosing one of five irregular past tense verbs to best complete the sentence and describe a certain picture

If carefully planned, therapy can be designed to focus on oral and written language simultaneously. This approach provides advances in several modes rather than waiting for oral language to be fixed and postponing the written mode even though it could have been addressed.

With this multimodal remedial rationale in mind, parts of Sentences and Other Systems from early elementary to adolescent levels can be borrowed, depending on the needs of the children. Of course, a thorough understanding of the program is required before any borrowing can occur. Three key aspects of Sentences and Other Systems that have been used with language disordered and learning disabled children are discussed here: (1) the teaching of the five basic sentence patterns, (2) the expansion of these kernel sentences into more and more complex structures, and (3) the program's approach to reaching the analysis of written intent, style, and narrative voice. Each of these aspects of the program, as used with the language disordered and learning disabled populations, has been altered and modified in any number of ways, as is analyzed next.

Modifications of the Five Basic Sentence Patterns

Instruction in use of the five basic sentence patterns is amenable to both oral and written language remediation with children who have language and learning difficulties. The rationale for using a kernel sentence approach as a basis for language teaching is the same as in the original Sentences and Other Systems program. The assumption is that sentences are composed of kernel elements that, when mastered, are used to build more complex structures. When children have evidenced oral or written language problems, remediation can follow the steps of normal acquisition. In writing, the children can practice the five basic sentence patterns by methods such as those in Exhibit 2-2.

The goal is to make the children comfortable and at ease in communicating in writing at the kernel sentence level. Should the pupils generate a more complex sentence, however, they are reinforced and encouraged to continue trying to use the most descriptive sentences possible. The point at the kernel sentence level is to reduce the complexity of the writing task, allow the pupils to experience and appreciate correct sentences, and develop a foundation on which to build more complex sentences. If they have difficulty with irregular past tense verbs or some other language structure, these can be highlighted in written as well as oral language. As in the Sentences and Other Systems program, oral practice also is used to precede sentences written on paper. That is, the children produce and compose a descriptive sentence orally, then write it on paper.

Modifications Involving Complex Sentences

As children demonstrate increasing success in using kernel sentences to describe pictures or retell stories, they are introduced to combining and

Exhibit 2-2   Suggestions for Adapting Sentences and Other Systems to Learning Disabled Populations

1. Copying a pattern from the teacher's model.
2. Copying a pattern and varying a key element to make a series of sentences based on the one pattern:

   The man jumped.   NP + VP
   The woman jumped.
   The dog jumped.
   THe fireman jumped.
   The cowboy jumped.
   The astronaut jumped.
   The cow jumped.

   The man threw the football.
   The girl threw the football.   NP + VP + NP
   The clown threw the football.
   The cowboy threw the football.
   The girl scout threw the football.

3. Looking at a picture, then an incomplete sentence pattern, then filling in the blank with a word that completes the sentence and correctly describes the picture:

   The woman carried a _____ .
   The captain turned the big _____ .
   The _____ rode a big horse.
   The clown _____ the ball.

4. Looking at two patterns and contrasting the meaning of each:

   The girl is pretty.
   The girl is sad.

embedding kernel sentences in a variety of ways to produce complex sentences. Thus, they receive instruction and practice in the use of conjunctions, adverbial movement, complements, and relative clauses. These elements can be taught by writing kernel sentences and "stretching them out" so that they include more information, or simply by encouraging oral discussion before writing and allowing the information that is to be communicated to be rehearsed, organized, and ordered mentally before the writing is done. A sentence combining approach (see Chapter 5) also has been used at this point with language disordered and learning disabled children. Thus, if they can learn to generate kernel sentences, they can proceed to combine these structures to produce more complex descriptive sentences.

Unlike the Sentence and Other Systems program, adaptations for language disordered and learning disabled children usually do not teach parts of speech by name, i.e., noun, verb, conjunction, adverb, adjective, and do not teach tree diagraming. This is not to say that it cannot or should not ever be done. There may well be some children who can do very well with sentence analysis of this sort. Typically, however, professionals have avoided such detail for a number of reasons:

1. Remediation is used to highlight the communicative nature of writing. The focus is on the meaning of the sentence and how it serves to communicate the author's intent. As such, the sentence is a whole and its parts are intimately combined and melded into a total, so it may not be appropriate with the language disordered and learning disabled populations to break the message back down into its component pieces.
2. Remediation is geared toward giving children a feel or intuition about correct and incorrect writing. By teaching sentence patterns, the actual labels are unnecessary. If the pupils are given appropriate instruction, they will internalize the consistencies among sentences according to meaning and function in the communicative act. They will indirectly learn the components of a sentence based on use and without the need to label them directly.
3. Language disordered and learning disabled children who have concommitant oral language problems already have demonstrated a linguistic deficiency. Somewhere in their language analysis or synthesis mechanism, they are not functioning adequately. Tree diagraming is a linguistic science. To require these children to step back and objectify language (decenter) by tree diagraming may be unreasonable. At the very least, it focuses attention away from the communicative function of language as a means of expression and generation and requires that it be analyzed and scrutinized in a scientific manner. Although it is a part of the Sentences and Other Systems program, a tree diagraming

component rarely is a standard part of a language curriculum for the language and learning impaired.

Modifications of Intent, Style, and Narrative Voice

The final aspect of the Sentences and Other Systems program to be described in its adaptation to language disordered and learning disabled children is the careful analysis of writing intent, style, and narrative voice. Although the meaning and comprehension of paragraphs and stories probably has always been a part of the curriculum for this population, the Blackwell et al. program offers a variety of helpful suggestions. Instruction is focused on deciding an author's purpose and intent in a written message. To do this effectively, the professional must provide the children with experience with a variety of types of writing such as humor, propaganda, straight biography, and fantasy. When the students can appreciate these forms of writing, they can attempt to mimic them by rewording them orally and in writing.

Just as in Sentences and Other Systems, journal writing is encouraged since it permits a number of extra learning experiences. Journal practice with first person narrative voice can illustrate the way in which this style differs from the third person. A journal permits special adventures or events to be recorded and relived at a later date or by another person. The pleasure of writing becomes a personal or shared experience. Practice is provided in fantasy writing, since journals and diaries dwell only on the past or the here and now. Fantasy writing projects to what might be possible and is stimulating to children's imaginations.

As in Sentences and Other Systems, children are provided with the experience of rewriting stories from a different character's perspective. This allows an in-depth analysis of point of view and intent in writing—"It may have seemed this way to X, but how would Y see and understand the problem?" In all these strategies is a core of identifying intent, style, and purpose. When reading a passage, the author's intent and purpose are investigated. When writing, the purpose and meaning of the written communication are isolated and used to order thought and develop the appropriate style.

These examples represent direct approaches of adapting Sentences and Other Systems to the language disordered and learning disabled populations. Obviously, creative professionals will adapt and borrow according to the individual children they service; however, these examples provide a general perspective on how parts of the program can be used with other than the hearing impaired.

EVALUATION OF REMEDIATION ASPECTS

The Sentences and Other Systems program represents a solid preschool through high school language curriculum for hearing impaired children and adolescents. Its writing component is designed to be comprehensive. However, the issue of transformational grammar as its core presents some difficulties. Since that element never was intended or designed to lend itself to instruction, the supposed transformational grammar base of the program actually is an attempt to devise a practical application of the theory. In that the instructional progression from simple kernel sentences to complex sentences is both logical and developmentally sound, the methodology appears to be appropriate.

The terminology, however, seems ill advised. If the notion of "teaching deep structure" can be avoided, the program can be said instead to focus on the meaning and intent—direct and indirect—of written language. The point is that reference to teaching theoretical constructs should be avoided.

In spite of these cautions, the route from simple sentence to complex sentence appears justified and has proved successful in terms of the effectiveness of Sentences and Other Systems. Hearing impaired, language delayed, and language disordered children need remedial attention to develop their first language, and this program appears to offer benefits in developing fluency in kernel sentences, followed by more and more complexity in manipulation of them. It is a matter of teaching the building blocks of a language, then the actual building.

The one problem with the kernel sentence approach comes in the writing mode with learning disabled children. In some pupils, oral language proficiency exceeds written language expression to some degree. To teach writing in short, simple sentences may be taking a step backward, since the children already may be using complex sentences orally. It may be better to order the oral sentences on paper than to require the five basic sentence patterns and then build complex sentences from that point. The goal may be to take the children's communicative intent and structure it, rather than go back to basic building blocks. As always with learning disabled children, however, there may be some who will benefit from a kernel sentence approach.

As noted, the Sentence and Other Systems program flows naturally from kernel to complex sentences. However, there is one caution. With language disordered and learning disabled children, the combining and embedding of kernel sentences into complex structures may be acquired more slowly than in the hearing impaired population. The hearing impaired have a sensory deprivation but in general can be assumed to learn language efficiently when they overcome or compensate for it. Language disordered and learning disabled children have demonstrated difficulties in the learning of language itself, so they may require a much longer time to master complex sentences.

The Blackwell et al. method provides a well-developed approach to teaching analysis and generation of a variety of narrative voices and styles. From the receptive stage of studying an author's writing to the expressive stage of producing a range of different styles, the program builds methodically. The benefit to all writing disabled populations is unquestionable.

The one aspect of the Sentences and Other Systems program that probably will not be adapted successfully with language disordered and learning disabled children is the sentence labeling and tree diagraming component. This approach still is used in many regular education classrooms and may be quite functional for those children and for the hearing impaired but may not be appropriate for those with language and learning difficulties. Those children need structure, but the question that arises is how effective is the act of labeling parts of speech in generating successful utterances?

Children with language difficulties need instruction in communication because they have a linguistic impairment. To require them to objectify language to the degree that they step back and analyze components (or for that matter remember or find meaning in the labels themselves) is quite questionable. Kernel sentences alone can provide an internal structure, complex sentences can be built on this base, and oral language proficiency can be used as a foundation for the writing mode. But labeling and tree diagraming may not be appropriate for this population.

Overall, Sentences and Other Systems represents a significant program for the hearing impaired and for children with language and learning difficulties. The merit of this approach already is becoming obvious to professionals around the country. It will be interesting to observe the increasing experimentation with this new approach.

BIBLIOGRAPHY

Bates, E. *Language and context: The acquisition of pragmatics.* New York: Academic Press, 1976.

Blackwell, P.M., Engen, E., Fischgrund, J.E., & Zarcadoolas, C. *Sentences and other systems: A language and learning curriculum for hearing impaired children.* Washington, D.C.: The Alexander Graham Bell Association for the Deaf, Inc., 1978.

Bruner, J. *Toward a theory of instruction.* Cambridge, Mass.: Harvard University Press, 1966.

Chomsky, N. *Aspects of the theory of syntax.* Cambridge, Mass.: MIT Press, 1965.

Chapter 3

The Myklebust System of Analyzing Language

The work of Helmer R. Myklebust has had significant influence on the field of language and learning disabilities. His system of organizing language modes into a developmental hierarchy has been widely accepted and applied as a basis and framework for differential diagnosis and remediation.

Although initially concerned with the total language system in his work with Doris Johnson (Johnson & Myklebust, 1967), in his most recent work (1973) Myklebust has focused more on the written expressive mode. His Picture Story Language Test (PSLT) (1965), described later in this chapter and in the evaluation unit in Chapter 11, has been well received by professionals and his remedial suggestions (1973) have had broad impact.

The approach does not constitute a set program but rather consists of a particular perspective or framework to use in the evaluation process, the interpretation of that analysis, and the planning and execution of remediation. Instead of prescribing precise procedures for the variety of written deficits, it describes the types of difficulties such children will experience and suggests kinds of activities and scope of remediation that may prove beneficial. A thorough knowledge of Myklebust's approach, coupled with clinical experience with language and learning disordered children, can result in the design of an effective instructional program. With further expansion and modification, the resultant program can be individualized for a particular child.

This chapter presents an overview of four aspects of the Myklebust system:

1. the rationale and underlying framework
2. the categorization of written expressive language disorder

3. the emphasis on the differential diagnosis
4. the suggestions for remediation

This is followed by a summary of Myklebust's research on incidence and type of writing difficulty in a variety of regular and special education populations.

RATIONALE AND UNDERLYING FRAMEWORK

Investigators have studied the two oral language modes and written receptive language for quite some time; however, little research has been done in the written expressive language mode, as noted in the Introduction to this book. Myklebust (1973) notes that the "study of the development and disorders of the written word in handicapped children has been neglected in special education" and that "even new and innovative programs incorporate little or no material on this facet of cognition and academic learning" (p. 55).

The result is that a large body of diagnostic and remedial information has accumulated for oral language and reading, but the instrumentation and programming for written expression have been scarce. School and clinical management of writing often has been haphazard, limited, or totally ignored. Fortunately, this state of affairs is changing because of the recognition of the need for more research and information on writing instruction and remediation. It was to meet this need that Myklebust began to study the written expressive aspect of language as it relates to children with language and learning difficulties.

The Three Types of Learning

The brain can be described as being composed of a number of semiautonomous systems, with learning taking place in three ways: through intraneurosensory, interneurosensory, or integrative processing and coding channels.

Intraneurosensory learning refers to what for the most part is occurring within a single sensory system—for example, a purely auditory learning experience. In fact, there may be little learning of this type since much of experience involves more than one sense. Interneurosensory learning refers to what occurs between and among sensory systems in an interrelated manner; for example, seeing and hearing a certain stimulus simultaneously will produce a two-faceted learning experience. Integrative learning refers to learning that results from the use of all sensory systems. Much of what is learned comes through the interneurosensory or integrative systems. In such learning, the brain receives the varied sensory inputs, integrates them, then formulates an appropriate output, if one is required. In other words, the brain decodes and encodes information. Language represents the result of all three types of learning, particularly the interneurosensory and integrative.

The Language Hierarchy

The hierarchical system of analyzing language, reviewed in the Introduction (Myklebust, 1960), consists of inner language, receptive, and expressive language. Inner language does not appear to be synonymous with the two others but rather precedes and focuses the development of other modes. It is the first language component to be acquired and is built on children's experiential base. That is, in manipulating objects, listening to their world, and other perceptual events, children pass through a variety of experiences. As they steadily build this knowledge of the world based on action and perception, they begin to represent the experience symbolically. They steadily develop a network of symbols, both verbal and nonverbal, whose meanings correspond with their world knowledge.

Language is a social event and the symbols the children build are unique. to their own personal experiences, yet equivalent enough to the community's definition so that these words can be used effectively for communicative purposes. In a position similar to Vygotsky's (1962), inner language can be defined as "the language with which one thinks" (p. 36). Children build an inner language system that represents experience symbolically, these words becoming the language of thought. Thus, the entire language system is based on experience with the world and the development of an inner language system.

Receptive oral language to some extent follows the acquisition of inner language and refers to the understanding or comprehension of language. It derives from inner language, since the children must discriminate, recall, retrieve, and temporally order what they hear and then associate it with their meaning base and knowledge of the world. If they lead to an interface and matching, they achieve meaningful comprehension; with a mismatch, their comprehension of auditory language is impaired. The acquisition of receptive oral language complements the ever-expanding inner language system, which in turn complements the increasing receptive oral language system. That is, the systems are mutually beneficial.

Expressive oral language follows the receptive oral developmentally. Comprehension for the most part precedes production in language acquisition. This is not to say that receptive oral language is developed completely before expressive oral language appears. Rather, comprehension appears first to some degree and continues to develop with production abilities. Logically, the reception of language would be a base for its expression, but there also is a mutually beneficial relationship between the two modes.

Receptive written language (reading) and expressive written language (writing) follow in order. Thus, in Myklebust's (1960) view, a base of experience leads to inner language, followed in order by receptive oral, expressive oral, receptive written, and expressive written language. Writing, then, can be viewed as the most complex mode of language.

A key aspect of this developmental hierarchy is that each of the progressively more difficult modes derives from its predecessor and paves the way for its own successor. In terms of written expression, a breakdown in the hierarchically lower modes will have some effect on writing proficiency.

When children enter school, it is assumed that they have a well-developed oral language system, both receptively and expressively. On this oral language base, the written language system will be built. As Mattingly (1972) describes it, the oral language system can be perceived of as a primary language loop onto which the secondary language loop (written language) is constructed. This relationship also is indicated in Exhibit 3-1. Receptive and expressive language in their primary form include listening and speaking behaviors—that is, auditory comprehension and oral production. The secondary system includes the skills of reading and writing.

In terms of Exhibit 3-1, and according to Myklebust's (1960) perspective, a problem in one or both of the oral modes (primary loop) may be the cause of children's reading or writing difficulties. More specifically, a disorder in receptive oral language (listening) probably would affect all of the three other modes in some way. A deficit in oral expressive language might or might not occur in conjunction with an oral receptive language disorder but would be expected to affect both receptive and expressive written language to some extent. In the same way, a written receptive language (reading) problem might or might not occur in conjunction with an oral receptive or expressive language problem but would be expected to affect written expression.

Written language expression, then, can be viewed as the highest form of language, built to some degree on competence in the other modes as well as the development of ability in the written mode itself. In other words, a written expressive language disorder may occur simultaneously with a breakdown in one or more of the other language modes or may signify a difficulty only in the written expressive element. Myklebust (1965) says that in reference to written expression, "not only is more intelligence required, but a higher degree of intersensory perception and facilitation are essential" (p. 4).

A REDESIGN OF JOHNSON'S AND MYKLEBUST'S SCHEMA

The authors of this text have elected to redesign Johnson's and Myklebust's (1967) stance as related to writing disorders. A disorder of written language may not be explained adequately as either (1) a breakdown somewhere in

Exhibit 3-1   Language Systems and Coding Processes

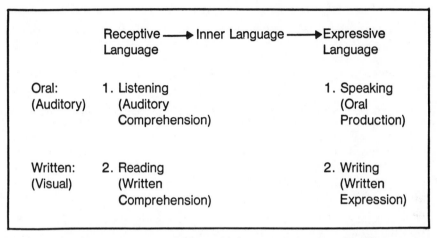

the language hierarchy below writing or (2) purely a disordered writing mode. Rather, writing may be said to encompass a redefinition of the previous requirements in auditory comprehension, speech, and reading. As illustrated in Exhibit 3 in the Introduction, writing involves different *kinds* of oral reception, oral expression, and written reception processes. The competency in these hierarchically lower modes is refashioned to reflect the demands of the writing task.

Hence, a writing disorder may reflect Johnson's and Myklebust's (1967) previously mentioned two explanations, but also can correspond to a breakdown in the way the hierarchically lower modes are redefined specifically for the writing task. Myklebust appears to have oversimplified the problem, for the difficulty may go far beyond his "either/or" explanation to a more subtle system of writing requirements and a totally new manner of using and integrating competency in the hierarchically lower language modes.

Prerequisites to Writing

Johnson and Myklebust (1967) have suggested that expressive written language has four basic prerequisites: auditory processing, visual processing, motor skills, and inner language. A number of skills have been identified as being key components of auditory processing:

- auditory memory: the ability to store auditory messages in appropriate form and retrieve and recall them when necessary

- syllabication: the ability to repeat words of more than one syllable in correct form

- syllable blending: the ability to listen to isolated syllables and pull them together into a word

- auditory discrimination: the ability to differentiate sounds and sound patterns

- following oral directions: the ability to listen to a series of directions and carry them out

- rhyming: the ability to take sound patterns and formulate rhyming words

- transduction of sensory information: the ability to transfer sensory information from one modality to another, such as identifying visual equivalents of an auditory message

The second prerequisite of written expressive language is visual processing. Its critical skills and abilities include the following:

- orientation and scanning: the ability to direct vision to a certain stimulus and attend selectively

- visual perception: the ability to discriminate between visual stimuli and to recognize and associate meaning with them

- visual memory: the ability to store and retrieve visual stimuli in correct form

- imagery: the ability to recall an experience with such perfection that a mental photograph actually is conjured up

The third prerequisite to written expressive language is adequate motor ability, including both gross and fine forms of motor coordination. Such skills as balance, handedness, laterality, directionality, or eye-hand coordination all have been found to be positively correlated with the reading and writing processes.

The final prerequisite Myklebust proposes for written language is adequate inner language processing. As discussed earlier, inner language represents the mental system of linguistic meaning associated with children's network of experiences with their world.

From Myklebust's underlying framework, it is an easy and logical step to the rationale of the system. Stated simply, the rationale is as follows: If children with problems can be evaluated in depth such that their ability in each language mode can be ascertained, the resulting language profile will provide the necessary information for the development of a remedial program.

In other words, an analysis of the integrity of a child's language system will identify the point at which a breakdown is occurring and therapy will need to be initiated at that point. The language profile, in a sense, categorizes or types the problem, after which further evaluation and remediation are appropriate.

WRITTEN EXPRESSIVE DISORDERS

As discussed earlier, Johnson and Myklebust (1967) divide the types of written expressive disorders into two fundamental groups: those related to problems in hierarchically lower language modes and those judged to be purely writing disabilities.

Relation to Disability in Other Language Modes

A problem in either oral language mode or in receptive written language may have a negative effect on writing. In terms of oral language disorders, the primary system of language learning and use is inefficient, implying that the secondary system—written language—is not soundly based on a well-functioning oral foundation and cannot be adequate. Whether the oral language problem is semantic, syntactic, or auditory perceptual, the result is a negative effect on the written language modes. A reading problem, in the face of an intact oral language system, also will impede writing proficiency since the receptive manipulation of visual language provides the base for the expressive.

Even more fundamental, a disordered inner language system will not order and code information appropriately. The result will be some degree of difficulty in all receptive and expressive language modes.

'Pure' Written Expression Disorders

In reference to learning difficulties of a "purely" written expressive nature, Myklebust describes three types: dysgraphia, revisualization problems, and difficulties in communicative formulation and syntax.

Dysgraphia refers to an impairment in which visual abilities and motor abilities by themselves are adequate but the integration of the two systems is deficient. Dysgraphic children cannot copy graphic symbols because they cannot remember the movements required to match the visual image.

Children with revisualization problems can copy a written model but cannot produce a written form spontaneously because they cannot recall the way a word should look. Both dysgraphia and revisualization involve beginning writing skills, illustrated by the prewriting component of the Total Writing Process Model (Exhibit 3 in the Introduction).

Children with problems in formulation and syntax can copy letters and spell words correctly but cannot generate appropriate sentences. Since they can perform beginning writing skills, their problem often is not observed until the middle elementary grades, after the writing basics have been introduced in the first and second grades. When they are expected to write paragraphs and stories, their abilities in writing break down significantly, and it is at that time that they usually are referred for remediation. Interestingly enough, if this formulation and syntax problem is purely in the written mode, these children will make writing errors that they do not make in their oral expressive language.

The most common errors by children in this population are "word omissions, distorted word order, incorrect verb and pronoun usage, incorrect word endings, and lack of punctuation" (Johnson & Myklebust, 1967, p. 229). As the research in oral language has shown, these are the very errors often noted in children with oral expressive language disorders. It is interesting that similar errors are observed in disorders of both expressive language modes.

Numerous programs already exist for children with dysgraphic and revisualization problems. The disorders of formulation and syntax, however, represent the crux of the difficulty for professionals. It is this aspect of writing remediation that has been largely ignored or avoided. The three components of the Total Writing Process Model and the resulting definition of the processes involved in efficient writing revolve around formulation and syntax, although the schema of language is changed from Myklebust's (1960) approach. In describing Myklebust's system of diagnosis and remediation, formulation and syntax are emphasized.

THE DIFFERENTIAL DIAGNOSIS

The differential diagnosis in language is geared toward investigating the integrity of the various modes so that remediation can be planned according to needs. The evaluation must be directed toward assessing the various systems semiautonomously and in a situation in which they all work together. In reference to written expression, the analysis must involve an investigation of the integrity of both oral modes and of the written receptive mode, in addition to a thorough evaluation of writing itself. Only in this way can the point of breakdown in the language hierarchy be identified. Thus, the differential diagnosis answers two general questions:

1. What is the child's ability in language modes that are hierarchically lower than written expression; that is, can the writing problem be linked to a more generalized language difficulty?

2. What is the integrity of the writing mode itself, if the problem is purely written—in particular, auditory perception, visual perception, motor skills, and aspects of formulation and syntax?

Through informal and formal evaluation, a profile is compiled of the strengths and weaknesses in total language ability so the type and character of the disorder become apparent.

SUGGESTIONS FOR REMEDIATION

In Johnson's and Myklebust's (1967) system, two general types of writing disorder exist: one associated with a language disorder in other modes and one specifically in the written expressive mode. In the case of a writing problem that is the result of, or at least is associated with, a disorder in one of the hierarchically lower modes, Myklebust advocates that therapy begin with the most basic language mode and proceed upward in the hierarchy or address the range of modes in a unified approach. In general, this is precisely what is being done in the field of language remediation at present. Work in the primary language system precedes or coincides with work in the secondary language system.

The pure writing problem represents a different perspective. As mentioned earlier, the prewriting abilities of children with dysgraphic or revisualization problems are addressed by many current programs. It is the formulation and syntax problem that is critically in need of more research and remedial instrumentation, and it is this subset of pure writing disorders that is described next in reference to Myklebust's approach.

Remediation for Formulation and Syntax Errors

Johnson and Myklebust (1967) suggest a series of three stages for remediating formulation and syntax difficulties in writing:

1. experience in recognizing and developing an awareness of writing errors
2. oral practice in ordering ideas and content (oral rehearsal)
3. actual writing experience proceeding through a sequence of four stages, ranging from concrete to abstract

The first stage comes from the view that children make errors in writing that they do not make in speaking, and if the written work is "refiltered" through the oral mode, the errors should be perceived readily. Johnson and Myklebust contend that this is precisely what happens with children in this population.

At Stage 1, the teacher can read the children's stories or paragraphs aloud, allowing the pupils to correct the errors verbally. The teacher can then correct the papers according to the errors previously identified and allow the pupils to reread their work. The obvious next step is for the children to begin to edit their own work by reading aloud paragraphs they have just written and allowing their intact oral language system to "guide" them in correcting the writing. Finally, the students are taught to proofread their written work silently, correcting errors they "hear" themselves read.

Further work in editing involves such activities as asking the children to choose which one of four sentences best describes a picture, with three of the sentences containing syntactic errors; or asking them to find the error in each of 20 sentences prepared in advance by the teacher. Again, the goal is to teach proofreading skills by relying on the auditory mode until an awareness of adequate written syntactic use becomes more evident. In the first stage, the pupils are developing only this awareness—they are not being asked to produce anything; that is, training is focused on the recognition of adequate written work and not on production as yet.

Before requiring the actual writing of paragraphs, the children are given guidance in ordering their ideas and thoughts and in working through what they want to communicate. Again at Stage 2, the auditory mode's integrity is relied upon. By helping the pupils choose an idea and having them rehearse aloud what they want to say, the children are utilizing their oral language skill in ordering their written work. Once they get a clear picture of what they want to say, the formulation of the total paragraph will be a less formidable task.

There are serious problems with Johnson's and Myklebust's (1967) approach at this point. In fact, research has not indicated that oral rehearsal improves written work (Sawkins, 1971; Graves, 1975). Writing is not "talk written down" but is qualitatively and quantitatively more complex and demanding than oral language. While oral rehearsal may organize a general idea of what children want to say about a topic, the specific requirements of the writing task are not improved by orally rehearsing the material.

The Transitional Phase

The major aspect of written expression in terms of content is the transition from concrete to abstract writing. In Stage 3, many children may have to be taught to write in concrete fashion before even considering work in more complex, abstract stories. Myklebust describes a four-level series of stages through which children can be taken to teach them to communicate in writing. These levels—Concrete-Descriptive, Concrete-Imaginative, Abstract-Descriptive, and Abstract-Imaginative—represent a progression from initial concrete writing to that characterized by abstract content and meaning. The term abstract refers to a topic that is removed from the present situation; that is, it is not bound by the existing context but rather concerns possibilities beyond the present situation.

The first level in the series, the Concrete-Descriptive, refers to writing about a subject that is readily observable. For children so impaired that they cannot readily generate an adequate sentence, instruction will have to begin at the most basic level. The children can be taught to look at objects and write one word, and later two, to describe them. As success is demonstrated, they are asked to write a complete sentence, for example, answering the question, "What do you do with it?" Later, pictures are used, with the children writing a sentence to a stimulus question such as, "What is X doing?" As can be seen, in every instance, the children are asked to generate a word, phrase, or sentence in writing to describe a concrete, tangible object or picture. Johnson and Myklebust (1967) suggest sentence combining techniques be used to teach the children to make more complex structures out of their simple sentences.

The next level in the sequence is Concrete-Imaginative writing, which refers to using the imagination to speculate on some small aspect of the concrete stimulus. For example, if the pupils are shown a picture of a girl opening a birthday present, speculation can be raised as to what is in the box. Then a sentence can be written that mentions the gift that was speculated to be in the box: "The girl saw a new dolly in the box." Again, the eliciting stimulus is concrete and is an object or picture held in front of the pupils. Myklebust notes that learning disabled children often find it difficult to speculate or generalize from the action in the picture. These children may be very bound to the "here and now," to what they can see directly. In such cases, they must be prompted and reinforced until they can generalize and write a little more abstractly.

The third level is the Abstract-Descriptive, in which the children add the elements of time and sequence to their story. The requirement is to learn to set the story in a particular frame of time and to order the events so that the flow is logical and appropriate. Johnson and Myklebust (1967) suggest the use of sequence pictures since they provide a clear, visual, beginning-to-end flow of events. Paired with writing sequence picture description stories, the children are taught to use transition words such as "then," "and," or "now." A diary also is useful in ordering events in the pupils' day in correct sequence. Toward the end of the Abstract-Descriptive level, the children are taught to write stories that have characterization and narrative. This is introduced by tape-recording the children acting out a play, then transcribing the narrative. From this point on, the children can be guided in constructing entire stories with a number of characters.

The highest level is Abstract-Imaginative, which focuses on "a plot, imaginative setting, occasional figures of speech, and some connotation of moral values" (Johnson & Myklebust, 1967, p. 237). By using open-ended sentences, the teacher can lead the child toward better written story development. Johnson and Myklebust describe how a simile can be taught. By choosing words that describe a color (in their example, Johnson and Myklebust use words that describe the color yellow), the children can fill in the blank so that they produce a simile, "As yellow as *gold,* As yellow as a *banana.*" At this level, the children also are required to learn first to prepare an outline to order their thoughts and the plot in its entirety before beginning the actual writing task. This permits the entire communicative intent to be thought through before the writing begins and averts haphazard development.

Problems at the Abstract Level

To any professional, it is obvious that Myklebust does not go into enough detail about disorders of formulation and syntax and seems to be almost casual about the smooth progress expected in the Abstract-Imaginative level of instruction. This abstract level is precisely the point at which many students break down. Myklebust is clear and the information is valuable at the three other levels of instruction, but he says little about the most difficult area.

He suggests that if teachers use open-ended questions, the children will perceive how to make their stories more complex. This may be true, but this technique has been used for quite some time and does not seem to be the total answer for generating and ordering writing of a complex nature. In the same manner, his suggestion for the building of a simile is intriguing, but a simile is only a minute part of the requirements for abstract writing.

Myklebust, in short, does not provide an overview or method of depth and substance. Adolescents and young adults around the country are plateauing at the abstract level and having great difficulty advancing in their writing skills. This probably is the most critical level at which more research and information for instruction is needed. Aspects such as sense of audience, complex sentence structure, and style come into play at this level. It most certainly is a point in the writing continuum in need of more focus.

This oversimplification of remediation at the abstract-imaginative level reflects Johnson's and Myklebust's (1967) corresponding handling of the category of pure writing disorder. Their theoretical framework simply is not detailed enough to support the depth of instructional programming needed.

Three-Component Analysis

On the contrary, the Total Writing Process Model (Introduction, Exhibit 3) provides that a specific writing disability be analyzed on three component dimensions. Students unable to produce quality written work could be demonstrating a problem in one or more of those three components, necessitating remediation aimed at those particular areas—not on a nebulous "abstract-imaginative" dimension. For example, if the breakdown occurs in addressing an audience appropriately, then therapy should focus on pragmatic writing issues; if the breakdown involves the structuring of sentences, therapy should emphasize syntactic features and organization.

In terms of such issues as punctuation, no precise suggestions are included in Myklebust's remedial approach other than to ask the children to point to various punctuation marks and "tell what they mean." This vague suggestion supplies little useful methodology.

Once the pupils are writing at the Abstract-Imaginative level, Johnson and Myklebust appear to be comfortable with a traditional grammar approach. They emphasize that this requires the learning of a second symbol system, which may be very difficult for learning disabled children. However, rather than suggest that traditional grammar not be used with such students, they propose that the texts chosen should be those that concretize the traditional grammar symbol system. They warn against having the children learn rules, but stress that they should understand the meaning of each part of speech on a conceptual level, as well as be able to define its use.

In view of the fact that language and learning disabled children experience great difficulty in learning the first symbolic system, much less the second one, Johnson's and Myklebust's acceptance of traditional grammar poses problems. Instead of advocating another approach to syntax, they suggest finding concrete traditional grammar textbooks for learning handicapped children, while admonishing teachers to make the children learn not the rules but rather the concepts behind the rules. It would seem that an alternate to traditional grammar would be a far better approach for children who have such needs. A number of alternate systems are available and are described in various chapters of this book.

A final issue discussed by Johnson and Myklebust (1967) is spelling, one of the most difficult skills demanded of children. It requires auditory, visual, motor, and memory skills of a very high level. They suggest that the teacher break up the spelling words into two lists: phonetic and nonphonetic. The phonetic words can be learned by activities such as having the children sound out the syllables of a word, fill in the missing syllable in a word spoken by the teacher, or write words, one syllable at a time, as the teacher slowly dictates them. Nonphonetic words are taught according to the methods used for revisualization of words: the target word is recognized from a group of words, the children must supply a missing letter, and finally must write the whole word. Johnson and Myklebust do not recommend oral spelling on the ground that it is a relatively useless skill and does not mean that the oral ability necessarily will translate itself into the correct motor ability.

Thus, Johnson and Myklebust propose a wide range of suggested thera-
peutic approaches and activities for use with children who have disturbances
in their ability to communicate expressively in writing.

Myklebust (1973) has utilized his Picture Story Language Test for extensive research on normal and handicapped children. He has studied the cognitive and language skills of these children at length, with some very
important results. An overview of his research and findings is presented next
to allow the entire perspective of writing deficits to be perceived.

RESEARCH IN WRITTEN EXPRESSIVE LANGUAGE

In one study (Myklebust, 1973), 747 normal children aged 7 to 17 were
selected from metropolitan, suburban, and rural areas. The Picture Story
Language Test (PSLT) (1965) was used to gather data on their written
expression. This test (see Chapter 11) yields scores on five factors of written
work: (1) the total number of words used in a story, (2) the total number of
sentences in a story, (3) the total number of words per sentence, (4) syntax,
and (5) abstract meaning.

Normal children's results on this test were not completely as expected. In
terms of total words, the urban and rural children scored below the suburban
at early age levels but similarly at older ages. This pattern was the same for
the total sentence calculation. Girls consistently wrote longer stories than
boys. Despite the difference in total words or sentences, the words per sentence
scores were similar in all three groups. Myklebust (1973) notes that this
finding indicates that the inadequate schooling often associated with urban
children does not affect this population on all written language factors.

The syntax of the normal children was similar in all three groups. In terms
of the level of abstract meaning used in the stories, the rural and particularly
the urban children fell below the suburbanites at early ages, the rural not
catching up until the 13-year level and the urban until the 15-year level. This
indicates a significant decrease in the ability of rural and urban children to
encode abstract meaning in written stories, although the gap closes in ado-
lescence.

These results suggest that within the different school environments there
were remarkable similarities as well as a number of significant differences
among the three groups. The words per sentence and the syntax were equivalent among the groups but the rural, and particularly the urban, pupils fell
below the suburban on total words and sentences and in the communication
of abstract meaning. This performance split, as far as the five subtests are
concerned, is reasonable if analyzed. Abstract meaning probably is conveyed
through the use of a greater total number of words and sentences—the longer
story can convey more information. An equivalent number of words per

sentence and syntax also are related, since a certain number of sentence skeletons or frames with a repeated syntactic structure may have been used frequently. From this standpoint, the major differences between the urban/ rural and suburban groups may be communication of abstract thought and meaning.

Myklebust (1973) conducted an additional study on the relationships between other language modes and the written expressive. Among normal children, receptive oral language overall was correlated positively with written language at the youngest age levels and with receptive syntax in particular through the 11-year age level. Expressive oral language was even more highly correlated with the written, decreasing to nonsignificance by the 15-year level. Both receptive and expressive oral language ceased to be significantly correlated at upper age levels, indicating that "as developmental maturation is achieved and cognitive processes become established, the interdependence of auditory and written language undergoes a change" (p. 16). This may be because of the children's ability to transduce from visual to auditory or vice versa and to use each system independently.

As to age and sex as they relate to written language, Myklebust found that females performed better than the males up to 17, when the sexes were equivalent for number of words, number of sentences, number of words in sentences, syntax, and abstract meaning. However, this particular ability level was attained by the females at 15 and then held constant, whereas males did not reach it until 17. The earlier maturation of females was evident from the 7-to-15 levels.

The data indicated that the two sexes used particular word classes differently. Girls used more nouns, pronouns, adjectives, adverbs, prepositions, and conjunctions than boys. As for articles and verbs, the groups were equal except for the future tense, which appeared late in both sexes but was used more by the females.

These results indicate that the richness of written language was evidenced more in female compositions than in males'; at no time did the boys use a word class more frequently than the girls. This increase in girls' written language fluency and quality is not without implications for instruction. It may be that boys require more emphasis on the use of the various word classes in written composition.

Reading Disabled Children

The handicapped children evaluated in the study evidenced performance and group trends in contrast to those of the normal children. The first group included reading disabled (dyslexic) children, aged 7 to 15, from a metropolitan area. In terms of cognitive abilities, these children scored below a normal control group, the lower scores becoming more pronounced as age increased. On a subtest performance, these students scored lowest on verbal tests; they often were above 90 IQ on the nonverbal. Overall, however, they scored lower than their normal peers, and the gap widened as they grew older.

On both parts of a receptive oral language test, the reading disabled children performed poorer than the normals and overall lagged by three to four years. On expressive oral language, they again scored three to four years lower.

On the reading tests, of course, the reading disabled children performed significantly poorer than the normals, with an even greater gap than on the oral language tests.

The results so far suggest that as a group, children who have reading problems demonstrate a significant language disorder. That their scores on the cognitive abilities test in many cases would be adequate on the nonverbal factors and depressed on the verbal ones further emphasizes the apparent language difficulties. A number of studies of the relationship of receptive and expressive grammatic language to reading ability and reading readiness show that a significant positive relationship does exist and that grammatic language may in fact be predictive of reading proficiency (Vogel, 1974; Semel & Wiig, 1975; Phelps, 1979).

On the Picture Story Language Test, the reading disabled children used markedly fewer total words and sentences than the normal students, performed below but closer to the norm on number of words per sentence, and again lower in syntax and communication of abstract meaning. Among the syntactic errors mentioned by Myklebust were verb tense, punctuation, and word order.

It is important to note that although all language modes were below the expected normal range, performance declined as the task requirement moved up the language mode hierarchy.

Mentally Retarded Children

In this study, educable mentally handicapped children were chosen from an urban environment. Not all the tests could be given to each child; however, the results in general indicated that this group was below normal on all tests. As expected, these children performed worse on written language tests than on oral language. Their performance on written expressive language was slightly better on a syntactical dimension than on length and abstract meaning, although overall written expression was below average.

Articulation Disordered Children

The children comprising the articulation disorder sample ranged in age from 7 to 13 years, came from a metropolitan setting, and excluded such disorders as stuttering, cleft palate, and cerebral palsy. These pupils as a group scored essentially adequately on cognitive abilities and receptive oral language. In expressive oral language and receptive written language, they were inferior to the normal children at the younger age levels but caught up at the oldest level. Their written expressive language ability was well below the normal group in total number of words and sentences and use of abstract meaning. They scored closer to the norm on the number of words per sentence and were markedly inferior in written syntax at the early ages but improved consistently, reaching normal limits by age 13.

These findings are of great interest to professionals who work with children who have articulation difficulties, which is one aspect of oral expressive language; Myklebust's results suggest there also is an impairment in their entire oral expressive language system. A similar impairment in written language, both expressive and receptive, also was noted. Of particular interest is the fact that these children were able to improve consistently and by the age of 13 became as proficient as their normal peers in oral expressive and written language ability. This seems to suggest a maturational factor or the need for the children in the articulation disordered population to receive alternate learning experiences at early ages in order to achieve in a manner equivalent to their normal peers.

Socially-Emotionally Disturbed Children

The results of the test battery for socially-emotionally disturbed children indicated that they were within normal limits on nonverbal cognitive measures but evidenced difficulties on the verbal items. Their receptive oral language performance was severely delayed at lower age levels, but caught up with the normals by the time they were 13 to 15. Expressive oral language test performance also lagged severely behind the normals; however, this ability did not increase to normal limits with age. Reading ability was below the normal range, and performance on the PSLT trailed the norm in every one of the five writing categories. In no case except syntax did the scores of the group even approach the normal.

Myklebust (1973) raises the critical question of whether these children should be judged and treated purely as individuals with social-emotional disturbances. The children in the sample came from a metropolitan public school system, and despite the fact that results may not be appropriately generalized to different populations, the cognitive and language deficiencies of these pupils should not be ignored because of their particular classification. That is, these children may need particular educational and remedial services beyond what often is given to socially and emotionally disturbed children. These pupils may require language evaluation and therapy.

Learning Disabled Children

The final group of handicapped children studied involved the learning disabled. They were selected from a metropolitan area and divided into two groups, one with a moderate Learning Quotient (Johnson & Myklebust, 1967) and one with a severe Learning Quotient. The Learning Quotient is a ratio between a child's potential for learning and the actual achievement. The performance of these learning disabled children on a series of in-depth reading tests indicated that they were below the normal range and that the subtest profiles for each group were very similar, differing only in degree of overall severity. That is, the breakdown of particular reading skill deficits ranked in order of most to least difficult were similar in both groups, the severe learning disabled group making lower scores overall.

The two most significant reading skill deficits for both groups were comprehension and vocabulary. On the PSLT, both the moderate and the severe learning disabled groups scored poorer than the normals, the most difficult factors being syntax and abstract meaning. These problems correspond to the comprehension and vocabulary difficulties just mentioned on the reading testing. Inasmuch as receptive written language is seen to precede expressive language, the basic vocabulary and comprehension deficits would affect processing of communication and would be expected to have an effect on written language, particularly abstract meaning.

This extensive study by Myklebust (1973) can be summarized as to writing by noting the following:

1. Reading disabled children were below normal on all factors of the PSLT, particularly on the total number of words and sentences and the use of abstract meaning.
2. Mentally retarded children scored below normal on all factors of the PSLT, particularly on abstract meaning.
3. Children with misarticulations at early ages scored below normal on all PSLT factors; at later age levels, performance on syntax improved and was equivalent to the normal group.
4. Children with socioemotional disorders scored below normal on all PSLT factors; only in syntax did they even approach normal.
5. Children with severe and moderate learning disabilities scored below normal on all PSLT factors, particularly in syntax and abstract meaning.

The impact of these results on remedial planning for handicapped children is profound. That the reading disabled would be deficient in written expression is predictable and accounted for by Myklebust's language hierarchy. Mentally retarded children, having reduced intellectual abilities, also could be expected to be deficient in written language—the highest language mode on the hierarchy and therefore the most demanding.

That children with articulation problems scored so low on written expressive is not totally surprising in view of the often reported reading difficulty in this population (Winitz, 1969). A deficit in reading can be predicted to coincide with a writing deficit. The findings for those with socioemotional disorders is somewhat surprising in the sense that these children often are characterized by both peaks and valleys in a wide range of abilities; yet this study found them consistently depressed in language. Finally, learning disabled children, with their high incidence of language difficulties, could be expected to have difficulties in written language.

It would seem that a differential diagnosis of any child suspected of having learning difficulties of any type should include an analysis of written expressive language. Concomitant remediation should be provided for any handicapped child with writing deficits. No matter the category, all of these children are viewed by Myklebust (1973) as evidencing a need for therapy in one or more language modes; that is, writing as well as reading or oral language may be in need of remedial attention. Thus, Myklebust has demonstrated clearly the need for written language to be a solid and consistent component of the remedial process for handicapped children. The "neglected mode of language" is as critical as any of the others and must be given a place in the special services area of focus.

EVALUATION OF MYKLEBUST'S REMEDIATION

The Myklebust (1960) system of analyzing language represents a synthesis of theory and practical application. The formulation of a provocative language mode hierarchy results in a logical transition to diagnostic and remedial suggestions. The entire approach revolves around the language hierarchy, from categorizing problems to initiating therapy. The language mode hierarchy has become a powerful force in the field of language and learning disabilities, and with reason, for it represents a unique systemizing of an abstract process.

The authors have redefined this hierarchy to better describe the written expressive language mode. The resulting schema offers an improved explanation of efficient writing and, by the same token, allows a "pure" writing disability to be analyzed more carefully than the somewhat more simplistic approach of Myklebust (1960). With a more in-depth framework of analysis, remedial management will be utilized more appropriately. The differential diagnosis suggested by Johnson and Myklebust (1967) has been used widely, as has his Picture Story Language Test (Myklebust, 1965). The emphasis has been on careful analysis and a detailed language profile.

In terms of remediation, Johnson and Myklebust (1967) describe three subsets of pure writing disorders. The subset involving formulation and syntax, composed of four levels ranging from concrete to abstract, appears sound up to the highest level. At that point, Johnson and Myklebust supply little solid remedial programming, a significant drawback in view of the fact that this is the area most in need of research and instrumentation. This lack may be related to the inadequacy of his definition of pure writing disorder, since the schema supplied by the Total Writing Process Model is significantly more amenable to remedial design.

Overall, Myklebust's program, in terms of a composite of all his books, provides a workable system of theory, rationale, categorization, differential diagnosis, and remediation. The system has had significant impact and influence on the field of language and learning disabilities and continues to be a powerful force.

BIBLIOGRAPHY

Graves, D.H. An examination of the writing processes of seven-year-old children. *Research in Teaching English,* 1975, *9,* 227-41.

Johnson, D., & Myklebust, H.R. *Learning disabilities: Educational principles and practices.* New York: Grune & Stratton, Inc., 1967.

Mattingly, I.G. Reading, the linguistic process, and linguistic awareness. In J.F. Karanzagy & I.G. Mattingly (Eds.), *Language by ear and eye: The relationships between speech and reading.* Cambridge, Mass.: MIT Press, 1972.

Myklebust, H.R. *The psychology of deafness.* New York: Grune & Stratton, Inc., 1960.

——————. *Development and disorders of written language,* Vol. I. New York: Grune & Stratton, Inc., 1965.

——————. *Development and disorders of written language,* Vol. II. New York: Grune & Stratton, Inc., 1973.

Phelps, D. *An investigation of the relationship between receptive and expressive grammatical competence and reading readiness.* Unpublished doctoral dissertation, University of Houston, 1979.

Sawkins, M.W. The oral responses of selected fifth grade children to questions concerning their written expression. *Dissertation Abstracts International,* 1971, *31,* 6287A-6288A.

Semel, E.M., & Wiig, E.H. Comprehension of syntactic structures and critical verbal elements by children with learning disabilities. *Journal of Learning Disabilities,* 1975, *1*(8), 46-51.

Vogel, S.A. Syntactic abilities in normal and dyslexic children. *Journal of Learning Disabilities,* 1974, 7(2), 103-109.

Vygotsky, L.S. *Thought and language.* Cambridge, Mass: MIT Press, 1962.

Winitz, H. *Articulatory acquisition and behavior.* New York: Appleton-Century-Crofts, Inc., 1969.

Chapter 4

The Phelps Sentence Guide Program

The Phelps Sentence Guide program utilizes an interactive approach to teach written expressive language from the simple sentence to the paragraph and story level. This program began as an adaptation of the Fitzgerald Key program (Fitzgerald, 1966) and was used with a language and learning disabled population at a major university training center. Its effectiveness in the early stages of use was demonstrated with handicapped children and adolescents and proved to be well received by students and public school personnel in outlying districts.

This demonstration of the program's effectiveness led to further additions, modifications, and expansions, resulting in a published version in 1980. The program has since been incorporated into a significant number of public school curricula and has been adopted by a variety of professionals in private clinical use. One interesting use that was not intended originally is with adult aphasics in therapy for written expression. Using the Phelps Sentence Guide program with this adult population has proved very successful.

RATIONALE, DESIGN, AND FIELD TESTING

The Phelps Sentence Guide program addresses the issues of sentence generation, structuring, imagery, and editing in children in both regular and special education. Accepting Myklebust's (1960) hierarchy of language (Chapter 3), Phelps-Terasaki and Phelps recognize that written expressive language is the highest and most demanding form of language. Errors in writing range from incorrect sentence structure to paragraphs with no cohesion.

Many current writing programs consistently seem to approach the teaching of writing from a "correction of a given" standpoint. That is, students are taught to alter or combine given sentences to equal a more complex construct. These approaches, although effective as far as they go, do not attack the issue of sentence generation directly.

It can be argued, of course, that a method such as sentence combining (see Chapter 5) will lead eventually to an intuition of what constitutes a complex and what constitutes a simple sentence. However, Phelps-Terasaki's and Phelps's program is designed to approach sentence formulation and internalization of structure directly. From the experimental version of the Phelps Sentence Guide to the published form, the intent has been to devise a structured, hierarchical program to teach generation, elaboration, and editing of sentences in a communicative context.

A key point is that other programs often neglect the communicative function of sentences and of the words and phrases that compose them. The Phelps Sentence Guide program utilizes a communicative context that emphasizes the purpose of writing, as well as structure and content.

Two key modifications of the first, experimental Phelps Sentence Guide program resulted in the published version. Before these modifications are described, the Fitzgerald Key modification is explained. As in the Key, the Phelps Sentence Guide consists of a left-to-right linear series of columns. Each column's heading corresponds to the word class whose members can be written in the column.

Unlike the Fitzgerald Key, however, the Phelps Sentence Guide does not use a geometric symbol system for elements such as the verb. Rather, the Guide uses a separate verb column labeled according to communicative function of verbing in the sentence. That is, the verb column is labeled "Doing." In addition, the Guide rearranges the linear order of word classes somewhat and uses discrete columns with vertical lines from the top to the bottom of the page. The Guide does not adapt any aspect of the Fitzgerald Key program itself, only a modification of its form.

The resulting Phelps Sentence Guide provides a visual representation of the structure of written language. This can be used to cue and order writing. Hearing impaired children have an auditory sensory dysfunction and benefit from the visual Fitzgerald Key. Language and learning disordered children may have an auditory system that, although normal in hearing acuity, does not process auditory information accurately to some degree. For such children, the Phelps Sentence Guide provides the visual compensation, support, and cueing needed to make up for the inefficient auditory system.

As with the hearing impaired, the visual cueing provides a concrete structure for writing that might otherwise be missing. Even language and learning disordered children without auditory processing impairment have been shown to improve with the program, simply because the visual cues enhance and blend with the auditory to make sentence structure more readily comprehensible. Visual cueing without the Sentence Guide—that is, without a concrete structure—is not so obvious. Somewhere along the line, children are expected to perceive that sentences have functional units that link meaning and use. If the pupils do not use normal learning channels or experiences to perceive how sentences are structured, and many language and learning disabled children do not (hence their difficulty), their written production will be inadequate and they will not appreciate the system behind sentences.

The Phelps program concretely illustrates sentence structure and the teacher or clinician guides the auditory and visual interface with the Guide's cueing system. Children in time internalize the correct structure of sentences, as well as the use, function, and ordering of sentence components. This internalized system replaces the one on paper, serving to order sentences mentally as it did visually on paper. The syntactic aspects of written language become fluent and more automatic. In other words, the children will have learned and internalized the system behind sentences.

The additional modifications of the original Phelps Sentence Guide program relate to work in learning theory and psycholinguistics. The oral language remediation, *Interactive Language Development Teaching* (Lee, 1975), was influential in the addition of the interactive aspects of the program. Lee's approach uses a carefully designed question and answer interaction between clinician and child. The teacher or clinician first completes a Developmental Sentence Scoring (Lee, 1974) technique on some of the child's oral language samples. The results provide a profile of the child's correct, incorrect, and omitted syntactic structures in eight categories: indefinite pronouns, personal pronouns, main verbs, secondary verbs, negatives, conjunctions, interrogative reversals, and WH questions.

The therapy plan is written to interface with the child's abilities and disabilities in the eight categories, and goals are designed to stabilize and expand the pupil's oral use of target structures. With flannelboard characters and objects, the teacher tells the child a story, using language structures that have been selected as goals for stabilization. Frequently throughout the story, the teacher asks the child a question that contains or focuses on a target structure and requires the pupil to formulate an answer that includes the structure. For example, "What will he do with the bike?" should be answered with a future tense sentence such as, "He will ride the bike." Only complete sentences are accepted, so the child will learn formulation and repetition of whole sentence units.

The beauty of this system lies in the fact that the teacher and child are involved actively and continuously, attention is maintained because the interaction must be monitored for a correct question/answer cycle to be completed, the clinician's questions set the structure of the responses and allow the key elements to be emphasized, and the pupil acquires facility in generating whole sentences within a controlled context.

This teacher-controlled interactive structure was added to the Phelps Sentence Guide program. When a sentence is incorrect or incomplete, the teacher questions the child, stressing column headings in the question. For example, "*Where* did the boy look?" or "What *can* the boy *do* with the fishing pole?" This careful questioning centers on the precise sentence element(s) on which the child's attention must be focused. In addition to incorrect or incomplete sentences, the teacher uses questions to focus on each word class and its role in the sentence. For example, in the sentence, "The clown is eating pizza," the teacher asks:

> *Who* is eating pizza?
> *What* is the clown eating?
> What *is* the clown *doing* with the pizza?

While asking the question, the teacher points to each corresponding column heading on the Sentence Guide. The child answers each question by reading the entire sentence. Since the teacher stresses the key element in the question, the child begins to associate each query with the corresponding information in the sentence. In time, the child makes an internal awareness and association between the following sentence components:

1. the word classes in general
2. the kinds of information the word classes contain
3. the items corresponding to the various word classes
4. the communicative function of each word class

In addition, since the sentences must be read in their entirety to answer the teacher's questions, the child is given practice and repetition in use of whole, complete written sentences, not fragments. Whereas in oral expressive language the speaker can and often will use phrases and fragments, written expressive language cannot be so encoded. In spoken language, the speaker can constantly gauge audience comprehension and given information and supply the new in any form—complete sentence or fragment. The speaker also wastes time in phrasing each sentence in complete form and instead speaks in sentence fragments; there is a tendency to be time efficient in spoken language.

In writing, since the audience's response cannot be gauged, the writer must be very clear; it therefore is regarded as unclear formulation to produce sentence fragments. This is but one of several major communicative differences between the two expressive modes. For this reason, it is imperative that written expressive language be learned, practiced, and stabilized in reference to sentence units, not fragments.

The final addition to the Phelps Sentence Guide program was the structuring of the program goals and levels. Bruner (1966) describes a curriculum approach in which rudimentary components of the entire scope are presented directly from the program's beginning. As competency increases, more and more aspects of the whole are added. Concrete material becomes increasingly more abstract and complex. Correct simple sentences are taught from the beginning and increased in complexity as work progresses.

The Phelps Sentence Guide program is divided into nine stages, each building and expanding on the previous ones. The nine are: (1) Introduction— Simple Sentences, (2) Expansion of the Subject, (3) Expansion of the Predicate, (4) Editing Practice: Basic Sentence Units, (5) Verb Tenses, (6) Editing Practice: Verb Tenses, (7) Paragraph Development, (8) Editing Practice: Paragraph Development, and (9) Advanced Applications. The content and focus of each level are controlled in scope so as not to overwhelm the child. When the descriptive subject is taught, the child writes sentences on a Guide that has preprinted predicates. The child need only concentrate on the subject that will best describe a picture and match the predicate. The pupil's attention thus can be focused on the key element and the child is not overwhelmed by a complex sentence generation task.

The Phelps Guide provides a visual system of structuring sentences, uses an interactive teacher-child dialogue that emphasizes components and their interface and communicative function in the sentence, requires repetition and practice in whole sentence units, and steadily builds written competency at each stage without overwhelming the pupil by the complexity of the task. It is an eclectic program, a combination of innovation and adaptation that has yielded a total that is much more than the sum of its parts. The program is cohesive and comprehensive, and teaches children to generate and appropriately order their written expressive communication.

PROGRAM OVERVIEW

As noted, the Phelps Sentence Guide program consists of the nine hierarchical stages listed earlier, beginning with the simple sentence and progressing to paragraphs and stories. The first stage focuses on teaching the basic sentence. Using a Sentence Guide (Exhibit 4-1), a visual structuring system is integrated with simple sentences that the child produces in describing a picture. Through questioning and continuing to increasingly higher program levels, the teacher expands sentences and shows the child how more information can be encoded by using additional sentence categories.

Exhibit 4-1   The Phelps Sentence Guide

First? Second? Next? Then? Last? Final? At last? Later?	Which? How many? What kind of?	Who? What?	How much? Which? How many? What kind of?	Doing? (Is, are, was, were, am, have, had, do, did, does)	What?	For what? To what? To whom? For whom?	When?	Where?	How? Why? If? For? Because? So that? Since?

Source: Reprinted from *Teaching Written Expression: The Phelps Sentence Guide Program* by Diana Phelps-Terasaki and Trisha Phelps by permission of Academic Therapy Publications, 1980.

The teacher uses Sentence Guide category headings in the question itself; for example, if wanting to prompt the child to use a reference to time, the teacher asks, "*When* did X do Y?" Simultaneously, the teacher points to the When column, indicating that this is where the child should write the answer. The child then does so, the teacher asks questions corresponding to sentence elements, and the pupil reads the entire sentence as an answer to each question. Thus, the communicative function of the When column and the other columns is associated with their roles in the sentence. The components are emphasized as they relate to each other, to their individual meanings, and to the sentence as a whole. The entire sentence unit, not a fragment, is practiced in response to the questions, and the pupil experiences the generative aspects of writing in a communicative context.

Other writing systems focus on altering or combining sentences, excellent ways to improve a given; however, those approaches do not address the generation of sentences directly. A given is refashioned, but not *such that* a sentence is generated. Working with imagery and sentence generation in the Phelps Sentence program leads to internalization of the Guide itself and to better decentering ability. The order and structure of written sentences becomes fluent and the subject and even the sentence itself are objectified and imaged.

Upper levels of the program emphasize such factors as the use of descriptive subjects and predicates, editing, sentence elaboration, imagery of more abstract topics, dialoguing, and the use of consistent tense. The program is effective because it improves writing as a whole in the following ways:

1. Through interactive questioning techniques, the child learns the communicative function of word classes and their relationship to the sentence and its meaning. At upper levels, the cohesiveness and thread running through entire paragraphs and stories are perceived and maintained in writing.
2. Through the use of a visual structuring system, paired with the questioning technique, the child develops an internalization of the order and structure of sentences and paragraphs.
3. Through the requirement of reading entire sentences in response to questioning, the child learns to recognize and use complete sentences in writing.
4. Through the use of limited focus at each stage, the child builds competency at each hierarchical level without becoming overwhelmed by too complex a task.
5. Through the use of all components of the program, the child learns to generate, elaborate, and edit written work.

6. Through the use of all components of the program, the child learns to objectify and image the message, thereby decentering self in writing and more efficiently addressing the audience.

The Phelps Sentence Guide program has been used by a variety of professionals in the special services: speech-language pathologists, resource teachers, and instructors in language and learning disability, remedial reading, and hearing impairment. The program also has been used in regular education classes at all public school levels from first or second grade to high school.

In the regular classroom, the children work in groups of eight to ten, beginning with Stage I (see next section) and proceeding through the eight other levels when indicated. The program moves smoothly at the elementary level if the children are assembled as in their reading groups. At the junior and senior high school levels, entire classes or parts of classes can use the program, usually in the English curriculum.

Special education professionals must tailor the program more carefully to the needs of every individual child. No "cookbook" approach can work with that population. In terms of the Phelps Sentence Guide program, one learning disabled child may spend many months at Stage II, while another will advance to Stage IV in 10 to 12 weeks.

Children in resource, language, or other remedial classes can be grouped according to their writing needs or can be worked with individually. For the program to be effective, its pace must be tailored to the needs of the children. If other programs are used in conjunction with the Phelps Sentence Guide, the goals of all of them should be coordinated and interfaced.

Despite this requirement of individualizing the program to the children using it, the Phelps Sentence Guide is easily worked into the curriculum of both regular and special education. To use the program effectively, the published version must be studied; however, an overview of the nine stages illustrates the progression of the work. The program is described in the context of teacher-child, not teacher-group, work. Group work is slightly different and is described in the published program.

PHELPS SENTENCE GUIDE PROGRAM STAGES

Stage I: Introduction—Simple Sentences

The purpose of Stage I is to allow the child to become familiar with the structure of the Sentence Guide and to develop fluency in writing simple sentences. The questioning technique is used to take a child's noninformative or incomplete sentence and expand its informational content. This is done by asking questions under some of the category headings that the child did not use. An introduction to imagery also is included.

The program is initiated by showing interesting pictures to the child. The pupil is asked to tell about them. The teacher puts the first sentence on the Guide, then asks questions that correspond to the sentence. The child reads the sentence alone or in unison with the teacher as an answer to each question. The basic procedure thus is illustrated, modeled, and experienced.

From here, the teacher uses questions to expand the information encoded in the child's sentence or to prompt the pupil to rewrite it in a better way. For example, if in looking at a picture the child says, "He's kicking it," the teacher writes that sentence on the Guide, then asks a Who, a Doing, and a What question in any order. A discussion follows on the informational content of the sentence, and the child is prompted to think of better ways to describe the "he" and the "it." The dialogue in Exhibit 4-2 illustrates the procedures just described.

In this way, the teacher, through questioning, expands the sentence already written or prompts the writing of a new one. This is a very basic level at which to begin writing.

Spelling in the program is taught via the Fernald (1943) or Stetson (1977) methods. These approaches are covered in the published version of the Phelps Sentence Guide program and so are not analyzed here. Briefly, they divide words into phonetic and nonphonetic groups, using specific procedures with each. A card file is compiled and continuously added to and reviewed.

Imagery is introduced at this level. The teacher hides a picture, asks the child to sit with closed eyes, and to listen carefully to the entire sentence and keep the words "paint a picture" in mind. The teacher says a descriptive sentence and gives the child time to assemble a mental representation. The teacher shows the original picture to the child, who matches it to the mental picture. The process is repeated, followed by a role reversal with the child hiding a picture from the teacher and leading the activity. This procedure ends with the teacher explaining that words, just like a paintbrush, can paint a picture in a listener's mind.

When painting a picture in someone's mind, the teacher gets one—either actual or mental—then says or writes words that describe it fully. The listener or reader then uses the words to paint a mental picture. The teacher explains that the key is for the child to get a picture on the desk or in the mind, step back and really look at it, then choose words that describe it well. Such activities help the child decenter, or become objective about, writing targets. Imagery and questioning techniques continue to be major aspects of focus throughout the Phelps Sentence Guide program.

Stage II: Expansion of the Subject

In Stage II, the child learns to write about a descriptive and informative subject. The possible categories are reviewed in relation to imagery. (Which

Exhibit 4-2 Dialogue in Phelps Sentence Guide

Teacher: Can you tell me something about this picture?

Child: He's kicking it.

T: O.K. Who is kicking it?

C: He is. (Points.) The boy is.

T: Write "The boy" in the Who column. Now, what *is* the boy *doing?*

C: He's kicking the ball.

T: Fine, write "is kicking" on the Guide here. (Points.) *What* is the boy kicking?

C: The ball.

T: Write "the ball" on the Guide. (Points to column.) Now, read the whole sentence back to me.

C: The boy is kicking the ball.

T: Good. *Who* is kicking the ball? (Points to Who column.)

C: The boy is kicking the ball.

T: *What* is the boy kicking? (Points to What column.)

C: The boy is kicking the *ball.*

T: What *is* the boy *doing* with the ball? (Points to the Doing column.)

C: The boy is kicking the ball.

T: Now, let's try to build a picture in our minds about this picture of the boy kicking the ball. How does the boy look in the picture? Close your eyes and tell me how the boy looks, where he is, and whatever else you "see" in your mind.

C: Well, he's a tall boy, and he's in the park.

T: Great! Now I know more about the picture you are describing. We'll write the new sentence right under the old one on the Guide. Where will you write "The tall?"

C: I'm not sure. . . . .

T: Well, "tall" tells you what kind of a boy was kicking the ball, so write "The tall" under the What Kind of column right here. (Points.) Then write the word "boy" under the Who column like in the other sentence.

C: Then do I write "is kicking" here again? (Points.)

T: That's right. And write *what* the tall boy was kicking in the What column. (Pauses as child writes sentence.) How about *where* the tall boy is kicking the ball? (Points to Where column.)

C: Oh, yeah. "In the park" goes there.

T: Fine. (Pauses as child finishes sentence.) Let's read the whole sentence together.

T and C: "The tall boy is kicking the ball in the park."

T: *Who* is kicking the ball in the park? (Points to Who column.)

C: The tall boy is kicking the ball in the park.

T: *What* is the tall boy kicking in the park? (Points to What column.)

C: The tall boy is kicking *the ball* in the park.

T: *Where* is the tall boy kicking the ball? (Points to Where column.)

C: The tall boy is kicking the ball in the park.

T: What kind of boy is kicking the ball in the park? (Points to What Kind of column.)

C: The *tall* boy is kicking the ball in the park.

T: What *is* the tall boy *doing* in the park? (Points to the Doing column.)

C: The tall boy is *kicking* the ball in the park.

T: You've done well. This sentence is even better than the one before. It paints a better picture in my mind when I read it.

girl did X? The redhaired, freckled girl did X.) The teacher prepares Sentence Guides in advance with sentences corresponding to pictures. In each sentence, the teacher writes a predicate on the Guide and the child's task is to supply a descriptive subject. Questioning continues for expansion and rewriting.

Stage III: Expansion of the Predicate

Stage III focuses on the predicate. Again, Sentence Guides are prepared in advance to correspond with pictures. Each sentence has a subject pre-written; the child's task is to supply a descriptive predicate. Questioning is used and imagery is stressed.

Stage IV: Editing Practice: Basic Sentence Units

Stage IV work emphasizes the child's recognition of the core of a sentence: the unity of a subject and a predicate. Inherent in this work is recognition of sentence fragments. Descriptive subjects and predicates continue to be stressed to avoid or reduce overuse of nebulous words such as "it." The program provides a number of ways to stabilize these points and to practice editing for incomplete or nondescriptive sentences.

One example is for the teacher to announce in advance that the child will read 20 sentences that may or may not have one of three types of errors, which are defined clearly in advance. Each sentence corresponds to a picture so that the child can better judge what elements are poorly described or are missing. The three errors targeted initially are:

1. fragments
2. nondescriptive subjects
3. nondescriptive predicates

When the child is alerted in advance as to what errors to look for, the complexity of the task is decreased—the pupil is less perplexed and more successful. The child and teacher then go over each sentence and discuss whether or not it is correct as it stands or needs changes. Error sentences then are rewritten on the Sentence Guide. Stage IV also includes activities focusing on state-of-being verbs.

Stage V: Verb Tenses

At this level, the child learns about and practices verb tenses. Initial work is in conjunction with the When column on the Sentence Guide. Language and learning disordered children often have difficulty with verb tenses and may require more time at this stage. Phelps-Terasaki and Phelps (1980) provide information as to the sequence of verb acquisition in normal children's oral language. This sequence is suggested as a guide for written work.

Stage VI: Editing Practice: Verb Tenses

Stage VI focuses on editing errors of verb tenses. Again, activities involve finding and rewriting error sentences. Editing also continues to include fragments and nondescriptive subjects and predicates.

Stage VII: Paragraph Development

Stage VII focuses on the initial work in paragraph writing. Sequenced pictures are used to order ideas (and images) concretely, and one sentence is generated per picture. Activities teach such connective words as "first," "next," "then," and "finally." Main idea sentences, appropriate selection of titles, and paragraph mechanics (margins, indentations, etc.) are introduced and practiced.

Stage VIII: Editing Practice: Paragraph Development

Stage VIII is devoted to editing paragraphs. Procedures are explained to stabilize correct ordering of events, appropriate titles and main idea sentences, accurate and consistent use of tenses, and proper sentence mechanics. Again, errors in prepared paragraphs are edited. In every case, the errors for which the pupil is to be on the alert are understood clearly in advance. Work progresses to the editing of the student's own paragraphs.

Stage IX: Advanced Applications

The final stage focuses on decentering and complex sentence development. Increasingly more abstract ideas are presented, and the child is taught to dialogue the pro and con of an issue or to create a mental picture of the content of a paragraph before writing the sentences.

Complex sentence development, or motivational sentence building, relates to adding subordinate clauses that communicate the "why" of an event. The student is guided in searching for or hypothesizing why a person or event is happening. Thus,

The small boy in black glasses is climbing the huge tree.

becomes the following sentence:

The small boy in black glasses is climbing the huge tree because he is new in the neighborhood and is bored.

Through a series of activities, the child learns to image more than just a mental picture—the pupil images motives, feelings, and reasons. This requires analysis of a total situation and of cause and effect relationships. This last stage is being expanded by Phelps-Terasaki and Phelps into a more in-depth program for older adolescents and young adults.

PHELPS SENTENCE GUIDE: PROGRESS EXAMPLES

To illustrate some of the positive data collected in reference to field use of the program, two examples are provided.

Example 1: A Boy 8, in Third Grade

The first example is a third grade boy, age 8, with moderate oral expressive language and moderate severe written expressive language problems. His reading and auditory comprehension were adequate; his was strictly a disorder of language expression. The teacher required that stories be written in class biweekly; this pupil repeatedly had received failing grades. The teacher did not provide instruction in written language; instead, she made an assignment, provided class time for the children to write, and graded and returned the papers. The following is a sample of one of this boy's written stories, dated September 1978, before he received written expressive language therapy.

SUMMER VACATION

My summer vacation was good because I had a good vacation. Swiming and riding my bike and have fun. I got a dog for my brithday too. It was fun.

This paragraph contains numerous errors of:

1. sentence structure and order
2. syntax and morphology
3. spelling
4. punctuation
5. mechanics
6. cohesion, clarity, organization, and unity

Although this child was able to structure thoughts to some degree, in that he kept to a single topic without digressing, the many errors detract immensely from the communicative efficiency.

Eight months later, following three one-hour oral and written language therapy sessions per week, this child wrote the following paragraph:

A TRIP TO THE PARK

My mother, my brother and I went to Galveston County Park. We went to spend the afternoon and have fun. First we played on the swings and slide. Then we watched some people in a canoe. Finally it was time to go home. It was a fun day.

Note the following improvements:

1. correct sentence structure
2. correct ordering of sentence
3. correct syntax and morphology
4. correct paragraph mechanics
5. use of connective "first," "then," and "finally"
6. correct spelling (the word Galveston had been worked on in therapy before this paper)
7. improved unity, cohesion, clarity, and organization

Although this composition still is relatively far from being descriptive and complex, the boy made remarkable progress in written expression. Interestingly enough, his oral language did not improve as greatly. It is hypothesized that in time, the consistent practice of written expressive structure will generalize in reverse—Myklebust's (1960) language hierarchy—and improve oral expression.

Apparently, since more time can be taken to compose and refine written than oral expression, this child finally received and used the time needed to analyze, practice, and acquire the structure of language expression. Slow, labored production in the written mode eventually led to more fluency. In time, this written structure did in fact seem to generalize to oral production. One year later, his oral output had increased markedly while his written expression continued to improve and be acceptable overall. The key point of interest is that written expression improved before oral expression, implying that written structure may have allowed the time to organize, compose, change, and visually monitor structure until fluency was achieved.

In oral communication, the message must be formulated and produced immediately; the speaker is not allowed considerable time to compose, alter, consider, and consciously work to formulate the message. These immediate time demands may inhibit language acquisition to some degree. Writing, since it allows time to study, fashion, and reshape, may allow the time for language structure itself to be studied, practiced, and internalized. The time demands reduce the pressure to produce language immediately, instead providing opportunities for thought and reflective formulation experience. Through the use of language instruction in the written mode, the internalized structure may order both expressive modes.

Example 2: A Boy, 16, in Eleventh Grade

The second example is a 16-year-old student in eleventh grade at a suburban high school. Following a semester of study of American literature, this student was assigned to write a paragraph analyzing Puritanism. Several novels and many lectures and class discussions prefaced this assignment so presumably the student had some degree of understanding of the topic. The task required that he order thoughts and compose a coherent paragraph. The following is what he wrote:

PURITANISM

The bad thing about it is the suffering so much guilt and anxiety. And wondering if you will be excepted (sic) into heaven or hell.

The following errors are readily apparent:

1. poor sentence development
2. poor sentence elaboration
3. poor paragraph development
4. poor informational content
5. poor sentence structure
6. word usage error (or spelling error?)

This student was found to have adequate oral expressive language and reading achievement within normal limits. The difficulty seemed to be a "pure" written expression problem. When asked to describe Puritanism orally, the youth did a far better job than his writing reflects.

This student received therapy with the Phelps Sentence Guide program for 12 weeks on a twice-weekly basis of 30 minutes to one hour each session. His English teacher provided the instruction during her off period. Work progressed rapidly. At Stage IX, the student received in-depth practice and guidance in dialoguing. A number of topics were discussed and dialogued, a position was chosen, the paragraph was outlined, and the final paragraph was written. Imagery was stressed.

From a point of not being able to follow these steps whatsoever, this youth progressed to a level of writing acceptability. This particular level in the program seemed to be the point at which written expression "clicked." He verbally explained on a number of occasions that he had learned how to "picture" a topic in his mind, allowing him to be able to write more fluently. At times, he even stopped working, said he needed to order his thoughts and images, and then continued writing. The following is an example of his writing at the end of the therapy period:

PURITANISM

Puritanism had many good and bad points. First, a good point was that the crime rate was low because crime is thought of as a very bad sin. Second, many good morals came from the Puritan's influence. Third, Puritans developed a strong faith for all their followers. Also, the Puritans worked hard for their community and for their religion. They respected businessmen since hard work kept a person living right. But Puritans had bad points such as not being tolerant. Puritans thought that they were the only correct thinkers because they didn't believe anyone else had anything to offer. Also, they looked down on poor people and called them lazy. They thought that poor people were poor because they didn't live right. Because of this, Puritans created guilt feelings in their followers. In summary, though Puritanism had many bad points, it had more good points.

The student improved his writing significantly in comparison to his earlier composition. It should be noted that during therapy he did not practice writing about Puritanism; rather, he was asked to repeat the earlier assignment at the end of the 12-week program. Because of scheduling difficulties, therapy was discontinued until later in the school year, but the two samples mark a clear increase in writing skills. Presumably, writing proficiency continued to improve.

In his second paragraph, the following are evident:

1. improved sentence elaboration
2. improved sentence development
3. improved sentence ordering leading to paragraphs with improved informational content
4. improved syntax
5. use of connectives such as "first," "second," "third," "also," and "in summary"
6. improved unity, cohesion, and logical development.

The Phelps Sentence Guide program proved very effective in teaching this youth to order and structure his written expressive language.

EVALUATION OF PHELPS SENTENCE GUIDE REMEDIATION

The Phelps Sentence Guide program offers a technique for teaching structure, elaboration, imagery, and editing to students from a single-sentence level to the writing of paragraphs and stories. The published version of the program did not become available until 1980, so time and experience in the coming years in a variety of professional situations are needed. That the experimental version of the program already has been used successfully in a context different from its original intent—that is, with adult aphasics—is proof of its versatility and effectiveness in a wide range of situations. The examples in this chapter attest to the usefulness of the program with language deficient students. The results in regular education settings also have proved positive.

As in the Fitzgerald Key program, the Phelps Sentence Guide provides a visual sentence structuring and ordering system that appears to become internalized in time so that written expression becomes more fluent and automatic. There also is evidence, and Johnson and Myklebust (1967) have noted this point, that for some children, competency in written expression may also generalize to the oral expressive mode. This reverse of the language hierarchy (Myklebust, 1960) seems to be related to the fact that more time is allowed for composition and refinement, as well as visual monitoring, in the written expressive mode. In time, written structure becomes internalized and automatic and it is at this point that the internal framework seems to generalize to the other expressive mode. This observation deserves further research and investigation, but has been observed clinically on several occasions by a number of professionals.

The Phelps Sentence Guide program gives the student effective structure in learning to expand and elaborate within a correct syntactical frame. The program teaches the student—first concretely and later more abstractly—to objectify sentence content into mental images that permit the person to distance self from topic in order to communicate more effectively with an audience. Since the program builds on a progressive mastery of skills ranging from simple to more complex, the student is not overwhelmed with the totality of generating written expression but can focus on certain skills within the context of written expression.

The Phelps Sentence Guide program is an eclectic system, composed of innovative and adapted components. It appears to be a solid, effective new contribution to the array of written expressive language approaches currently in use. In any case, the Guide represents one of the few purely written expressive language remediation programs yet developed.

BIBLIOGRAPHY

Bruner, J. *Toward a theory of instruction.* Cambridge, Mass.: Harvard University Press, 1966.

Fernald, G. *Remedial techniques in basic school subjects.* New York: McGraw-Hill Book Company, 1943.

Fitzgerald, E. *Straight language for the deaf.* Washington, D.C.: The Volta Bureau, 1966.

Johnson, D., & Myklebust, H.R. *Learning disabilities: Educational principles and practices.* New York: Grune & Stratton, Inc., 1967.

Lee, L. *Developmental sentence analysis.* Evanston, Ill.: Northwestern University Press, 1974.

——————. *Interactive language development teaching.* Evanston, Ill.: Northwestern University Press, 1975.

Myklebust, H.R. *The psychology of deafness.* New York: Grune & Stratton, Inc., 1960.

Phelps-Terasaki, D., & Phelps, T. *Teaching written expression: The Phelps sentence guide program.* Novato, Calif.: Academic Therapy Publications, 1980.

Stetson, E. Unpublished paper, University of Houston, 1977.

Chapter 5

Sentence Combining

The sentence combining school of instruction in written expressive language is a widely used approach currently receiving much research attention. This instructional system focuses on teaching students to combine simple sentences into more complex structures. The combining task is taught in a number of settings according to a variety of rules or combination methods. For example, embedding a simple sentence in a larger construction illustrates one method; conjoining two simple sentences with a conjunction is another. The core of this approach is the combining of several smaller sentence units into a single larger sentence unit.

Sentence combining is based on a transformational-generative perspective of language. This grammar system has been a dominant force in the analysis of syntactic language and has been used as a base for many reading and oral language remedial programs. In sentence combining, a particular system and a series of grammatical rules are perceived to be used in building complex sentences. These rules account for the combining of core ideas and sentences into appropriate end products that are the most efficient for communicative purposes. Thus, core units are transformed according to rules into the end units.

This chapter explains the sentence combining approach to teaching writing. First, the transformational-generative grammar base is described, followed by the methodology, a review of some of the research, and concluding with an analysis and critique of sentence combining instruction.

THEORETICAL BASIS OF SENTENCE COMBINING

The advent of transformational-generative grammar (N. Chomsky, 1957) revolutionized the theory underlying sentence complexity. Prior to his work, language complexity was thought to be derived from additions to main or core clauses. For example, a complex sentence with a descriptive subject used to be conceived of as a basic noun clause to which a number of modifiers had been added. The additions further explained the noun clause itself. Chomsky's efforts, however, resulted in defining the modifiers of a noun clause as additions that were combined from several basic kernels into a more complex structure. That is, a series of kernel sentences were combined, conjoined, or embedded to result in a complex structure reflecting its component kernels. Chomsky's transformational-generative grammar marked a clear breaking away from the status quo. The following points further illustrate the differences in conception:

1. Prior to Chomsky, the main clause was perceived to direct and focus the entire sentence.
2. Prior to Chomsky, the main clause was perceived to precede all additions, which occurred as a result of enlarging the scope of the main clause.
3. Prior to Chomsky, the additions were perceived to relate only to the main clause, not to the underlying language utterance.
4. Prior to Chomsky, sentence complexity was defined as an enlargement of the scope of the main clause. This growth was the result of additions radiating from the utterance itself, expanding laterally to include modifications dependent upon the main clause. The main clause was perceived to be the given, and complexity followed this given.

Transformational-generative grammar proposes a different theory for the origins of both sentences and sentence complexity. This theory develops a relationship between deep and surface structure by means of transformational rules. The major points and tenets of transformational-generative grammar are outlined briefly.

The Kernel Sentence and the Proposition

A language utterance in its smallest and most basic form is expressed as a kernel sentence, or even as a proposition. This kernel sentence is the most basic structure in the communicative chain and is the element most intimately linked to the original thought. The kernel sentence is formed by following a series of phrase structure rules or procedures—abstract processes used to form the utterance. The simplest phrase structure rule is that a sentence is composed of a noun phrase and a verb phrase, or S = NP + VP.

A lexicon, or mental dictionary, is used to supply the words for the abstract categories involved in the phrase structure procedure. That is, the phrase structure rules serve to create a "skeleton" sentence into which the lexical units are placed. This skeletal structure serves two purposes:

1. It acts as a frame for inserting words, in a slot-filling manner.
2. It is "slanted" toward the lexical items it needs because it is so closely related to the underlying idea.

In other words, the skeletal sentence, built by phrase structure rules, is formulated in such a way that it is prepared in advance for the lexical units appropriate to the communicative intent.

A kernel sentence, composed of phrase structure procedures concretized through lexical or word units, is active, simple, direct, and indicative. The kernel sentence or proposition is a basic utterance minus modifying and descriptive units. Each kernel sentence or proposition corresponds to a single unitary idea and is close to the speaker's essential and original interior language thought or conception. Thus, the kernel sentence can be termed the deep or underlying structure or formulation of the sentence.

This deep structure of the sentence is the part most directly related or closest to the actual meaning or intent of the utterance. Once a deep structure is generated, operations may occur that transform the emerging sentence into its resultant surface structure. This surface structure may not actually emerge overtly but can be produced in spoken or written form.

Surface Structure

The concrete or overt form of the sentence, including all transformations, can be termed its surface structure. This surface structure, in speech, is given a phonetic and articulatory interpretation yielding its pronunciation. The surface structure, in writing, is given an orthographic interpretation yielding the written sentence. The surface structure also has a semantic interpretation, yielding the meaning of the sentence to the person receiving the utterance.

Ambiguity results when the surface structure is interpreted as other than that formulated by the deep structures of the communication. This ambiguity is related to a mismatch between the communicative intent of the message and its surface form.

Competence and Performance

N. Chomsky (1957) differentiates between competence and performance in language utterance. He defines competence as individuals' innate or given ability to generate deep structures and then communicate them. It is their language capacity, an internalized system of rules, of which they are unaware.

Deep structure is not taught or learned; it is, like thought, a capacity, an expression of individuals' abilities as humans.

Chomsky defines performance as the actual application of an individual's competence. It is the end product of the expressive communicative cycle, given all the day-to-day interferences that may limit a listener in interpreting it on a surface structure level. These variables can range from mental conditions and fatigue to nonstandard grammatical forms that interfere with the semantic and syntactic meanings that the person sought to communicate.

For example, a person who is very tired may "garble" a message and not communicate efficiently. Performance errors are not indicative of deep structure faults but of transformational mistakes or of performance factors. All of these factors—deep structure, surface structure, transformational rules, etc.—are related in the communicative cycle. The relationship among the components in oral language is illustrated in Exhibit 5-1.

Exhibit 5-1   Oral Language Relationships

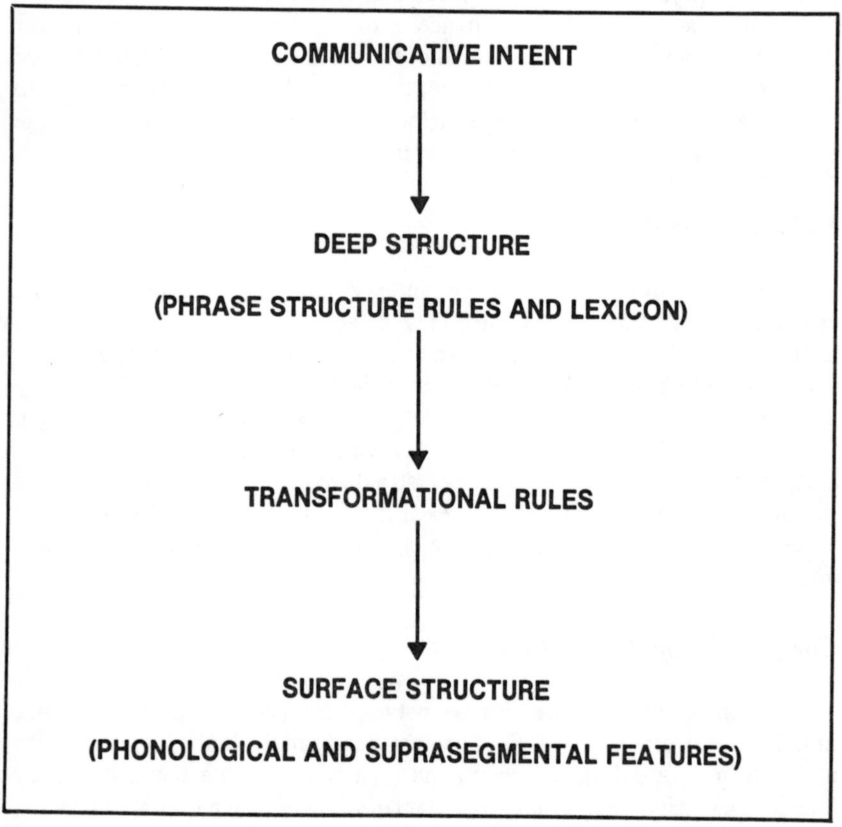

COMMUNICATIVE INTENT

↓

DEEP STRUCTURE

(PHRASE STRUCTURE RULES AND LEXICON)

↓

TRANSFORMATIONAL RULES

↓

SURFACE STRUCTURE

(PHONOLOGICAL AND SUPRASEGMENTAL FEATURES)

Suppose the individual has a desire to communicate a particular message. The deep structure of the message is built by phrase structure rules and the lexical entries. Then, if appropriate, transformational rules are added to produce the surface structure. This surface structure is interfaced with its phonological features and characteristics, and an articulation program is followed. The result is the oral production of the message.

Relationship of Deep and Surface Structure

The use of a tree diagram makes the relationship of deep and surface structures even clearer (Exhibit 5-2).

A kernel sentence or proposition, then, contains two basic units: an NP and a VP. Before it emerges from deep structure as a surface structure utterance, the kernel may undergo several transformations. For example, the passive transformation changes the original active kernel sentence, through a series of steps, into a passive structure. For example, "The car hit the train" becomes "The train was hit by the car." A proposition is always originally active; to become passive, a transformation must occur.

The question transformation changes the original indicative kernel sentence into an interrogative surface structure: "You will go" becomes "Will you go?" A proposition is always indicative; to become interrogative, a transformation must occur. Emphatic and imperative transformations also alter the deep structure by adding emphasis, "They go. They do go."; or by deleting an understood subject, "You get out. Get out." A proposition always is a simple, not complex, construction.

In summary, a proposition or kernel sentence is simple, indicative, and active in its origin and conception. Through any of a number of transformations, it is changed into a particular surface structure. Transformational-generative grammar focuses on the process of sentence formation rather than on analysis of the resultant end product. In so doing, linguistic relationships become clearer, suggesting general patterns that underlie most languaging.

Simple and Complex Sentence Generation

The rationale behind complex sentence origin essentially is the same as the procedures for simple sentence generation. Clark and Clark (1977) prefer the term proposition rather than kernel sentence. They define proposition as what expresses a basic unit of meaning, a basic unitary proposal, that sometimes occurs prior to kernel sentence projection. Like a kernel sentence, a proposition has a verbal unit and a noun unit. The following sentence illustrates the difference between proposition and kernel sentence as proposed by

Exhibit 5-2   Tree Diagram of Deep and Surface Structures

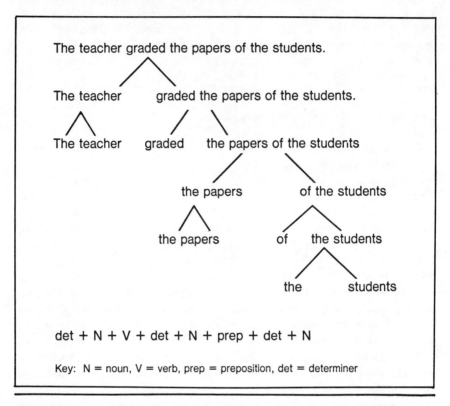

Key: N = noun, V = verb, prep = preposition, det = determiner

Clark and Clark. It is a simple kernel sentence: simple, indicative, and active; however, it contains four propositions:

The fast red car speeds around the big curve.

1. The car is fast.

2. The car is red.

3. The curve is big.

4. The car speeds.

When these four are combined, they yield a simple kernel sentence. Proposition 4 is the base upon which the three others are arranged. Each proposition contains a unique idea or meaning component:

Proposition 1 - fastness of car

Proposition 2 - redness of car

Proposition 3 - bigness of curve

Proposition 4 - speed of car

When these four meaning components are combined, they yield the simple kernel sentence: The fast red car speeds around the big curve.

These propositions are the underlying structure of meaning that is expressed on the surface in linear units of syntax and phonology. Three important conclusions result:

1. Simple sentences use combinations of propositions to generate more effective simple sentencing. Obviously, language production that can combine four propositional units of meaning into one surface utterance is more efficient than speaking in short, simple sentences.
2. Such an utterance also is more ordered in that, as in the example above, the speaker has chosen Proposition 4 as the one on which to arrange the three others. Had the speaker expressed all four propositions independently, the individual would have made no cognitive choice as to the relative emphasis of one proposition over another. Combining propositions allows the speaker to create meaning beyond that of using lexical units plugged into phrase structure rules.
3. In contrast to language theory prior to Chomsky, transformational-generative combinations are surface unions of underlying meaning units plus cognitive ordering. The main clause does not occur first and then become enlarged linearly; rather, all propositions or ideas originate as equal meaning units until acted upon by the speaker. The main clause is not independent of additions; instead, the speaker combines propositions into complex utterances. Thus, combining propositions not only yields more efficient sentencing, but also demands cognitive ordering.

COMPLEX SENTENCE THEORY

The methodology of complex sentencing is identical to that in combining propositions into a kernel sentence. Just as simple sentences result from combined propositions, so do complex sentences result from combined propositions and kernel sentences. Such complex combinations are more efficient and reflect cognitive ordering by the speaker, just as simpler combinations also reflect efficiency and order. Complex sentencing results from three procedures: coordination, embedding, and complementation. Each procedure unites two or more kernel sentences, each composed of at least one underlying proposition, into a complex structure.

Coordination

Coordination links ideas that are equal to each other in emphasis. Not only are the ideas equal in origin and in thought but also the speaker chooses to link them as equal in emphasis in surface structure. Coordination also is efficient in that it eliminates extraneous or redundant words. The following two propositions can be combined into one proposition:

1. John laughs at lunch.

2. John smiles at lunch.

Combination: John laughs and smiles at lunch.

A compound predicate combines the two kernels by deleting extraneous words, thus yielding a more efficient utterance. Cognitive ordering places "laugh" first but on an equal standing of emphasis with "smile."

The words that serve as coordinating conjunctions/connectors are as follows: and, but, nor, for, so, and yet. The most common of all the conjunctions is "and." This word unites sentences without distinguishing time, as do the words "yet" and "so;" or distinguishing result, as does the word "for;" or distinguishing choice, as do the words "or" and "nor;" or distinguishing contrary options, as does the word "but."

Since coordinating connectives are simply a link between two or more propositions, their use implies cognitive structuring of language relationships. The following two propositions function adequately independently but when combined suggest a relationship not expressed when considered alone:

1. John smiles during lunch.

2. Mary laughs during lunch.

Combination: John smiles during lunch, but Mary laughs.

Combining the two propositions suggests a relationship or sequence of events that unites two hitherto independent propositions into a new proposition different in semantic context. The step of combining propositions requires cognitive action.

Adverbial connectives also combine propositions into new relationships in which the propositions still maintain equality of emphasis. These connectives, however, more clearly delineate relationships between the propositions. Adverbial connectives include words such as the following: however, nevertheless, moreover, on the other hand. The following unrelated propositions, when linked by an adverbial connective, not only become more efficient but also demonstrate a cognitive ordering of relationships and ideas that transforms the earlier propositions into a new language utterance:

1. She wins the contest.

2. She cries.

Combination: She wins the contest; nevertheless, she cries.

Combining the two propositions creates a new relationship between the propositions not part of the propositions independently.

In the following sentences, the connectors "and," "therefore," and "when" radically alter the kernel propositions to produce new semantic arrangements:

I cried and fell down.

I cried; therefore. I fell down.

I cried when I fell down.

Embedding

Embedding is the second method of generating combined propositions or complexity in sentence production. Embedding occurs when one sentence or proposition is included within another sentence or proposition. Several propositions can be embedded to yield one simple sentence, illustrated by, "The fast red car speeds around the big curve." The same procedure can be used to create complex as well as simple sentences. The following two sentences can be combined into one sentence by embedding:

1. The man is a doctor.

2. The man works in a hospital.

Embedding: The man who works in a hospital is a doctor.

Proposition 2 was embedded into Proposition 1. In so doing, Proposition 2 became a dependent clause on the surface structure, dependent upon the main clause structurally and semantically in terms of surface structure. However, the dependent clause is not the less important clause but rather has been so related to the first proposition as to almost merge within it. But an important point results. In transformational-generative grammar theory, propositions retain their underlying relationship to meaning regardless of their syntactical surface structure arrangement. The speaker has so ordered language production as to subordinate one proposition in emphasis but has not removed the underlying equality of propositional meaning in the deep structure relationship. Proposition 2 is dependent only in terms of surface structure.

Sentences thus do not become complex because the speaker begins with one sentence and adds surface refinements; they become complex when the speaker combines underlying propositions into surface complexities, yielding new semantic components. Complexity results from a combining of underlying meaning units into new cognitively ordered arrangements. Traditional grammar defines complexity as a broadening and refashioning of surface arrangements, leading to surface choice of a more "important" meaning attributed to one clause over another. Transformational grammar maintains the essential propositional meaning but alters surface syntactical structure to create new relationships and meanings.

Relative adjective and subordinate adverbial clauses are the two major embedding methods that yield sentence complexity. Clark and Clark (1977) refer to such combination procedures as relativization, which they define as the attachment of one proposition to a constituent of another proposition for the purpose of modifying that constituent part by restricting or qualifying it. The following is an example of relativization:

1. The girl cuts the cake.

2. The cake is a gift.

Relativization: The girl cuts the cake that is a gift.

Proposition 2 was turned into a relative clause that qualified and restricted the word "cake" to specify a gift cake.

Relativization by restricting and qualifying creates more efficient sentences as well as newly ordered relationships between propositions that entail new meaning units. Relativization by definition involves combining simple sentences into complex ones as well as by combining propositions into simple sentences. Modification can occur within noun, verb, prepositional, and possessive phrases. The process merely becomes more "complex" when producing complex sentences.

Embedding and relativization can follow relative pronouns such as who, whom, whose, which, and that, or subordinating connectives such as when, because, if, since, and although. The example above illustrates relativization using a relative pronoun "that;" the following example illustrates relativization using the subordinating connector "when:"

1. The boy eats lunch.

2. The boy is hungry.

Relativization: The boy eats lunch when he is hungry.

Proposition 2 was embedded at the end of Proposition 1 by specifying and limiting when the boy "eats lunch."

In summary, relativization and embedding create more efficient sentences as well as new meaning relationships through cognitive structuring of the parts. Subordination differs from relative adjective clause subordination in the following two ways:

1. Adverbial subordination generally does not require deletions as does relative clause subordination. In the former, the kernel sentence retains its essential underlying structure.
2. Adverbial subordination generally is not embedded within a kernel sentence but either precedes or follows in its entirety the kernel proposition to which it is attached.

Essentially, children more easily acquire mastery of subordinate adverbial clauses than of relative structures. Research by Hunt (1965) indicates that by the fourth grade, children can use a wide variety of complex transformations in their speech; they simply do not do so with great frequency. The frequency of such usage increases significantly with age, primarily because of cognitive development. The young child approaches complex sentencing by following what Clark and Clark (1977) describe as the principle of not rearranging or interrupting linguistic units if at all possible. This principle leads to the assumption that when relative or subordinate clauses are involved, children evidence greater choice and ease in using them in combinations that do not interrupt the designated major proposition of their sentence. For example:

1. Relative clauses that follow objects are easier to master than those that follow subjects and interrupt the sentence.

   a. The man who wears white is a doctor.

   b. The man is a doctor who wears white.

   Sentence b is acquired earlier because it involves the least amount of rearranging.

2. Adverbial subordinate clauses that follow the main clause are easier to master than those that precede the main clause. Children assume the first event should be the main clause and that the second ordered event is the subordinate clause.

a. If we open the door, flies will come in.

b. Flies will come in, if we open the door.

Sentence b is acquired earlier because it assumes a time ordered relationship of main clause first and subordinate clause second.

Complementization

The third method of obtaining sentence complexity is by complementization, defined by Clark and Clark (1977) as filling in the empty part of one proposition with another proposition. Complementization involves combining propositions into more efficient units by cognitive arrangement. Several procedures that lead to complementization are the use of *that*; the use of *for* . . . *to*; the use of possessive *'s* . . . *ing of* . . .; and following *Wh* words, such as what, why, and where. Given a sentence "Something is sad" as an example of complementization, ideas are used to fill in the empty unit "something" as follows:

1. *That* the baby cries is sad.
2. For the baby *to* cry is sad.
3. The baby*'s* crying is sad.
4. *What* the baby is crying for is sad.

Children acquire complementization easier in cases where it is marked clearly as such—for example, following *that* or a *Wh* word. Children also assume that the closest noun to be complemented is the subject of the complement. C. Chomsky (1969) has reported interesting results in testing comprehension of children with the following two sentences:

1. Kevin told Will to go out.
2. Kevin promised Will to go out

Young children assume that the second sentence has the same meaning as the first since they expect the subject of the complement to be the one closest to it. Hunt (1965) reports that children have the most difficulty in syntax in mastering the use of a noun relative clause or a complex nominal phrase. He reports that measuring the frequencies of these elements in a given situation yields a fairly reliable index of a student's grade level and/or academic standing in that grade in terms of high, middle, or low ability. Sentence complexity derived by complementation is the most difficult method of establishing combinations leading to syntactic complexity.

Compounding, relativization, embedding, and complementization account for the variety of ways sentences can be elaborated, ranging from descriptive simple to complex combined ones. In transformational-generative grammar, such elaboration follows the combining of propositional meaning units into larger constructions.

Following this brief overview of the basis underlying transformational grammar, attention now is directed to the remediation process resulting from this theory. Given that sentence complexity derives from the combination of propositions, a linguistic approach to remediation was devised entitled sentence combining.

THE SENTENCE COMBINING APPROACH

The T-Unit

A major tenet of sentence combining is that complexity increases with age. Hunt (1965) developed the term T-unit, defined as a main clause plus any clausal or nonclausal attachments. He counted the frequency of T-units as well as the number of words per T-unit occurring in student writing. Dividing the number of words by the number of T-units yielded a number that he termed the T-score. T-scores increased significantly, though slowly, with age. Such measurements enabled Hunt to determine norms for T-scores for children at certain grade levels as well as for skilled adults. The adults were selected on the basis of being competent in magazine writing. Through analyzing the T-units derived from writing samples by the children and the adults, Hunt determined the following:

1. Children increase the number of words per clause as they mature.
2. Children increase the number of clauses per T-unit as they mature, but at a certain point—apparently twelfth grade—the number becomes and remains fairly stable. Obviously, a sentence cannot go on forever.

Based on his research, Hunt postulates that the best indicator of syntactic maturity was the number of words per T-unit. Children in fourth grade had an average of 8.6, eighth graders 11.5, and twelfth graders 14.4. Skilled adults, on the other hand, averaged 20.3. Further, Hunt reports that the number of relative clauses quadrupled from fourth to twelfth grade. He determined that no other form of subordination increased as markedly. Language research has shown that relative clauses are particularly difficult to master because they require deletions as well as rearrangements of the main clause. He also notes that the increase in complementization was a very significant determiner of the differences between grades and abilities. Hunt concludes that older writers used more sentence combining involving relativization, compounding, and complementation.

Hunt (1970) later compared the amount of sentence combining evidenced in free writing samples to that in given writing combinations. Given writing combinations involved a set number of very basic kernel sentences that the students were instructed to combine into "better" sentences. In comparing the T-scores of the writing samples, he finds the following:

1. Students exhibit the same general syntactic characteristics in free writing as in given writing.
2. Clause length is sensitive enough to differentiate between ability groups within a grade, such as high, middle, or low. Clause length also discriminates well between grades.
3. Younger students require more T-units to communicate a certain meaning in their writing than do older writers, who produce more content in fewer T-units.
4. Older writers add meanings to the given writing based upon the new relationships they created with combining procedures. Complex combinations create a meaning apart from the original deep structure of the propositions. This cognitive ability not only to use more complex syntax but also to create shades of meaning through such devices demonstrates the differences between writing abilities.

The following example shows how the same sentences might be handled by students at different levels of writing ability, using grade levels as determined by Hunt (1965):

Example A

The man finally opened the door. The door was tall. It was red. It was heavy. He fed them the food.

(5 T-units, 4.2 words per T-unit, performance below average fourth grade level)

Example B

The man finally opened the door. The door was tall, red and heavy. He fed them the food.

(3 T-units, 6.0 words per T-unit, performance below average for a middle-level eighth grader)

Example C

The man finally opened the tall, red, and heavy door to feed them the food.

(1 T-unit, 15.0 words per T-unit, performance above average for high-level twelfth grader)

Sentence Combining and the T-Unit

Given the Hunt measurement device, Mellon (1969) devised a program to teach sentence combining to determine whether it would raise the T-unit scores of children. His program has no relation to rhetoric or composition curriculum units but is designed separately as linguistic practice. He stresses that he is enhancing syntactic expression, not writing. His exercises are geared to linguistics, not composition. He determined that his grammar practice must meet two conditions:

1. The result must be a sentence exhibiting the best possible model of syntactic maturity; therefore, the exercises are to be structured and prearranged so that the outcome will be a predetermined excellent and mature syntactical construction. For the study to be acceptable, the student must be led to formulate syntactically fluent and mature responses. The student should not work on immature syntactic patterns.
2. The student's entire attention should be directed toward the linguistic combinations at hand, not toward the added need to create new content or context within which to practice. Therefore, all of the content is provided to the students; they need only practice their new skills on the given content. Their focus thus is not to be split among many variables or needs.

Mellon's procedure requires the children to study a series of kernel sentences, after which they are given directions for combining them into one new unit and writing it out in completed form.

Mellon argues that practice in sentence embedding will carry over into the student's own expression. As such, the student orally practices the problem until all elements are embedded, creating one complex sentence. The pupil then writes out the ensuing complex sentence from memory of the previous oral steps.

Mellon (1969) suggests that students intuitively know what is right and what is wrong in grammar. Given the sentences, "The boy is tall" and "The boy is happy," students naturally will combine them into "The tall boy is happy" and not into "The boy happy and is tall." In this way, sentence combining allows for individuals' intuitive knowledge of their language to be the determiner of the final, combined sentence. Unlike traditional grammar, the child with normal oral language will be error free in using the combining approach. Since the exercises are considered to be grammatical and not compositional, the complexities of discourse are avoided. The problems are isolated from interference from composition or writing practice. Mellon includes particular transformation problems illustrating each of the transformations being taught. His nine lessons for complex transformations are:

1. Sentences within sentences
2. Sentences as nouns: fact clauses
3. Sentences as nouns: question clauses
4. Sentences as nouns: gerund and infinitive phrases
5. Sentences as nouns: derived noun phrases
6. Sentences as noun modifiers
7. Sentences as noun modifiers: modifying phrases
8. Sentences as noun modifiers: pronoun modifiers
9. Building noun modification

Mellon's lessons, then, are constructed primarily to give practice in nominal combinations, for he states that based on the work by Hunt (1965) it is the increase in nominal constructions that is most sensitive to maturity and age changes.

Nominal Constructions

Nominal is a term that describes the word or word groups that function as subjects, direct objects, indirect objects, objects of the preposition, and other noun functions. Nominals break into two categories (Hunt, 1965): headed and nonheaded. A headed nominal is one in which the combining transformations refer to the same word. For example, in the following two sentences the word the modifiers restrict is the same; each proposition is headed by the same nominal.

1. The man is angry.

2. The man is hungry.

Combination: The man is angry and hungry.

Man is the headed nominal for both angry and hungry. However, in non-headed nominals, the combining process does not work so simply. Nonheaded nominals are similar to complementation as discussed earlier but produce noun clauses, verbals, or appositives. In complementation, a phrase or clause is embedded in response to a vacant or empty noun, usually designated as *something*.

1. The man knows *something*.
2. The mailman delivers the letter.

Complementation: The man knows that the mailman delivers the letter.

There is no direct connection lexically between the two sentences; thus, nonheaded nominals are considerably more difficult and more sensitive to the measurement of efforts of instruction. Mellon focuses primarily on such non-headed combinations.

Concentrating on specific practice for each skill enumerated in his lesson plans, he ends with general practice in which the student is given ten or so simple propositions to combine into one complex expression.

He divides seventh graders into three groups: an experimental team using sentence combining techniques, a control panel using sentence parsing based on traditional grammar, and a placebo unit using literature and composition. Over a nine-month period, Mellon measured their syntactic maturity as obtained from free writing of essays in one-hour periods. He found that the experimental group wrote 32 percent more (nonheaded) nominals than did the control group. The experimentals gained a T-unit lead representing almost a year and a half over the control group. However, that lead is only .75 words per T-unit—a small increase upon which to base significance.

Mellon cautions that the increases are so small to begin with that researchers must not rule out differing levels of cognitive development as the explanation for the performance differences. Nonetheless, his study offers strong evidence of a relationship between sentence combining and syntactical maturity in student free writing situations following practice.

The Effect of the Oral on the Written

Miller and Ney (1968) report a second study researching the effects of oral sentence combining on student writing and syntax. Using fourth graders, they found that the experimental group wrote more words, used more practiced structures, and increased in syntactic maturity as defined by T-units. However, this study is based upon only 24 students, a very small number from which to generalize the data to other populations. Both writing samples upon which growth is measured also are based on a film that had sound.

Students could have followed the film style, syntax, and lexicon rather than generating their own structures. They could have learned what to imitate rather than what to generate. Despite these drawbacks, the study provides interesting data to support the effectiveness of sentence combining instruction on children's writing.

O'Hare (1971) also researched the efficacy of sentence combining, measuring syntactic growth based on six factors:

1. words per T-unit
2. clauses per T-unit
3. words per clause
4. noun clauses per 100 T-units
5. adjective clauses per 100 T-units
6. adverb clauses per 100 T-units

Figures for these six levels of maturity were computed for each of the seventh grade pupils in a Florida high school by analyzing the first ten T-units from each of a student's ten compositions; five essays were used as preexperiment essays and five as postexperiment writing. Eight experienced English teachers graded overall writing quality between the control and experimental groups based on ideas, organization, style, vocabulary, and sentence structure. Spelling and punctuation were corrected before submittal to the judges.

O'Hare found that the experimental group experienced significant growth in all six areas of syntactic maturity and scored T-units above the mean established by Hunt for twelfth graders. In addition, O'Hare found that such practices were more efficacious for high IQ students than for those with low IQ's, although the latter also gained significantly. He reported that the experimental essays were better in a proportion of .70 to .29 as compared to the control group's.

However, O'Hare's study involved only a small group of students from a Caucasian, middle-class high school, making the generalization of results to other populations difficult. Nonetheless, his findings also are impressive.

Curriculum Sources and Methodology

There are two textbooks devoted to instruction in sentence combining. Strong (1973) directs his exercises and scope primarily at school-age pupils. Daiker, Kerek, and Morenberg (1979) focus on college-age students. However, both textbooks follow a similar format:

1. Both offer a multitude of exercises.
2. Both are subdivided into chapters that build specific syntactical skills.

The major chapters in the latter book (Daiker et al.) are the following:

1. relative clauses
2. participles
3. appositives
4. absolutes
5. prepositional phrases
6. subordination
7. coordination
8. noun substitutes

Each chapter (Daiker et al., 1979) has approximately eight exercises to reinforce and illustrate the target skill. The exercises are inventive, creative, and interesting. Much thought has gone into the arrangement of the potential essays by grouping five to six similar propositions. The student is led indirectly to certain groupings of ideas. By partitioning the kernel sentences into groups, the student tends to try to rewrite that propositional unit into one complete sentence.

Daiker et al. contribute an important addition because their exercises fit together to make a compositional whole. Upon conclusion of the assignment, the student has a well-constructed essay, ranging from narration to exposition to persuasion. The final product becomes an example of good writing—even if the student's sentences are simplistic syntactically. The essay has coherence, emphasis, and unity as given; the student need add only syntactic maturity to polish the writing. The essay topics cover a variety of interesting areas: "The Pepsi Generation," "Karate," "Tattooing," "Dressed to Kill," and "Dracula."

Compositional Goals

Daiker et al. also move beyond specific syntactical goals to include compositional goals, which they define as strategies for effective writing, focusing on the following:

1. rearrangement—to foster unity
2. repetition—to foster clarity of compositional content
3. emphasis—to foster the controlling idea
4. coherence—to foster use of transitions
5. tone—to foster clarity of writer's intent

They use the same format as before in addressing these rhetorical issues: eight exercises, each devoted to an interesting topic to reinforce each target skill. Again, students are virtually led to produce the final polished essay illustrating the target skill. Daiker et al. conclude their text with exercises on revising poor paragraphs and clarifying or editing preliminary notes before writing.

The Writer's Options (Daiker et al., 1979) is a well-formulated and well-constructed manual for teaching linguistic competence through a sentence combining remediation approach. Although geared for college students, it certainly is applicable to advanced high school students. Because of the essay format—an extended amount of discourse—the text is too complex for beginning writers.

To support their thesis, Daiker et al. field-tested sentence combining instruction in an experimental program with entering university freshmen. They reported a significant increase in the students' syntactical maturity, calibrated by using Hunt's T-units as well as rhetorical improvement as measured by the entire composition.

Explorations and Targets

Strong (1973) directs his efforts toward the intermediate and the high school student. His chapters reflect simpler target skills and rely upon easier propositions for combination, reflecting the abilities of a younger age group.

Strong divides his text into two parts. The first, Phase I, "Explorations," contains 77 exercises. Each exercise provides from 14 to more than 100 kernel sentences organized around one central topic. The topics range from "Street Scene" to "How Whites Look to Blacks" to "Ski Dreamer." The topics are interesting, relevant, and consciously designed to attract adolescent attention.

Following each exercise, Strong offers concise suggestions for combining the sentences: "Sentences 10-12 and 13-14 can be combined into one longer sentence" (p. 10). As the program develops, the suggestions move beyond combination to composition possibilities. For example, following "The Carver" is the suggestion to "write a detailed description of someone you have seen deeply absorbed in something he likes doing" (p. 115). The purpose behind Phase I, according to Strong, is to "develop a feel for the patterns of Written English" (p. 157).

In Phase II "Explorations," Strong targets eight sentence constructions:

1. sentence in two levels
2. sentence in two levels with base clause in the middle
3. sentence in two levels with absolutes
4. multilevel sentence
5. multilevel sentence with base clause in the middle
6. sentence with two base clauses and two levels
7. sentence with two base clauses and multilevels
8. sentence combining the base clauses.

He illustrates each target by first showing the student the many kernel sentences, then the target sentence that results from combining the kernels. The student is given grouped kernel sentences with which to imitate the model. Following specific practice with each of the eight target transforms, the student applies the new skills by practicing on 13 general topics as in Phase I. Phase II thus provides practice in copying and imitating a model.

Strong's text is well thought out and easy to use with adolescents. He provides interesting topics, well-illustrated targets, and plenty of practice. As with the Daiker et al. (1979) model, the strength in a sentence combining test is not only the number of exercises but also the underlying plan that accounts for a "better" end product sentence regardless of how completely the student transforms the kernels.

However, exercises in his eight target areas are complicated and seem to require an arbitrary arrangement of kernels to match a model rather than to produce a natural process.

Centrality of Themes

Numerous exercises are used to reinforce their ability to feel comfortable with and use the new skill. In both the Strong and Daiker et al. texts, all the sentences are organized around central themes. The practice examples are independent of a larger composition whole. Sentence combining methodology is simple, clear, direct, and easy for the instructor to administer and for the students to follow.

In short, the theory behind both textbooks is that skill developed from practice in combining given like propositions into complex ones will transfer to student-generated propositions. Thus, each book offers a wide variety of exercises to practice combining simple propositions into more complex utterances or texts.

Sentence combining methodology involves the choice of a target skill followed by numerous exercises to develop facility in using that skill. If, for example, the target skill involves conjoining predicates, the methodology is as follows.

Students are shown examples of combined predicates to illustrate the skill. They then are given groups of related propositions to combine into a compound predicate sentence. For example, they might be asked to combine the following two propositions into one sentence:

The nice boy runs quickly.

The nice boy jumps hurdles.

Combination: The nice boy runs quickly and jumps hurdles.

REVIEW OF THE RESEARCH

The major research studies testing the sentence combining method are those by Mellon (1969), Miller and Ney (1968), O'Hare (1971), and Daiker et al. (1978), Stewart (1978), and Combs (1976). All report improvements in using sentence combining with experimental groups when compared to control groups. The ages in these studies ranged from seventh graders to college freshmen. Care was taken to account for intervening variables such as differences in population, teacher influence on ability, and reliability in composition analysis.

Combs (1977) notes that even two months after completion of the program, a significant number of essays still were chosen by teachers who were rating them as being of better quality than the control section. O'Hare (1971) also reports positive judgments as to improved quality of composition. However, Marzano (1976) challenges the results of the composition evaluations by questioning the reliability of forced choice ratings.

Thus sentence combining continues to raise disturbing questions that mitigate its proposed complete efficacy as remediation. Ney (1976) discovered that his experimental project with college freshmen did not support the effectiveness of sentence combining practice and written language improvement. In response, Daiker et al. (1978) maintain that Ney spent only about ten minutes of class time for sentence combining as opposed to other experimental projects that involved extensive in-depth practice ranging from two hours a week to a solid six-week curriculum. Ney, however, disputes Daiker et al. (1978) by stating that college freshmen should only need ten minutes of class time for practice. Ney argues that the principles being taught required only that amount of time. To spend more time, he feels, is wasteful of precious college time, and is useless. In short, if the remediation is sound, Ney argues, then the student does not need to spend substantial time on it—theoretically, the students intuitively know the transformational rules; they just need awareness of how and when to use the process.

Time, then, is a factor worth considering. Intensive sentence combining remediation programs require large amounts of time (an hour and a half or so out of five hours of language arts class). If the student intuitively understands the combining process, Ney's point is clear: why so much time? A secondary consideration is the stability of improvement in the experimental groups. For example, Combs (1976) cautions that although his research supports sentence combining as an effective remediation program, in a post-test two months after the practice, his students lost half of the gains demonstrated in an immediate posttest.

The question arises: does practice in sentence combining increase syntactic maturity because the students merely imitate the curriculum, or do students "own" the skills, thus being able to generate their own complex utterances? Does the imitation fostered by practice transfer to new cognitive schemes? In short, how much time is needed to build new cognitive schemes?

Ney (1976) says ten minutes of class time is too little to elicit significant syntactical change, implying that sentence combining does not tap the student's intuitive language knowledge as readily as some have maintained. Apparently, sentence combining requires extensive time. Not only is it time consuming, but Combs reports that sentence combining improvements are not stable, again implying that sentence combining practice does not produce reliable new cognitive schemes that the student now uses in place of earlier immature syntax. Does sentence combining actually enable students to use intuitive language skills in a more overt or conscious manner?

Ney (1978), in response to the criticism engendered by his negative results, maintains that a good control teacher has more effect on student compositions (teaching no sentence combining) than a poor sentence combining instructor. Sentence combining, then, needs a good teacher to sell its results; in and of itself perhaps, it may not be so efficacious. Perhaps positive attention—not any particular type of instruction—is as effective as a special type of instruction.

Yet many of these research results do demonstrate that sentence combining does have a marked effect on syntactic maturity as measured by T-units. Ney's (1976) focus is on decomposing complex sentences into kernels as well as the reverse—building kernels into complex sentences. Daiker et al. (1978) argue in response that decomposing, by emphasizing analysis after the utterance rather than practice to produce it, does not teach sentence combining as a tool. Instead, such practice merely teaches a nonpractical theory that is not applicable to student writing. Ney (1980) concludes that he prefers games of composition to sentence combining. Daiker et al. firmly maintain that adequate time coupled with composing exercises will yield improved syntactical results in student writing.

But the issue is not so easily resolved. The first flush of excitement over a new remediation program has died down, leaving time for sober new appraisals. The issue has even led to parody, as when Malone (1980) testifies to the benefits of sentence fragment combining that (1) offers longer fragments—even two years above grade level, (2) offers longer discourse with no wrong answers, (3) follows natural inclinations, and (4) is loved by students.

EVALUATING SENTENCE COMBINING VARIABLES

An evaluation of the proposed benefits of sentence combining can be grouped under three headings: measurement, generation, and cognition.

Measurement

Sentence combining derives its strength as an effective remediation program from the increases it produces in measured T-unit length. However, San Jose (1978) reports that the norms of T-unit length established by Hunt (1965) really cannot be considered norms because research has not adequately established developed mental syntactical trends. Such norms also are derived from very small and fairly homogenous populations, leading to generalization to a broad array of populations based on much less than adequate norming procedures.

O'Donnell (1976) points out a major limitation of using Hunt's T-unit length as an indication of structural maturity: there are no data to show how T-unit length measures structural complexity. Although research supports Hunt's contention that clause length and clauses per T-unit increase with age, merely measuring *more* by T-units does not necessarily report quality. Length of syntactic units can be achieved in numerous ways, not all of which require as much syntactical maturity as others. T-unit length does not measure differences in complexity; it measures only differences in length predicated on the faulty assumption that length implies maturity.

Thus, much of the research supporting sentence combining uses a measurement device that does not differentiate kinds of complexity but rather assumes that length equals complexity. Common sense indicates that some highly complex.sentences may be very short; and, conversely, some totally simple constructions can be very long. Researchers are attempting to devise a measurement device that calibrates more than length.

Crowhurst (1979b) agrees that Hunt's T-unit norms are misleading because students vary their syntactic complexity to fit the chosen mode of discourse. Crowhurst (1979a) also finds that students use greater syntactic complexity when writing argument or exposition than when producing narration or description. In fact, she reports that the range of T-unit length for tenth graders writing in different modes varies considerably: narration 11.15, description 12.81, and argumentation 14.26. Given that Hunt (1965) assigned a norm of 11.5 for grade 8 and 14.4 for grade 12, the unreliability of Hunt's T-unit lengths becomes apparent. Crowhurst (1979a) finds great variation when assigning different modes. Using Hunt's norms, Crowhurst's tenth grade students could be considered either disabled and at the eighth grade level or advanced and at the twelfth grade level, depending on the topic. Apparently the norms used are not as valid as was considered earlier; the writing task often can elicit different levels of syntactic complexity.

Crowhurst (1979a) also makes a strong case for avoiding the term "syntactic maturity," declaring that Hunt's (1965) conclusion that "greater syntactic complexity is to be equaled with greater syntactic maturity and that merit or value attaches to the feature" is false. Instead, she maintains that mature writers have greater syntactic resources at their disposal that they use according to the nature of the task. She concludes that complexity does not equal maturity, although maturity may contain complexity.

DiStefano and Howie (1979) also criticize T-unit length as not considering either depth of modification or idea development. Instead, they have developed their own system of weighing certain sentence parts to determine the extent of the expansion of ideas.

Maimon and Nodine (1978) also report that syntactic complexity varies with the mode used; their students use fewer complex sentences when writing in the analytic mode than when combining using given kernel sentences. They theorize that the difficulty of the topic constrains the use of sentence complexity—the students must attend wholly to the content.

Generation

A second problem with sentence combining research is illustrated by Lunsford (1979), who maintains that "sentence combining drills will often fail to transfer new patterns into the basic writer's own writing—unless the sentence combining work helps build inferential bridges" (p. 43). Lunsford maintains that when a student is working below the cognitive level necessary to abstract a principle from drill work, then generalize the principle and apply it, the drill work will not be successful. Transfer does not occur unless the student can cognitively grasp the principle.

Lunsford places greater emphasis on inferential reasoning and conceptualization to ensure that drill work is productive. She offers an important cautionary point: sentence combining must begin or reach where the student is cognitively; it does not function in a cognitive void, although much of the literature focuses on external drill apart from internal meaning units. In short, drill with given propositions does not necessarily transfer to produce student-generated complex propositions.

Cognition

A final problem with sentence combining drill also addresses the cognitive domain. Hunt (1970) reports that mature writers, although using the same initial propositions as less mature and younger writers, produce semantically different compositions because, through the use of transitions and arrangement of ideas, they create and fashion new content as well as syntax. Complex sentence combining generates a meaning apart from the original propositions. Merely giving students practice in combining drills does not mean they can, as a result, create new content from the refashioning of syntax.

The semantic, conceptual side of language complexity often is overlooked or considered an eventual natural result following syntactical arrangement. On the contrary, syntactical arrangement may follow cognitive refashioning and reshaping, syntax being the external graphic representation of the newly complex conceptualizations.

O'Hare (1971), however, feels that style is primarily syntactical, that the same content can be expressed by both skilled adults and by high school writers with the adults merely fashioning images that lack the more concrete representations of the students. But a careful reading reveals that the skilled writer has done more than refashion syntax: the expert has created new content different from that expressed by the students.

Pluses and Minuses

In short, sentence combining may provide practice and may increase ability in combining syntactical units but this does not necessarily imply drill, or increasing skill in cognitive modifying, or refashioning information that gives new, more, or different meaning to syntax changes. Sentence combining focuses on syntax, not semantics. Although O'Hare argues that when students are asked whether a complex sentence produced by combining makes sense, such questioning merely clarifies the syntax transformations within their given frame—such a query does not lead to cognitive creation, nor could it. Rearranging surface parts into a new construction is not the same cognitive skill as generating new syntactical units to reflect more complex conceptions and thoughts about the world. Rearrangement does not always equal generation.

Daiker et al. (1979) do attempt to bridge the gap between syntax and semantics in their sentence combining textbook. They include an entire section on rhetoric or compositional theory as well as exercises on emphasis, arrangement, unity, and tone to help students develop meaning skills for use in writing. But the question is not resolved: do exercises in thematic unity help students generate complex conceptions that are objectified in complex sentences? A complex sentence is more than a new surface arrangement of parts; it is a newly created, newly envisioned conception of new cognitive relationships expressed in surface complex sentence form.

O'Hare (1971) maintains that students have the semantic skills to write complex material; they just need to be released from crippling syntactical chains. Once given syntactical skill, their semantic abilities can flower. Students can create with their new syntactical skills confidently and freely, needing only guidance in improved syntactical use to be able to communicate their intent.

Christensen (1967), although not a proponent of sentence combining, proposes that "solving *how to say* helps solve the problem of *what to say*" (p.

7). In other words, when given a form, students' language abilities can fill in the content naturally; the form gives them a pattern upon which to build semantic content.

Syntax First, Then Cognition?

This reasoning assumes that syntax shapes content, much like the proverbial cart before the horse. Does not content precede syntax, content being the force that shapes the resultant syntax? Does practice in combining sentences actually make one *think* more complexly? Cognition is more than an increase in the number of skill steps students can perform in composing sentences. Syntactical complexity also does not always mean semantic complexity, and syntactical simplicity does not always mean semantic simplicity.

Hemingway writes simply, but his meaning is not simple; he would be considered a syntactically immature writer by sentence combining standards. Yet within his simplicity of syntax is great depth of meaning. Complexity can be either or both semantic and syntactical; sentence combining approaches this issue from a purely syntactical point of view, overlooking the fact that complexity can be encoded in simple direct sentences as well as in complex structures.

The point here is that sentence combining assumes that complexity can be achieved by syntactical rearrangement without developing the underlying semantic intent that directs the focus of the expression. Students become adept at imitating sentence combining patterns without necessarily owning those patterns, thus accounting for Combs's (1977) cautionary note in reference to the stability of sentence combining gains over time.

Students can be taught to imitate and to use transition and combining words such as "despite," "however," and "although" as well as embedding procedures without intuitively owning the cognitive ordering that such words entail. Language is a vehicle for communication of thought, style, personality, philosophy, and world view. Simply practicing surface rearrangement does not necessarily mean individuals have learned new methods and ways of ordering their intent. Intent is encoded in surface structure and governs its direction.

Sentence combining assumes that students intuitively will grasp the cognitive or meaning changes encoded in a variety of surface structure patterns. For many this may be so, but it certainly is not a given.

SENTENCE COMBINING EVALUATED

Sentence combining involves a linguistic approach to written language remediation. As such, it focuses on language utterances and, through drill practice, reforms simple expressions into more complex ones. Based on transformational-generative grammatical theory, sentence combining defines complex syntax as resulting from multiple embeddings and combinations of simple propositions into more mature constructions.

From Hunt (1965) comes an analysis of a hierarchical development of certain syntactical combinations that increase with age, yielding a more complex or mature style. Syntactical maturity is measured by T-unit lengths, calculated by determining average number of words per T-unit. Sentence combining exercises give students guided practice in producing complex utterances by joining several propositions into a more mature whole. Current research studies support an improvement in student T-unit lengths and a high frequency of certain embeddings following sentence combining practice.

On the positive side, sentence combining can give students practice in developing fluency with certain linguistic patterns. Reinforcement through drill practice helps students in owning these new patterns. The use of sentence completing as measured by T-units also seems to enhance student compositions as a whole.

However, sentence combining focuses on surface rearrangements, assuming that the underlying cognitive explanations and reasons will follow; but rearrangement is not generation, for imitation of language patterns is not the same as creation of new semantical constructs expressed through syntactical codes.

Sherwin (1969) questions whether transformational sentence combining is anything more than a controlled method of writing-to-teach-writing. He asks whether sentence combining derives from any grammatical background and suggests that research has not supported the transformational-generativists' claims that posit a link. Instead, he feels sentence combining is merely a limited form of writing-to-teach-writing—structured composition exercises rather than intuitive grammatical practice. Sherwin's point illustrates the problem raised by reviewing the sentence combining research: are these more than controlled imitation exercises to improve composition? Does imitation build adequate cognitive bridges to lead to stable improvement?

Sentence combining does not address the needs of the audience, thereby omitting an important dimension of communication. It also does not consider the rhetorical needs of the modes of discourse, again omitting an important dimension of communication. For what it does—give practice in new linguistic patterns—it seems to do well. But a realistic appraisal must be cautionary and not attribute to sentence combining more than it can deliver.

BIBLIOGRAPHY

Chomsky, C. *The acquisition of syntax in children from 5-10.* Cambridge, Mass.: MIT Press, 1969.

Chomsky, N. *Syntactic structures.* The Hague: Mouton Publishers, 1957.

Christensen, F. *Notes toward a new rhetoric.* New York: Harper & Row Publishers, Inc., 1967.

Clark, H.C., & Clark, E.V. *Psychology and language: An introduction to psycholinguistics.* New York: Harcourt Brace Jovanovich, 1977.

Combs, W.E. Further effects of sentence-combining practice in writing ability. *Research in Teaching English,* Fall 1976, *10*(2), 137-149.

_____."Sentence-combining practice: Do gains in judgments of writing 'quality' persist?" *The Journal of Educational Research,* July-August 1977, *70*(6), 318-322.

Crowhurst, M. The effect of syntactic complexity on teachers' quality ratings of written compositions. Paper presented at Conference on College Composition and Communication, Minneapolis, April 4-7, 1979a.

_____. On the misinterpretation of syntactic complexity data. *English Education,* December 1979b, *11*(2), 91-97.

Daiker, D., Kerek, A., & Morenberg, M. Sentence-combining and syntactic maturity in freshman English. *College Composition and Communication,* February 1978, *29*(1), 36-41.

_____. *The writer's options: College sentence combining.* New York: Harper & Row Publishers, Inc., 1979.

DiStefano, P., & Howie, S. "Sentence weights: An alternative to the T-unit." *English Education,* December 1979, *11*(2), 98-101.

Hunt, K.W. *Differences in grammatical structures written at 3 grade levels: The structure to be analyzed by transformational methods.* U.S. Office of Education, Cooperative Research Project 1998. Tallahassee, Fla.: Florida State University, 1964.

_____. *Grammatical structures written at 3 grade levels.* Research Report 3. Champaign, Ill.: National Council of Teachers of English, 1965.

_____. Syntactic maturity in school children and adults. *Monographs of the Society for Research in Child Development,* February 1970, *35*(1, Serial No. 134), 1-67.

Lunsford, A.A. Cognitive development and the basic writer. *College English,* September 1979, *41*, 38-46.

Maimon, E.P., & Nodine, B.F. Measuring syntactic growth: Errors and expectations in sentence combining practice with college freshmen. *Research in Teaching English,* 1978, *12*(3), 233-244.

Malone, J. Sentence-fragment combining: A miracle. *English Journal,* January 1980, *69*(1), 15.

Marzano, R.J. The sentence-combining myth. *English Journal,* February 1976, *65*(2), 57-59.

Mellon, J.C. *Transformational sentence-combining.* Research Report 10. Urbana, Ill.: National Council of Teachers of English, 1969.

Miller, B.D., & Ney, J.W. The effect of systematic oral exercises on the writing of fourth grade students. *Research in Teaching English,* Spring 1968, *2*, 44-61.

Morenberg, M., Daiker, D., & Kerek, A. Sentence-combining at the college level: An experimental study. *Research in Teaching English,* October 1978, *12*(3), 245-256.

Ney, J.W. The hazards of the course. Sentence-combining in freshman English. *The English Record,* Summer/Autumn 1976, *27*, 70-77.

_____. Counterstatement. *College Composition and Communication,* October 1978, *29* (3), 303-04.

_____. A short history of sentence-combining: Its limitations and use. *English Education,* February 1980, *11*(3), 169-177.

O'Donnell, R.C. A critique of some indices of syntactic maturity. *Research in Teaching English,* Spring 1976, *10*(1), 31-38.

O'Hare, F. *Sentence combining: Improving student writing without formal grammar instruction.* Research Report 15. Champaign, Ill.: National Council of Teachers of English, 1971.

San Jose, E. Notes and comments. *Research in Teaching English,* February 1978, *12*(1), 91-92.

Sherwin, J.S. *Four problems in teaching English: A critique of research,* Scranton, Pa.: International Textbook Co., 1969.

Stewart, M.F. Freshman sentence-combining: A Canadian project, *Research in Teaching English,* October 1978, *12*(3), 257-268.

Strong, W. *Sentence combining: A composing book.* New York: Random House, Inc., 1973.

The Total Writing Process: Attention to Audience and Mode

UNIT INTRODUCTION

Component 2 of the Total Writing Process Model encompasses the cognitive and pragmatic abilities necessary for individuals to fully address their writing to the appropriate audience using the chosen mode of discourse. The individuals must be able to analyze and evaluate their composition in reference to an internal guide model. This guide leads the students to an awareness of the requirements of their purpose and topic in order to communicate successfully.

The internal guide results from the students' cognitive abilities to distance themselves from the topic far enough to be able to evaluate the strengths and weaknesses between the fit of their given compositions and the envisioned needs of the audience or mode. The students' ability to distance themselves also from their audience so they can perceive its needs independent of their own is critical for successful mastery of Component 2 and so that their purpose in communication will be achieved.

If the intended audience is the individual student, the need for decentering decreases significantly. However, communication generally implies a link to someone other or outside of self; in such cases, decentering or objectivity achieves critical importance.

This unit has two chapters. Chapter 6 involves audience awareness and the psychological basis for decentering, its benefits, and current research and plans that attempt to increase students' decentering skills. None of these plans are formulated into a full-fledged theoretical and methodological program; rather, they are specific lesson programs designed to help students differentiate self-needs from audience needs in communication. Many of these programs focus on oral language since there has been little research on written language in this area.

Chapter 7 involves mode awareness, the rhetorical basis for the writing act, and the requirements of each rhetorical mode. This chapter compares the pragmatic needs in speech to the pragmatic needs in writing. It focuses on the methods of instruction suitable to ensure a composition that fits its desired purpose. Again, no full-fledged programs are available; rather, specific curricular techniques are formulated to enable students to achieve the purpose of their composition: to communicate an idea effectively.

This unit reviews the cognitive demands of both audience awareness—decentering—and of mode awareness—revision. Component 2 of the Total Writing Process Model is under conscious control of the students. This component implies revision, restructuring, reshaping, and reformulation of the initial written message into a newly designed one meeting the needs of audience and mode. These requirements are external to the students and demand their ability to decenter in order to be able to address these needs effectively.

Before presenting the two chapters in this unit, pragmatics in the context and development of oral language are described since the vast majority of research and attention has been on the oral mode. The study of pragmatics is relatively new and represents a composite of a diverse group of disciplines such as philosophy, psycholinguistics, and speech-language pathology.

The research serves as a basis for presenting the pragmatic writing approaches. Indeed, in the future, oral language research will probably be used more and more as a foundation and guide for the study of pragmatics and writing. The interface between pragmatics in the oral and written modes appears considerable. If written expressive language development actually mirrors the oral, as suggested in Chapter 2, then pragmatic development may be assumed to be similar to some extent in the two modes.

At this point, however, the definition and development of pragmatics in the oral mode serve as a reference for the written mode. Pragmatic development in oral language therefore is introduced first in this unit to establish a frame for comparing the limited and initial work in written pragmatic ability when reading Chapters 6 and 7.

OVERVIEW OF PRAGMATICS IN THE ORAL MODE

Bates (1976) defines pragmatics as being based on the rule system relating to the use of language in context. Language takes place in a social context; it is a communicative activity that reflects and uses the context of conversation.

As McLean and McLean (1978) point out, not only do adults use language as a means of achieving social or communicative goals but also children themselves first acquire and develop language as a way of obtaining similar objectives. Hopper and Naremore (1978) define communication itself in a pragmatic sense by calling it a "dynamic interplay between learning bits of grammar and bits of appropriate usage" (p. 62). Bloom (1978) divides pragmatics into two aspects: the goals or functions that language serves and the influence on language of linguistic and nonlinguistic contexts. Fillmore (1974) defines pragmatics as a three-part system uniting "linguistic forms and the communicative functions these forms are capable of serving, with contexts or settings in which given forms have given functions" (p. V-1).

Thus, pragmatics can be viewed as a communicative activity that allows certain goals or functions to be served and that takes place in a social context. The question to be answered in analyzing children's language development is not simply what semantic and syntactic forms they use but rather the "content and form" (Bloom, 1978) and how they express this aspect in actual communicative contexts. Just as rules for syntax can be isolated and studied, so can pragmatic rules and rituals be—although the pragmatic issue is less direct and more elusive overall than the syntactic.

Pragmatic rules are based on such factors as who the speaker is, who the listener is, what the topic is, where the conversation takes place and under what conditions, and the use/misuse of the given-new interaction (Hopper & Naremore, 1978). Individuals tend to use different forms of communication with their boss than with their children. Their sentences to the former may be formal and respectful but to the latter may be informal and direct. Topics such as religion and politics can turn a low-key, easy communicative interaction into a heated argument. Communication in some surroundings, such as in a church, may be totally different from the interplay around a backyard pool. The mental and physical conditions of the speaker and listener can influence the conversation. Finally, poor perception or judgment by speaker or listener may impair or impede the interface of given and new information in a conversation.

The Given-New Strategy

The given-new strategy (Clark & Clark, 1977) is a dynamic interplay between speaker and listener. The speaker assesses what the listener knows about a topic and therefore does not have to have explained, then adds the new information to this base. The listener takes in the new information generated by the speaker and anchors it to what the person already knows about the topic. As such, there is a constant and mutual assessment, appraisal, and judgment process taking place. Should the speaker assume that the listener knows much more than is the fact, the conversation may be over the listener's head. For example:

> Speaker: John is a gifted child.
> Listener: Who is John?
> Speaker: He's Matt's son.
> Listener: Matt who?
> Speaker: Matt, my next door neighbor.
> Listener: Oh. Is John a youngster or an adult?

The reverse also is true. If a speaker assumes that a listener knows much less about a topic than is the actual fact, the conversation may be redundant, boring, and a partial waste of time.

Pragmatics therefore is communication considered within its social context. It involves a composite of a variety of linguistic and nonlinguistic aspects. The study of its development in children has been very recent. Miller (1978) has pointed out that over the last 30 years, the study and treatment of language has shifted considerably. In the 1950s and early 1960s the emphasis was on phonology—the sound and sound combinations of the English language. The accurate production of speech sounds, rhythm, and inflection was highlighted. In the late 1960s and early 1970s, the emphasis shifted to syntactic issues. Triggered for the most part by Chomsky's (1965) work, the focus was on syntactic and morphological development and on transformational-generative grammar. In time, it became obvious that transformational-generative grammar was not the total answer either, and the research shifted to semantic considerations. The most recent issue involves the definition, study, description, measurement, and treatment of language within a pragmatic framework.

Bates (1976) is one of the first to attempt to analyze pragmatic development in children, using a Piagetian framework. Her approach is divided into three pragmatic components: performatives, presuppositions, and conversational postulates. The development of these components is traced in children through the use of observations and informal assessment techniques. Each of these is discussed before the developmental sequence is presented.

The Performative Component

Performatives are associated with utterances in terms of the goals or functions language will serve. The development of the term "performative" from its narrow original reference to its final meaning constitutes a fascinating example of philosophical refinement. This sequence is traced briefly.

Austin (1962) explains that at one time sentences were thought simply to state facts or describe a certain situation. He also describes ethical propositions: sentences designed to elicit a certain emotion, command conduct, or influence in other ways. One subgroup of ethical propositions consists of performatives—sentences that actually encompass an act simply by their being pronounced, for example, "I pronounce you man and wife," and "I sentence you to ten years in jail." Just saying these sentences is an act—a speech act.

Austin states that a performative by its very nature must be in the first person, present tense. With further study, however, it became obvious that some performatives had no subject or verb, such as the baseball umpire's statement, "Out!" He noted that by saying a sentence with such verbs as "promise," "thank," and "warn," the speaker actually performs the acts encoded in the sentence. Hence, the speaker is promising, thanking, or warning because this is what the individual says is occurring. The utterance still is reducible to first person, present progressive tense, however. In uttering, "Out," the umpire actually is saying, "I declare you to be out." Looking for underlying performatives, Austin discovered that all sentences encode speech acts. "I declare that I am sorry" can be reduced to "I am sorry." And so the argument goes. Any spoken sentence can be reduced to an underlying form that encompasses a speech act. Thus, anything that is said constitutes a speech act, with an underlying subject (I) and object (you).

Illocutionary Acts

Searle (1969) goes even further to state that there exists a core of nine performatives (he calls them illocutionary acts) into which all performatives can be reduced. Searle identifies these illocutionary speech acts as requesting, informing, questioning, promising, advising, warning, thanking, greeting, and congratulating. An illocutionary act is chosen on the basis of the speaker's goals and motivations. A speaker may use a direct act or an indirect speech act. For example, a person speaking to a boss probably will cloak an imperative by substituting a request: "Shut the door" becomes "Can you shut the door?" Each illocutionary act is built on a number of felicity conditions or factors that allow the utterance to be successful. The breaking of a felicity condition causes the utterance to be defective, so the communicative goal may not be reached.

Every illocutionary act has its own set of felicity conditions, and a single goal can be encoded in a number of different speech acts. For example, the imperative "Pass the salt" can be cloaked in four different sentences, each representing a different method of encoding:

desire—"I would like to have the salt."
reasons—"Why don't you pass the salt?"

ability—"Can you pass the salt?"
future action—"Will you pass the salt?" (Clark & Clark, 1977, p. 125).

Thus, these examples show how a particular intent can be voiced directly, as in the imperatives, or indirectly through a number of speech acts.

Indirect meanings can be implied through the manipulation of felicity conditions of direct speech acts. Searle (1969) gives examples of the felicity conditions he feels are implied in a *sincere* promise:

1. Normal input (aural) and output (oral) mechanisms [are involved.]
2. The promise is encoded in a sentence.
3. A future act is predicated.
4. The listener would prefer that the speaker do the promised act rather than some other act.
5. The speaker and listener do not assume that the speaker will do the promised act under normal circumstances.
6. The speaker intends to do the promised act.
7. The speaker recognizes that by sincerely promising the act, he is obligating himself.
8. The speaker allows the listener to recognize this obligation (pp. 57-61).

An insincere promise would vary, according to Searle, in that Number 6 would state that the speaker intends that the utterance make the speaker responsible for planning to do the promised act. If the speaker does not do as stated, the promise becomes defective. Therefore, the felicity conditions change according to the factor of sincerity.

An illocutionary act occurs in conjunction with suprasegmental phonological features, verb moods, and extralinguistic contexts. These features, moods, and contexts allow for further cues as to indirect meanings. The illocutionary act thus achieves its goal either directly or indirectly.

Breaking the Cooperative Principle

Indirect illocutionary acts can be implied by breaking the cooperative principle (Clark & Clark, 1977), which states that the speaker will be truthful, clear, relevant, and concise in utterances. If one of these maxims is broken and if the context supports it, an indirect act is implied. For example, if a person is eating soup that is too hot and says, "What we need is some hot soup," the context will support the sarcasm. The listener will not say, "Oh, your soup isn't hot enough?" The latter will not assume the speaker is telling the truth and following the cooperative principle; rather, the listener will know that the soup is steaming hot and will understand the sarcasm. The speaker probably will have used suprasegmental phonological features such as an intonation characteristic of sarcasm. Illocutionary acts thus can be direct or indirect, based on suprasegmental phonological features, extralinguistic context, felicity conditions, and adherence to cooperative principle.

Searle describes a locutionary act as simply the physiological movements for producing speech and a perlocutionary act as the effect of an illocutionary act on the listener. The locutionary act is interpreted according to meaning, which revolves around grammatical, semantic, and suprasegmental features. An illocutionary act involves the specific act encoded. A perlocutionary act actually is a nonlinguistic response to an illocutionary act. The illocutionary act has a goal intended to be achieved with the listener; however, the response may or may not match the goal.

Performatives (illocutionary acts) are elements of a three-part cycle: locutionary acts to illocutionary acts to perlocutionary acts. The normal child develops the first two acts over time; the perlocutionary act, of course, depends on the listener in large part. Bates's category of performatives implies locutionary and illocutionary acts.

The Presupposition Category

Bates's (1976) second category of pragmatics is presuppositions, which she defines as the speaker conforming to the topic-comment relationship shared between speaker and listener. Children develop psychological presupposition skill before moving on to such aspects of communication as indirect meaning. That is, early on, children assume a shared topic and make only a comment (zero anaphora). Later the child learns to "control his own procedures of taking for granted as symbolic structures in themselves" (p. 27), combines topic and comment in utterances, and later still learns to understand and use implied or indirect meanings.

Piaget divides language into communicative and noncommunicative dimensions. Noncommunicative language is characterized by an egocentric quality, defined as such because the child "is centered about himself and fails to take into account the other's point of view" (Ginsburg & Opper, 1969, p. 90). These authors cite evidence that this egocentric quality is phased out slowly between the ages of 4 to 6, at which point socialized, nonegocentric communication becomes the major dimension. As the ability to presuppose is developed, children's language becomes appropriate in its topic comment and achieves its communicative intent more efficiently. Bates is clear in saying that the meaning intended by the children is the same whether or not they succeed in communicating effectively. The children may intend a particular meaning but because of poor presuppositional ability be unable to communicate effectively.

Conversational Postulates

Bates's (1976) final category is conversational postulates, which refer to implications of conversation, or indirect speech acts, in general. The cooperative principle and felicity conditions already discussed are two aspects of conversational postulates. In addition, indirect speech acts are communicated by using sincere polite forms, sarcastic polite forms, and/or dialectal, stylistic, and playful violations.

Pragmatic Development in Oral Language

During the sensorimotor period, Bates suggests that children progress in the use of performatives, propositions, and presuppositions. From birth to 8 or 9 months, they use behaviors that do not signal particular intentions but are interpreted as a signal by adults, such as smiling. Between 9 and 13 months, children intentionally use motor and vocal gestures to signal illocutionary acts of a primitive nature.

Bates asserts that this "illocutionary period" corresponds to Piaget's Stage 5—using novel means to attain familiar goals. Although words may not be spoken during Stage 5, children use what Bates terms protoimperatives and protodeclaratives. By using gestures and nonmeaningful sounds, children can signal a preverbal imperative. For example, a child holding up a toy phone for the mother to talk into may say "Hah," meaning, "Talk into this phone!"

A protodeclarative is a preverbal declarative that directs an adult's attention to the children or something in the real world. The children may exhibit self (show off), show objects to adults, or give or point to objects. To get adult attention, the children may use adults as tools in obtaining an object or use things as tools to get objects that then are shown to the adult. At this stage, presuppositions are composed of nonverbal ways of attending to or pointing to novel aspects of the environment. That is, the children presuppose almost everything is assumed by their audience and use nonverbal means to focus on novel aspects of a situation.

In progressing to Piaget's Stage 6, the children become capable of symbolic thought and begin to use words. They insert referential words or propositions into performative frames that so far have been used only nonverbally. The children still presuppose almost everything is assumed by their audience (zero anaphora). This one-word stage continues to represent a "split-level" (Bates, 1976) approach to using presuppositions. That is, children use a verbal one-word comment that is built on a topic that is present in the immediate context. An adult who is aware of the context can guess at the topic and see how the children's comment fits. Thus, children don't just randomly name things; they are using topic-comment speech in its earliest form.

Bates takes the view that a symbol refers to both "an act and an object, in that all mental objects are derived from the child's actions upon the world" (p. 11). Children do not passively allow the world to encode data in their minds; rather, they actively go out and interact with the world, making sense and coding data based on these interactions. Thus, knowledge is an interactive process. "Through assimilation and accommodation, the child is able to achieve a dynamic and balanced interaction that is the source and substance of its knowledge" (p. 11). Children do not "know" the world as it actually is but only know what their interactions with the world have taught them. One child's interpretation of the world will be different from another's; both are based on individual actions.

According to Bates, "a symbol or representation is the internal reenactment (re-presentation) of the activities originally carried out with objects or events;" that is, symbols are created from an "action blueprint" (p. 11). In this view, the mental symbols owned by children are related directly to the actions that allowed the symbol to be encoded. As knowledge and symbols are expanded, the original blueprint may not be linked directly to the symbol except through an intricate labyrinth of associations and chunkings.

A particular person's meaning for a word will be highly individualized and dependent on that individual's action patterns, associations, and mental relationships made between action patterns. However, despite the highly individualized internalized meanings of words, the community's definition also is included in these concepts. To communicate with others, the community members must "own" a common denominator of meaning. Superimposed on this common denominator are the children's individual meanings.

Referring vs. Meaning

Bates distinguishes between the acts of referring and meaning. She relates reference to the words and phrases a speaker uses because they stand for something in the real world or in the person's mental world. Meaning refers to the viewpoints, mental sets, or mental operations that a speaker wants to impose or create in a listener. A word may refer to a mental symbol unique to a person's actions in the world, while meaning is a term reserved for the intent of the speaker in creating an attitude in the listener. Bates uses Piaget's term "figurative learning" to describe children's building of propositions (which are made from symbols) and reserves the term "operative learning" for pragmatics and the "mapping of a proposition into sounds, embedding it in higher propositions, or calling it up indirectly in the form of presupposed or entailed information" (p. 12).

Children's single-word utterances can stand for imperatives and declaratives, or can be a category of sign-referent relations called indexes (Peirce, 1932). Indexes relate to signs that are associated with their referents because they actually participate in the referent, as "smoke indexes fire" (Bates, 1976, p. 91). Later, the children develop the ability to identify and discriminate between icons (which have a direct, physical resemblance to the referent) and symbols (related to the referent by arbitrary links decided on by the language community).

Children who begin to use two-word and three-word sentences soon tend to more operative knowledge. Those who have joined, moved, and imbedded objects in earlier operative functions now can join sentences with conjunctions, move words around in a sentence, and imbed sentences as linguistic operative functioning. Bates suggests that the increasing figurative and operative abilities are responsible for the growth from one-word to three-word sentences, since children must objectify what they know about a situation in order to make it the object of their communicative scheme.

Three Stages of Metapragmatics

In the preoperational period, Bates identifies three stages in the development of metapragmatics (the ability to talk about talk, whole speech acts, or aspects of a speech act). First, children encode the pertinent people in a speech act, but not the shifting roles of speaker and listener. They use demonstrative pronouns (this, that), but not shifting personal pronouns (he/him, she/her). They employ some nonoptional locatives ("put" is nonoptional because it requires an object and a place or container, "play" is optional because it requires no additional objects), use no conjunctions, and have zero anaphora (no surface structure implying reference or relationship to preceding discourse).

In the second metapragmatic stage, children begin to use conjunctions, adverbs, and noun modifiers that add the utterance onto a previous fact—linguistic or contextual. Thus, "I want another cookie" implies an earlier cookie was obtained; "And I do this" implies a relationship to another previous action. Sometimes adverbs such as "now," "then," or "not now" appear. Children also use simple present and some regular past tense verbs.

The third stage of metapragmatics relates to (1) talking about speech acts, (2) the use of a variety of time adverbs, (3) mastery of regular past tense verbs, (4) inclusion of a range of conjunctions, and (5) (taking more time to master but beginning to be used at this stage) varying personal pronouns, verb inflections, and shifting roles of speaker and listener. Bloom (1978) states that more difficult speech acts, such as promising or warning, do not develop until the second half of the preoperational period, at around age 5. In a survey of research, Bloom also finds that the speech act most used by 3-year-olds is requesting.

Word order also becomes an issue in the preoperational period. Bates observes a series of steps in word order acquisition in which the children:

1. use a comment-topic strategy (subject final)
2. alternate between topic-comment and comment-topic strategies
3. follow a subject-verb-object ordering rigidly
4. use adult word orderings.

Gaining or Holding Attention

Commenting on methods of gaining or maintaining adult attention by children 2 to 3 years old, Bloom (1978) states that they employ primitive forms that are equivalent in use to adults' methods. Children this age may repeat "Mommy, mommy, mommy . . ." ten times until attention is received. Or they may ask "O.K.?" several times to assess attention to what was said. These early forms are equivalent in use to the adult's "Get it?" or "Do you know what I mean?" By the end of the preoperational period, children should be able to manipulate direct performatives and presuppositions but still need to acquire conversational postulates.

At the concrete operational period, the last Piagetian period described by Bates, the focus is on relating children's knowledge of conversation and reversibility to their pragmatic language abilities. Indirect speech acts require the children to be capable of reversibility, a knowledge that takes time to develop fully. Understanding and use of conversational postulates continue through the primary years. Bates (1976) gives two reasons for the children's having to "own" the concept of reversibility in order to manipulate indirect speech acts.

First, these indirect speech acts require children to be able to consider or take the position of both speaker and listener—encoder and decoder. For example:

I know I mean X. The listener will hear Y but has sufficient additional information to know that I mean X (p. 214).

Second, the children must accurately maintain an utterance while moving from performative, to proposition, to presupposition, to conversational postulate, and back to the utterance. For example:

X becomes Y but is still X (p. 214).

Bates traces the use of counterfactuals (conditionals) in Italian children to demonstrate the refinement of this pragmatic construct in the concrete operational period. In Italian children, a conditional verb inflection is reserved only for counterfactuals, while in English, modals are used to indicate not only counterfactuals but other forms as well. This counterfactual development in Italian children therefore is separate and more amenable to study.

The Italian counterfactual is "always pragmatically ambiguous" (1976, p. 221). The sentence "If it were raining, I would stay home" in Italian "can be used either in a situation in which the speaker does not know it is raining, or in a situation in which he knows that it is raining" (p. 221). In any case, the listener cannot assume that the speaker assumes that it is raining. The counterfactual can be used pragmatically for indirect speech acts such as polite sentences or "hedges." In other words, "the counterfactual serves to block the invited inferences of indicative 'if/then' statements: The listener may not infer that either the antecedent or consequent are true, but he also may not infer that the speaker is *necessarily* ignorant" (p. 222).

Counterfactuals in Action

A research project was designed to assess Italian children's use of counterfactuals: asking them to identify a picture of a monkey, tell what the monkey is doing (eating a banana), identify their own names, and then answer what they (the children) would do if they were monkeys and what the examiner would do if a monkey, i.e., "I would eat the banana" and "You would eat the banana."

Bates found three clear stages in the development of the use of counterfactuals:

1. the indicative stage, ages 2 to 3 years, 11 months, in which children use no response or the simple present indicative ("I eat a banana");
2. the alternative stage, 3 years 11 months to 5 years 6 months, in which the children use the present indicative and some conditional inflections, but a variety of other verb forms as well—all being used interchangeably and probably equivalent in meaning to them at this point;
3. the conditional stage, ages 5 years 6 months to 6 years 2 months, in which the conditional is used the most frequently.

Bates sums up the study with several conclusions:

1. Although errors characteristic of the first two stages continue through the third stage, the conditional seems mastered by the age of 6.
2. Until the conditional stage, all the various verb forms (including the conditional) appear to be used interchangeably and share an equivalent

meaning base, while in the third stage, an awareness of the pragmatic value of the conditional becomes apparent.

3. The counterfactual "will require an ability to know when and why it is necessary to signal the unreality of a situation. The child must be able to predict what kinds of inferences a listener might draw unless otherwise warned" (p. 249). In other words, the children must decenter and take the position of the listener, this role-taking ability being seen in this pragmatic instance at a time "2 years prior to the boundary for concrete operations" established earlier by Piagetian researchers (p. 249).

It is interesting that a language ability would be a precursor to role taking and decentering skills in other cognitive tasks, although this may be due to the way the children have operationalized these elements. Thus, a clear developmental pattern in the acquisition of conditionals was observed in the Italian children. Although these factors are more difficult to measure in the English language, it could be hypothesized that similar results would be obtained in a similar experiment. By 6 years of age, children are decentering and taking the listener's perspective in order to be polite or "beat around the bush;" however, this role-taking ability is not fully developed as yet.

Combining Form and Function

In terms of indirect speech acts encoded in polite terms, Bates describes form and function as being combined in nine distinct ways.

1. an imperative as an imperative
2. an imperative as an interrogative
3. an imperative as a declarative
4. a declarative as a declarative
5. a declarative as an interrogative
6. a declarative as an imperative
7. an interrogative as an interrogative
8. an interrogative as an imperative
9. an interrogative as a declarative

The imperative, interrogative, and declarative each can be expressed as the function of itself or cloaked in one of the two other forms. For example, an imperative can be spoken directly, "Leave," as an interrogative, "Would you please leave?" or as a declarative, "I'd like you to leave." Until the age of 3-1/2 to 4 years, the first stage in the development of use of indirect speech acts based on politeness, children are unaware of indirect speech acts. If they choose to direct the listener's activity, they use an imperative; if they need an answer, they ask a question; if they choose to focus the object of a listener's act, they use a declarative. Any utterance that seems to be indirect at the first stage is explained by their having learned the structure by rote within the context of the performative.

In the second stage, children can distinguish between the surface form of an utterance and its underlying performative function, allowing them to use a variety of syntactic forms to communicate and correspond to the function. Interfacing with this new ability is the children's increasing skill at taking the listener's perspective, although this decentering still is not well developed. The children still cannot utilize utterances that serve a function hidden from both form and content.

In the third stage, children can use form and content in any way that will serve them. They decenter and role-take better and thus can "deceive, wheedle, seduce, and persuade" (p. 292) more effectively. By considering their audience, they can judge how to mask their function or how direct to be. Bates hypothesizes that until children are solidly concrete operational (around 7 or 8 years), they will not be smooth and competent in role taking and the many types of indirect speech acts.

Bates suggests that by around 3 years of age, children have a very general concept of what politeness means. This understanding is particularly directed toward the knowledge that politeness may allow a goal to be obtained, whereas not being polite may cause the goal to be lost. Bates points out that psychoanalytic theory places the concept of morality (posttoilet training) at about this time, and that this is the age at which children can talk about speech acts (metapragmatics). With such understanding, children's recognition of the value (good/bad, polite/impolite) and associated speech act will be facilitated. Children of this age use the word "please," lower their intonation, and reduce the dimensions of a request ("May I just play with it for a minute?" or "May I just have one tiny cookie?").

More difficult polite forms require decentering skill, and so develop through the preoperational and concrete operational periods. Bates finds some indications that concrete operational children process pragmatic information by analyzing function (declarative, imperative) and manner (polite) independently. At earlier periods, this division is not obvious.

Thus, pragmatic development begins at a very basic level and progresses to more complex dimensions. From a protoperformative base, children acquire direct performatives, presuppositions, and conversational postulates. The developmental sequence results in conversational fluency on direct and indirect planes.

PRAGMATICS AND WRITING DEVELOPMENT

Bates' work clearly has shown the way in which pragmatic development interfaces with cognitive development in general. It is important to note that children must be concrete operational before they can be expected to generate and appreciate indirect and subtle language effectively. Apparently, this ability is relatively efficient by 7 to 8 years of age. Of course, children vary and some are competent earlier or later than others. At this point, however, the indirect and subtle aspects of language are more a function of semantic development, i.e., to appreciate a political satire requires political knowledge. If the children's decentration, which occurs at the concrete operational level, provides the oral base for ability in presupposition and conversational postulates, the question is raised as to when this decentration shows itself in writing. Presumably, that will appear later than the oral ability, since the written language mode is built on proficiency in the oral. The sequence of pragmatic development orally is as follows:

1. direct speech acts, function (declarative, etc.) only
2. syntactic and morphological components; semantic aspects
3. presuppositions
4. conversational postulates, indirect speech acts, function (declaratives, imperatives, etc.) and manner (polite), all processed independently.

If pragmatic development in writing reflects this sequence, students can be expected to learn direct written modes and sentence structure, followed by an increasingly more efficient sense of audience, and finally an ability to write with implicature, satire, and other indirect or unique styles. This observation remains to be studied and supported or rejected by research in pragmatics and writing.

SUMMARY

This developmental overview has been detailed in the hope that readers will become aware of the research in pragmatics to date and perhaps realize that this information offers tremendous potential for further study on both pragmatics and writing. Investigators only now are beginning to regard pragmatics in reference to writing, and information within the oral mode should provide direction and the base on which to build studies.

The oral base must be investigated first, since it is the natural foundation for writing, but information now exists that can and should be used in the context of pragmatics and writing. Written language has not yet received the research attention it requires; however, the choice of mode and the planning and analysis of effect on audience have been utilized to some degree in hypothesizing possible instructional programs. These pragmatic approaches are described in this unit as they currently are manipulated instructionally.

BIBLIOGRAPHY

Austin, J.L. *How to do things with words.* Oxford, England: Oxford University Press, 1962.

Bates, E. *Language and context: The acquisition of pragmatics.* New York: Academic Press, 1976.

Bloom, L., & Lahey, M. *Language development and language disorders.* New York: John Wiley & Sons, Inc., 1978.

Chomsky, N. *Aspects of the theory of syntax.* Cambridge, Mass.: MIT Press, 1965.

Clark, H.C., & Clark, E.V. *Psychology and language: An introduction to psycholinguistics.* New York: Harcourt Brace Jovanovich, 1977.

Fillmore, C. Pragmatics and the description of discourse. *Berkeley Studies in Syntax and Semantics,* 1974, No. 1, VI-25.

Ginsburg, H., & Opper, S. *Piaget's theory of intellectual development: An introduction.* Englewood Cliffs, N.J.: Prentice-Hall, Inc., 1969.

Hopper, R., & Naremore, R. *Children's speech: A practical introduction to communication development.* (Second Edition) New York: Harper & Row, 1978.

McLean, J., & McLean, L. *A transactional approach to early language training.* Columbus, Ohio: The Charles E. Merrill Publishing Co., 1978.

Miller, L. Pragmatics and early childhood language disorders: Communicative interactions in a half-hour sample. *Journal of Speech and Hearing Disorders,* 1978, *43*(4), 419-436.

Ochs, E., & Schiefflin, B. *Developmental pragmatics.* New York: Academic Press, 1979.

Peirce, C. *Collected papers.* (C. Hartshorne & P. Weiss, Eds.). Cambridge, Mass.: Harvard University Press, 1932.

Piaget, J. *The language and thought of the child.* Cleveland: Meridian Books, The World Publishing Co. First published, 1926.

Searle, J. *Speech acts: An essay in the philosophy of language.* London, England: Cambridge University Press, 1969.

Chapter 6
Audience Awareness

EGOCENTRISM AND ROLE-TAKING TERMS

Research in developmental communication has attributed young children's relatively poor performance to factors of egocentrism (Piaget, 1926; Piaget & Inhelder, 1967), inability to take the role of the other (Flavell, 1975), or to lack of sensitivity to the needs of the listener (Glucksberg, Krauss, & Higgins, 1975; Dickson, 1980). These explanations seem inadequate for several reasons:

1. Performance is not the result of an inability; performance reflects some sort of ability.
2. These explanations do not account for age and individual differences in young children's performance.
3. Definitions of egocentrism and role taking are circular: you are "egocentric" if you do not "take the role of the other" and you are "unable to take the role of the other" because you are "egocentric." A definition of the term "sensitivity to the needs of the listener" is equally as elusive. What does it mean to be "sensitive to the needs of the listener?" Does sensitivity require a speaker's *conscious* awareness of what the listener needs to know before any feedback is received?

Whatever it means "to be sensitive to the needs of the listener," studies (Mueller, 1972; Maratsos, 1973; Garvey & Hogan, 1973; Shatz & Gelman, 1973; Menig-Peterson, 1975; Sachs & Devin, 1976; and Meissner & Apthorp, 1976) suggest that young children can demonstrate this notion.

For example, Mueller (1972) reports that 3- , 4- , and 5-year-olds are more explicit verbally when communicating with a person who could not see as compared to one who could. Garvey and Hogan (1973) note that pairs of children between the ages of 3½ and 5 communicate with each other in a manner consistent with the verbal or nonverbal behavior of their partner. Shatz and Gelman (1973) find a difference in the way 4-year-olds speak to 2-year-olds and to adults that is appropriate to the differential characteristics of the listeners (e.g., 2-year-olds receive shorter, more attention-demanding utterances). Sachs and Devin (1976) observe that 4-year-old subjects speak differently to dolls that are designated as being age 2 or 4. In fact, Keenan, Schiefflin, and Platt (1976) portray the child entering school as in command of topic-comment propositions. That is, children are able to engage a listener into attending to an event and once having signaled attention, proceed to comment on it.

If research has demonstrated children's ability to take the role of their listener into account, then why does the term "egocentrism" hang on, especially in the context of written expression? To answer this question, the origin and definition of role-taking terms must be examined. Then the focus proceeds to a model of cognitive development that can go beyond a description of written language performance to provide a functional model against which to discuss the demands of written expression—Pascual-Leone's Theory of Constructive Operators. Finally, approaches to written remediation are discussed.

ORIGIN, DEFINITION OF ROLE-TAKING TERMS

Role-taking ability is defined by Flavell (1975) in terms of two general forms of social-cognitive behavior:

> (1) the general ability and disposition to "take the role" of another person in the cognitive sense, that is, to assess his response capacities and tendencies in a given situation; and (2) the more specific ability to use this understanding of the other person's role as a tool in communicating effectively with him. (p. 1)

According to Flavell, an important part of what is involved in effective communication can be conceptualized as a coding-then-recoding process, in which the recoding component is "monitored" by role-taking activity. Thus, speakers first encode a referent for themselves, then attempt to discern the listener's role attributes that are relevant to the referent, the set of nonreferents, and the potential message(s). On the basis of this, the speakers attempt to recode the message to suit the listener. The recoding may be identical to the speakers' initial self-encoding or it may involve either a modification of that or an entirely new message.

Empirical support for Flavell's notion of self-encoding comes from Glucksberg, Krauss, and Weisberg's (1966) work with speaker-listener pairs in the 4- to 5-year age range. In general, these children are either unmotivated or unable to communicate information about novel visual patterns to another child. A 4-year-old might say "It goes like this" and trace the design with a finger when asked to describe the design to a listener who could neither see nor be seen by the child. But when familiar pictures are used instead of novel designs, the children's performance is much better. Glucksberg, Krauss, and Higgins (1975) attribute the youngsters' inadequate performance on the novel stimuli to their inability to take their listener into account in encoding it. In Flavell's terms, the subjects' messages are self-encoding and so familiar stimuli present no problems since all have agreed consensually upon names. To test the self-encoding hypothesis, Glucksberg et al. (1975) use the encodings provided by the children when communicating with them about the novel forms. The results show quite clearly that their performance improves significantly when the messages employ *their own* encodings (although these same messages communicate very little to others). Glucksberg et al. (1975) interpret these results as supporting Flavell's theory of self-encodings.

Theoretical underpinnings for Flavell's notion of self-encoding come from Piaget's notion of egocentrism and Vygotsky's (1962) concept of inner speech. In his early work (1926) Piaget observes that the utterances of children below the ages of 7 or 8 are inadequate communicatively, even when the intent to communicate is evident. He terms such utterances "egocentric speech" and speculates that they are derived from the youngsters' inability to appreciate others' differing points of view. He contrasts "egocentric speech" with "socialized speech" that is characteristic of older children and adults, in which the listener's point of view is taken into account in the formulation of the message. Piaget finds that after age 7 or 8, children gradually rid themselves of the egocentric illusion and begin to use role-taking techniques to make their communications adaptive. The decline in egocentrism is believed to result from reinforcement—often negative, it appears—issuing from interactions with peers.

But in his later writings (Piaget & Inhelder, 1967) Piaget speaks of the decline of egocentrism in terms of the growth of perspectivism. Perspectivism refers to the ability to coordinate one's own point of view with that of another in a spatial sense. Piaget assesses perspectivism in his famous "three mountains" task in which a child facing a three-dimensional display of mountains is asked to choose pictures representing what another person sees from different locations. Flavell has integrated the intellectual and social sides of Piaget's egocentrism concept.

Two 'Routes' to Communication

According to them, generalized egocentrism can affect a child's communicative output via two "routes": (1) insensitivity to the listener's role attributes; and (2) perceptual, cognitive, and linguistic deficiencies. Flavell admits that egocentrism is not the only factor that sets limits on these abilities. The "insensitivity route" contains the social component of Piaget's concept of egocentrism, while the "perceptual, cognitive, and linguistic route" contains the intellectual component. According to Piaget, the fact that children continually are bound by their own points of view adversely affects their perceptual and cognitive discriminations as well as their comprehension and use of the language. It would be nice if research could prove the separability of these two routes, but the likelihood is remote that communication failure is due to nothing but inadequate perceptual-cognitive-verbal equipment or to nothing but an inability to discriminate the other's listener role attributes.

Flavell declares that Piaget makes a persuasive case for the vital part that a generalized egocentrism plays in children's initial self-coding of the communication's raw materials. But, he adds, Piaget does not describe the characteristics of the initial self-codings or the subsequent recoding for external communication. Flavell finds Vygotsky's (1962, especially Chap. 7) distinction between inner speech (speech for oneself) and external speech (speech for others) pertinent to his notion of self-coding and recoding inasmuch as it asserts that one's private self-coding of events is a decidedly unedited, communicatively inadequate affair and that an extensive recoding is necessary for external communication. According to Vygotsky, speech during the early, preschool years is at once private and social, with no real differentiation, as Flavell would say, between self-coding and coding for others. Between the ages of 3 and 7, however, the two functions gradually diverge. Vygotsky notes that "speech for oneself originates through differentiation from speech for others" (p. 133). Social, communicative speech remains overt and presumably becomes more elaborate and complex as mastery of the language is achieved. Private speech, or "innerspeech," as Vygotsky calls it, progressively becomes more covert until it evolves, to a large extent, into "thinking in pure meanings" (p. 149).

Because of its characteristics of abbreviation and condensation, inner speech is an unfit vehicle for communication. It seems to be an efficient and nonredundant language for communicating data to and for oneself but would require extensive recoding to meet the informational requirements of an external listener:

> It is evident that the transition from inner to external speech is not
> a simple translation from one language into another. It cannot be

achieved by merely vocalizing silent speech. It is a complex, dynamic process involving the transformation of the predicative, idiomatic structures of inner speech into syntactically articulated speech intelligible to others. (p. 148)

Vygotsky's conceptions, perhaps even more than Piaget's, point up the wide gulf that is liable to exist between speaker and listener. It is difficult enough for adults to bridge this gulf. To answer the question of whether or not children can be aided in acquiring this bridging skill, the social-cognitive requirements of role-taking must be assessed in relation to the cognitive developmental level.

Cognitive Development, Role-Taking, and Communication

Flavell (1975) sees role-taking activity as comprising five social-cognitive components: (1) *existence,* the awareness of perspectives in general; (2) *need,* knowing that an analysis of perspectives is called for; (3) *prediction,* the ability to discriminate the task-relevant role attributes; (4) *maintenance,* the ability to maintain over time the inferences yielded by this analysis; and (5) *application,* the ability to apply these inferences to a particular situation (i.e., how to translate what one knows about the other's listener role attributes into an effective verbal message).

Using two tasks in which second and sixth graders communicate information about a game and about visual displays, respectively, Cooper and Flavell (mentioned in Glucksberg, Krauss, & Higgins, 1975) report that the variance in second graders' performance is accounted for by variance in general role-taking abilities (the first three components listed above), while the variance in sixth graders' performance is related to variance in task-specific role-taking abilities (the last two components above).

Glucksberg et al. (1975) point out that one's ability to infer from this study of relationships between role-taking ability and communicative behavior remains obscure because both abilities are drawn from the same set of behaviors. They give as an example the fact that one measure of task-specific role-playing is the extent to which two versions of a story differ; one version is told to a child, the other to an adult. They point out that operationally role-taking ability here is primarily communicative ability. For Glucksberg et al. (1975) the underlying reason for young children's relatively poor communication performance is their failure to edit. That is, youngsters do not modify their messages in socially appropriate ways.

This notion of "editing" or "comparing" is part of a two-stage stochastic choice process model derived by Rosenberg and Cohen (1966). This model postulates that speakers sample randomly from their repertoire of names for the referent. The names sampled then are compared for applicability to the referent and nonreferents. When the speakers estimate that the name has greater applicability to the referent than nonreferents, there is a high likelihood that they will emit it. When the sampled name is estimated to be more applicable to the nonreferents, the speakers are likely to reject the name and sample a new one. This process continues until a name that meets the comparison criterion is sampled and used.

The problem with this model is that it is so idealized that its usefulness in explaining or predicting performance is limited. A more realistic picture is a network of interacting speaker, listener, stimuli, and feedback variables. A description of this model with respect to referential communication performance is presented by Foorman (1977, note 1; 1980). To extend this model to written expression, the theoretical perspective—Pascual-Leone's Theory of Constructive Operators—is discussed next.

THE THEORY OF CONSTRUCTIVE OPERATORS

Juan Pascual-Leone first presented his Theory of Constructive Operators in his doctoral dissertation at the University of Geneva in 1969. Since then he and others have supported and elaborated upon the theory through extensive writing (Pascual-Leone, 1976; Pascual-Leone, Goodman, Ammon, & Subelman, 1978; Ammon, 1977). Central to Pascual-Leone's theory are three elements: (1) the Piagetian notion of scheme; (2) the notion of a "field of activation;" and (3) the notion of scheme boosters.

According to Pascual-Leone (1969), schemes are the "mental blueprints" for action that guide behavior. Schemes perform three kinds of functions: figurative, operative, and executive. Figurative schemes represent experience as reproduced in memory or as conceived perceptually. Operative schemes, on the other hand, transform experience according to a set of rules:

> If, for example, a subject were to look at two different photographs and to judge that they were of the same (but unknown) house one would say that he did so by applying an operative scheme representing a "sameness" function ("If two objects are alike in all relevant aspects, they may be presumed to be the same") to the figurative schemes representing the features of each of the photographs in question, and that he generated a new figurative scheme representing the fact: "These two photographs are actually of the same house." (Case, 1974, p. 545)

Executive schemes are the internal representation of the plans that control behavior. To a large extent executive schemes determine the activation of particular figurative and operative schemes. All schemes operate under an initial set of conditions (i.e., a releasing component) and a subsequent set of conditions that they can generate (i.e., an effecting component). A subset of a subject's repertoire of schemes is a "field of activation." This field can be analogized to a "panel of light bulbs" (Pascual-Leone, 1974), much like a sports stadium advertisement board, in which patterns of light are activated according to the executive plan of the computer program.

The factors that determine whether a scheme is included in a subject's field of activation are known as "scheme boosters." The main scheme boosters, or operators, are: C-learning operator, L-learning operator, M-operator, F-operator, and A-operator. C-learning, or content learning, accounts for the modification of individual schemes as a function of experience. L-learning, or logical learning, accounts for the rule or structural learning that can be applied beyond situations of specific content.

The M-operator is similar to Piaget's and Inhelder's (1967) field of centration and to notions of mental (or focal) attention and short-term (or working) memory. The M-operator is the mental energy available for organizing schemes. Its magnitude is "the maximum number of activated schemes which can be coordinated at any one time" (Case, 1972, p. 287). The important thing about M energy is that its power increases with age in steps that correspond to each one of Piaget's developmental substages (Exhibit 6-1).

The two other operators or scheme boosters are F and A. The F-operator is what Piaget refers to as "field effects" and is responsible for the relative weight a subject gives to cues in the perceptual field. Often there are salient perceptual cues present in a problem that tend to activate an inappropriate

Exhibit 6-1 Functions of the M-operator

Age (in Years)	Developmental Substage	M Power
3-4	Early operational	e + 1
5-6	Late preoperational	e + 2
7-8	Early concrete operational	e + 3
9-10	Middle concrete operational	e + 4
10-12	Late concrete—early formal	e + 5
13-14	Middle formal operational	e + 6
15-16	Late formal operational	e + 7

Key: e = amount of space occupied by the executive scheme; numeral = maximum number of additional schemes that can be coordinated at a particular substage.

executive scheme if given too much attention. The A-operator refers to situation-bound or situation-free affective factors that can influence the activation weight of perceptual-motor or cognitive schemes.

The Interactions Explained

The Theory of Constructive Operators explains the interaction of schemes and scheme boosters in terms of general organismic principles. A major principle is called schematic overdetermination of performance. According to this principle, many schemes may be activated in a given situation but the subset that "wins" the competition will involve the pragmatically compatible schemes whose individual tendencies sum to the greatest weight. Thus, a subject's performance reflects not only schemes necessary and sufficient to the particular act but also the competing schemes not applied.

The Theory of Constructive Operators' notions of repertoire of schemes and scheme boosters provides a useful construct with which to explore the activation of factors influencing the use of a specific discourse mode in a particular communicative setting. Because the theory developed out of a desire to make Piagetian theory functional (Case, 1974), this new theory provides the mechanism by which predictions can be made as to when (i.e., at what age) a particular structure will be acquired as well as what kind of subject will obtain the structure first. The mechanism for prediction is that of task analysis. This involves a careful analysis of complex task performance in terms of the successive subskills prerequisite for success. Each step of the analysis requires one mental transformation.

Case (1972) points out three prerequisite conditions to succeeding in a task: (1) a tendency to maximize use of available M; (2) an appropriate repertoire of schemes; and (3) a tendency to prohibit the activation of incompatible schemes by starting only those that are consistent with the majority of relevant schemes. The Theory of Constructive Operators has been applied in analyzing a variety of logical operational and verbal tasks (Pascual-Leone & Smith, 1969; Case, 1972, 1974, 1975; Foorman, 1977, Note 1; de Ribaupierre & Pascual-Leone, 1979; Pulos, 1980; Furman, 1980; Goodman & Pascual-Leone, 1980). Scardamalia (1980) and Bereiter (1980) have applied the theory to written performance.

In applying the theory to an analysis of written performance, there must be a reminder of the obvious but important fact that written language, unlike oral language, is not based on speaker-listener interaction. Written language has no external feedback loop except to the extent that the writer is capable of self-editing. Consequently, the writer must act autonomously in planning and executing a message framed by a particular discourse mode and structured by skills of handwriting, spelling, and punctuation. The task of writing can be divided into two sets of variables: writer variables and task-related variables of topic and mode of presentation.

Writer Variables

The neo-Piagetian constructs "repertoire of schemes," "scheme boosters," and "executive controlling behavior" are useful in accounting for variability in performance attributable to factors emanating from the writer. The writer's understanding of the task instructions—executive schemes—clearly influences the nature of the composition. There often is the feeling that the task instructions in classroom composition assignments are not interpreted by the student writer in the way that the teacher intends. This problem became clear in the cognitively complex task of two referential communication interactions in which the stimulus materials were the same but the instructions differed slightly (Foorman, 1977). In one instance the instructions were, "Tell me everything you can about that picture." These instructions invited many personal associative descriptions of which the following (from a 6-year-old boy's description of a dog) is the most extreme. (Listener comments are added parenthetically.)

> It looks like Brownie. (What's Brownie look like?) Brownie just looks like a little dog . . . like a dog that . . . that (inaudible) . . . that's big. (Really?) And this looks like Soda and Rootbeer got ran over by a car. I really liked those two dogs. Soda's really alone now. (That's too bad). So when I come to school here I always walk down I see Soda and I play with her for a few minutes. (That's nice.) She's lonely.

This child seems to be performing a task other than the one the experimenter had in mind. In the Theory of Constructive Operators' terminology, the A-operator appears to be influencing the activation weight of certain schemes in the child's repertoire. In an attempt to clarify the purpose involved, another referential communication task was conducted, using the same materials. There were several different scenarios for the children to play: Dogs concerns describing a lost dog; Cars, describing a lost car; and Faces, describing a lost person. The instructions included a scenario about how the boy had lost his dog (or, for the other stimulus materials, lost his friend, or his car had been stolen). The child goes to the authorities (the dogcatcher or the police, both played by the experimenter) to describe what is lost or stolen. These instructions seemed to help motivate and orient the child to the goal of the task.

One 6-year-old girl began her description of each dog and car item with a dramatic lament, "Ooo, my dog is lost!" or, "Oh, my car is lost!" But by the last stimulus set—Faces—the task purpose seemed to have faded and she began to describe all universal features. The tendency to do that had been evident since the first set of stimuli was introduced but had been governed by the scenario-boosted task purpose. Increasing fatigue on the child's part and the experimenter's failure to rehearse the scenario strongly during the last set of stimuli undoubtedly contributed to the loss of the task purpose in favor of the youngster's own agenda of listing universal features.

In the second item of Faces the child's opening comment of "A man's lost!" was met by the experimenter's question, "What's he look like?" This question opened the doors for any universal feature that the child wanted to mention (e.g., nose, eyes, forehead), regardless of its relevance to the task of differentiating referent from nonreferents. But that opening comment of "A man's lost!" does suggest that the child remembered the ostensible goal of the task, at least at the beginning. It appeared that changes in the executive controlling behavior could occur from moment to moment within the same item.

Another subject in this same pilot study—a 5-year-old boy—could keep the task purpose activated in his head throughout the experiment but could describe only two features. His two-feature descriptions followed a similar pattern, which was not influenced by any listener feedback as to the adequacy of the description: *hair length* for Faces, wheels and *length* for Cars, and *orientation* and *tail* for Dogs. Factors of saliency, previous learning experience, or affect seemed to be at work. In Theory of Constructive Operators' F-, C-, or A-operators were possible scheme boosters here.

3 Other Aspects of Writer Variable

Three other important aspects of writer variable are the neo-Piagetian construct M energy, cognitive style, and the extent of the speaker's vocabulary. As mentioned earlier, M energy is the mental energy available for coordinating schemes. The M-operator, then, provides energy for focusing on nonsalient and nonemotional aspects of the task. The 5-year-old just described did not appear to have sufficient M energy for overcoming the influence of perceptual saliency and affective factors. But an older child, with a greater M-capacity, might be expected to be able to boost schemes more appropriate to the tasks.

The term "cognitive style" refers to general stylistic schemes that determine the F-operator's domination of the executive function. The cognitive style most relevant to referential communication task, whether in an oral or written mode, is that of field dependence-independence. Speakers who are *de*pendent on the perceptual field have a difficult time extracting, from a part of the field of information, material that is relevant to the task. Field *in*dependent speakers, however, pull relevant information out of the perceptual field with little difficulty. In addition to individual differences in field dependence-independence that cut across levels of M energy, there is a developmental tendency in this cognitive style. That is, with increasing age there is a gradual shift from field dependence to field independence. This shift is related to the developmental increase in M energy. In short, with increasing age a child will have more M energy available for boosting schemes that are independent of the perceptual field.

The remaining aspect of writer variable is vocabulary repertoire. A large vocabulary is an obvious advantage to a speaker in a descriptive-recognition task. In Theory of Constructive Operators' terminology this vocabulary repertoire is part of C-learning or content learning.

To summarize these writer variables, the nature of what a person is writing appears to be influenced by the individual's understanding of the task (the executive), the scheme boosters M-, F-, A-, C-, and L-operators, and the writer's cognitive style and vocabulary repertoire.

Task-Related Variables

In the case of written expression, task-related variables refer to familiarity with the topic and genre. Obviously, familiarity with a topic will influence activation of the writer variables. A certain degree of familiarity will call forth an executive plan that can access available vocabulary and organize this content into logical structures that conform to conventions of handwriting, spelling, and punctuation. At the most automatic level, the topic may entail enactment of conventional scripts (Schank & Abelson, 1977). These scripts are so routine that an opening frame such as "Once upon a time . . ." structures the level of modes and array of slots that follow.

But whether sufficient "psychological distance" (i.e., relative field independence and affective separation) can be maintained with a familiar topic depends greatly upon the amount of available mental energy for boosting task-relevant schemes at the whole-text level. Planning at the level of the entire text is reminiscent of Piaget's notion of "reflective abstraction" (Piaget & Inhelder, 1969) and information processing's simultaneous bottom-up and top-down planning (Rumelhart, 1975, 1980). In the Theory of Constructive Operators, such an all-encompassing view requires an executive notion of the composition's theme as well as specific executive strategies for writing and evaluating different sections. In oral communication, the speaker's auditory output as well as listener responses provide feedback that may be instrumental in prompting revision of plans. In written expression, however, an executive procedure is required that allows the writer to write, read, and evaluate without breaking the flow of the process itself.

In addition, evaluation may require suppressing one version of the composition in favor of a new one that maintains the intended meaning. Such flexibility in scheme activation and modification exerts demands on available mental energy. When the observer fails to see this evaluation procedure in the writer's performance, the reason for failure is not necessarily clear. In other words, the observer does not know whether the writer is failing to build mental representations of relevant features or is able to build them but simply does not realize their relevancy to the communicative task at hand.

The interpretation of writing difficulties as emanating from a mediation or production deficiency is crucial to the choice of remediation techniques. It is unlikely, however, that difficulty with writing stems from a production deficiency alone. Bereiter and Scardamalia (1980) find that even the contentless prompt of encouragement to write more results in greater written production. Rather, it appears more likely that writing difficulties result from the interaction of a mediation deficiency with the other psychological variables discussed above under writer variables. That is, a mediation deficiency may result from lack of appropriate executive plans, or mental energy for boosting the content relevant to the topic, or the logical structures for organizing the material in meaningful ways.

One way for a teacher to approach the problem of a mediation deficiency in written expression is to simplify the task by changing genres. If a student is having difficulty with a narrative or argument mode, the teacher can try switching to an imaginative mode. The writer can be asked to pretend to be on another planet. Perhaps this imaginative genre in its openendedness can reduce constraints of conventional vocabulary and spelling, thereby increasing writing output.

Another method is for a teacher to encourage what Bereiter and Scardamalia (1980) call "metamemorial" and "goal-directed searches." The purpose of metamemorial searches is to access relevant semantic content before implementing goal-related searches. For example, if the goal is to describe the effect of jogging on life style, the teacher might implement several large scale memory searches under such headings as aerobics or exercise and health. The difficulty with proposing memory searches as an effective writing aid is that the information most readily accessed is likely to be at too general or too particular a level. Or, as Foorman (1977) discovered by priming relevant information before a referential communication task, the primed material is not necessarily transferred to the task at hand. Without an executive plan linking the accessed information to the related task, the speaker/writer may fail to see the relevance of the primed information to the new work.

In sum, written expression demands a set of mechanical skills such as handwriting, punctuation, and spelling that are executed within a discourse plan constrained by task variables of topic and genre and writer characteristics of processing space, vocabulary repertoire, cognitive structures for organizing information, affective involvement, and task understanding. Remediation of writing difficulties, therefore, not only must address the me-

chanical elements, it also must consider the metadiscourse knowledge required of the task in relation to the writer's cognitive capabilities.

COGNITIVE DEFICIENCY AND REMEDIATION

Current approaches to written language improvement can be evaluated in
terms of how well such theories address the nature of writing and the learning
characteristics of the writer. The abstract nature of written language has
been discussed, a nature that because of its independence from context requires a qualitatively different level of cognitive processing than any other
language mode. Such a new level of cognition requires, according to Olson
(1977), a facility in placing meaning within the text in a logical, reasonable,
and objective manner.

Bruner (1966) categorizes knowledge into three modes that can apply to
written expression: (1) the iconic, or "mental picture" of experience; (2) the
enactive, or the how-to-do narration or description; and (3) the symbolic, or
the analysis that utilizes abstract relations. Bruner maintains that much
writing is deficient simply because the student does not have facility with the
symbolic use of knowledge. A deficiency in these cognitive representations of
knowledge can remain undetected—until a student writes. A person could
have abstract reasoning abilities and still be egocentric in writing style, relying
on other language coding abilities for compensation. Only in the writing task
itself will such a cognitive disability become apparent.

The referent is removed in writing, requiring the writer to assume an
empathetic stance toward the reader. The failure to do so underlies the
deficiencies in cognition listed earlier. Only when the writer steps from "self"
and addresses an unknown and "unknowing" reader will the writer begin to
use the essential skills necessary to communicate with the reader: logic, reasoning, objectivity, and analysis. Without a sense of audience, the writer feels
no need to relate, explain, and expand ideas internally so as to communicate
externally apart from the individual's own experiences. The writer must actively place meaning in external written expression rather than in an assumed
shared set of experiences. Perhaps this active awareness of audience accounts
for the difference in reflective and reactive writers: reflective writers have a
sense of audience to whom they address their compositions, thus accounting
for their greater expressive success, whereas reactive writers do not decenter
well in their composition. Bereiter (1980) states that "epistemic writing
emerges when the person's skill system for reflective thought is integrated
with his skill system for unified writing. The creation of a literary work then
becomes, in addition to whatever else it may be, a personal search for meaning" (p. 88).

Based on their work with primary school children, Rosen and Rosen (1973), reporting on children's inability to address an audience, feel they are better able to communicate ideas as mimes than through written language. As mimes, children know that they have to be explicit or the audience never will guess their intent; the elimination of verbal language forces them to compensate by addressing the needs of the audience. As soon as the children begin using written language, they promptly assume the receptors share their language code and lose their earlier communicative intent and audience awareness. The Rosens feel that dramatic techniques are excellent in helping children learn how to address an audience, a sense that then generalizes to writing. They feel a writer, like an actor, must be a "predictor of reactions and act on his predictions" (p. 268); writing is essentially a carefully planned monologue that can communicate without the actor. Children can learn how to address an audience, thus opening the way for comprehension to be more logical, expressive, and expansive—higher cognitive skills that follow the ability to cognitively address an audience outside of self.

Problems of Speaker Styles

Bannatyne (1971) states that nonegocentrism is but one style or code of language usage; the speaker has several other styles to use to fit other communicative needs. However, an impairment in this particular code disables the person's written expression. Vygotsky (1962) and Bruner (1973) argue that such an inability limits and constrains thinking in its abstract and symbolic form. Flavell (1975) discusses methods to compensate or remedy this cognitive problem.

Flavell describes various techniques to aid students in decentering and in recognizing different conceptual or perceptual points of view. He discerns that the speaker creates an image of "listener role attributes" that is used as an active monitor to organize, shape, or recode if necessary. Flavell (1975) reports success in increasing nonegocentric stance by practicing with 6-year-olds in learning how to role play. Cazden (1972) states that since role-playing abilities develop in elementary school, a child's capability will be affected positively if given "a range of situations in which he is forced to consider alternative points of view in order to achieve his communicative intent" (p. 204). Not learning such skills in the elementary grades may seriously cripple students who cannot develop such abilities on their own.

In secondary schools, role playing may lose the "punch" that comes from the play ability of children. An alternative device may be dialoguing, expanded to expository writing and topics involving controversial points of view. The student writes both sides of the proposition, with an intention to explore the topic fully but not necessarily to resolve the issue.

Metacommunication Ability

Thus, a sense of audience goes beyond the writers' own perspective, forcing them to address their audience with all the cognitive skills necessary to communicate. Awareness of the need to activate these skills in communicative interactions is what Flavell (1980) terms metacommunication ability. Role taking or dialoguing are tools to help students in decentering so that they will place meaning outside of themselves and into their text. Writing topics that force students to encounter an audience outside of self obviously are of great merit and value in instruction and remediation.

Three types of writing exist: expressive, poetic, and transactional. Britton defines transactional writing as "a means to an end outside of itself. The form it takes, the way it is organized, is dictated primarily by the desire to achieve that end efficiently" (1971, p. 212). It points away from the speaker, uses logic and reasoning, and includes analysis and theorizing. This is the style of writing that increases cognitive complexity and broadens thinking. It is the style that Bruner says "promotes growth of mental operations" (1973, p. 47).

Gere (1977) criticizes transactional topics because she feels students should not be expected to write in such a manner since they cannot do so effectively when not "involved." Students should write exclusively or primarily for personal reflection and enjoyment, not for a restricted and nonsympathetic audience. Gere suggests that even colleges should favor expressive writing rather than forcing students to write essays, laboratory reports, research papers, and other transactional forms that they cannot master. She feels that if students can write expressively, then they can go naturally to transactional writing because they will have mastered expressive writing. Success is the criterion; students should never be given an assignment they cannot master.

However, Bruner (1966) maintains that writing assignments must not be limited to what students can do—that this does not create enough stimulus for cognitive growth. He says that only in times of conflict does the "child make sharp revisions in his way of solving problems" (1973, p. 11). Practice in expressive writing also appears to have no relationship to improvement in transactional writing skills.

'Ownership' of Ideas

In transactional writing, students learn to "own" an idea that comes from outside their own "self" by actively incorporating new knowledge, making relationships, and formulating hypotheses. In so doing, they must cognitively encounter the new ideas or thoughts rather than merely express what they already "own." Transactional writing yields a different type of knowing—an intellectual owning, not a "feeling" or subjective owning. Certainly the degree of owning may be higher in expressive writing because the subject is the students' own feelings, but such a response involves little active cognition. Students can "own" transactional topics—become motivated, be interested, and care—but it is a qualitatively different kind of owning. As stated earlier, oral discussion can help students organize and understand their topic, but the writing process is aided by practice in placing meaning in the text by means of transactional assignments.

To restrict writing to what is easy, unstructured, and low in cognitive growth potential is inappropriate; to justify it in motivational (not cognitive) terms is unsound. Certainly expressive writing has a place in generating ideas, words, phrases, and interest; but written expression is more than listing and requires practice, particularly in later school years. Involvement and owning the task obviously are important and the degree of owning is higher when the subject is the students' own feelings, but current stress on creative expression at the expense of expository writing as a remediation has little basis in an understanding of the nature of written expression.

Rather than increasing expressive writing, greater attention should be given to transactional writing with teacher guidance, because the instructional benefits are more significant than those that come from expressive writing. Moreover, Bereiter and Scardamalia (1980) suggest that "it is not enough just to teach background knowledge and how-to-do-it strategies for dealing with problems as students spontaneously represent them. Something should be done to enable students to construct and function within more complex problem spaces" (p. 82). They offer (pp. 90-92) "procedural facilitation as an instructional model of learning within 'complex problem spaces.'" They suggest seven procedural facilitations where the executive demand is high and the writer's representational knowledge exceeds procedural knowledge:

1. Mimic mature executive processes by providing simplified routines and surrogate tasks;
2. Minimize attentional demands;
3. Minimize choices;
4. Structure procedures so as to focus on mature tendencies such as the evaluation-revision process rather than immature tendencies of mechanics.
5. Facilitate awareness of covert cognitive processes so as to facilitate access to them when needed;
6. Label tacit knowledge of discourse elements, such as setting, character, moral, cause (for the narrative mode);
7. Employ procedures that can be adjusted in terms of cognitive complexity.

Bereiter and Scardamalia are encouraging "procedural facilitation" over "substantive facilitation," where the teacher takes on the responsibility of processing information. By keeping the responsibility for processing information with the writer and at the same time facilitating the procedures to be used, the teacher can provide instruction that will serve the demands of the task at hand and, it is to be hoped, the demands of future assignments.

BIBLIOGRAPHY

Ammon, P.R. Cognitive development and early childhood education: Piagetian and neo-Piagetian theories. In H.L. Hom & P.A. Robinson (Eds.), *Psychological processes in early education.* New York: Academic Press, 1977.

Bannatyne, A. *Language, reading and learning disabilities.* Springfield, Ill.: Charles C. Thomas, Publisher, 1971.

Bereiter, C. Development in writing. In L.W. Gregg & E.R. Steinberg (Eds.), *Cognitive processes in writing.* Hillsdale, N.J.: Lawrence Erlbaum Associates, Publishers, 1980.

Bereiter, C., & Scardamalia, M. From conversation to composition: The role of instruction in a developmental process. In R. Glaser (Ed.), *Advances in instructional psychology* (Vol. 2). Hillsdale, N.J.: Lawrence Erlbaum Associates, Publishers, 1980.

Britton, J. What's the use? A schematic account of language functions. *Educational Review,* 1971, *23*(3), 205-219.

Bruner, J. *Studies in cognitive growth.* New York: John Wiley & Sons, Inc., 1966.

_____. *The relevance of education.* New York: W.W. Norton & Co., Inc., 1973.

Case, R. Learning and development: A neo-Piagetian interpretation. *Human Development,* 1972, *15,* 339-358.

_____. Structures and strictures: Some functional limitations on the course of cognitive growth. *Cognitive Psychology,* 1974, *6,* 544-573.

_____. *Motivation, experience and intellectual development.* Unpublished manuscript, 1975.

Cazden, C. *Child language and education.* New York: Holt Rinehart Winston Inc., 1972.

Cohen, B.D., & Klein, J.D. Referent communication on school age children. *Child Development,* 1968, *39,* 567-609.

de Ribaupierre, H., & Pascual-Leone, J. Formal operations and M-power: A neo-Piagetian investigation. *New Directions for Child Development,* 1979, *5,* 1-43.

Dickson, W.P. (Ed.). *Children's oral communication skills.* New York: Academic Press, 1980.

Flavell, J.H. Cognitive monitoring. In W.P. Dickson (Ed.), *Children's oral communication skills.* New York: Academic Press, 1980.

Flavell, J.H. *The development of role-taking and communications skills in children.* New York: Krieger, 1975.

Foorman, B.R. *A neo-Piagetian analysis of communication performance in young children.* Unpublished doctoral dissertation, University of California, Berkeley, 1977.

_____. Language development in the K-3 classroom: Using the referential communication paradigm. *Psychology in the schools,* 1980, *17,* 278-283.

Furman, I. *M-demand of problem-solving strategies in Piaget balance-skill task.* Paper presented at the American Psychological Association convention, 1980.

Garvey, C., & Hogan, R. Social speech and social interaction: Egocentrism revisited. *Child Development*, 1973, *44*, 562-568.

Gere, A. Writing and WRITING. *English Journal*, 1977, *66*(8), 60-64.

Glucksberg, S., Krauss, R.M., & Higgins, E.T. The development of referential communication skills. In F. Horowitz, E. Hetherington, S. Scarr-Salapatek, & G. Siegel (Eds.), *Review of child development research* (Vol. 4). Chicago: University of Chicago Press, 1975.

Glucksberg, S., Krauss, R.M., & Weisberg, R. Referential communication in nursery school children: Method and some preliminary findings. *Journal of Experimental Child Psychology*, 1966, *3*, 333-342.

Goodman, D., & Pascual-Leone, J. *M-stages and stage transitions:* A developmental trace study. Paper presented at the American Psychological Association convention, 1980.

Keenan, E.O., Schieffelin, B.B., & Platt, M.L. Propositions across utterances and speakers. *Papers and Reports on Child Language Development* (No. 12). Stanford University California Committee on Linguistics, December 1976. (ERIC Document Reproduction Service No. ED 161 298).

Maratsos, M.P. Nonegocentric communication abilities in preschool children. *Child Development*, 1973, *44*, 697-700.

Meissner, J.A., & Apthorp, H. Nonegocentric and communication mode switching in black preschool children. *Developmental Psychology*, 1976, *12*(3), 245-249.

Menig-Peterson, C.L. The modification of communicative behavior in preschool aged children as a function of the listener's perspective. *Child Development*, 1975, *46*, 1015-1018.

Mueller, E. The maintenance of verbal exchanges between young children. *Child Development*, 1972, *43*, 930-938.

Olson, D. From utterance to text: The bias of language in speech and writing. *Harvard Educational Review*, *47*(3), 1977, 257-282.

Pascual-Leone, J. *Constructive cognition and substance conservation: Towards adequate models of the human subject.* Unpublished manuscript, 1974.

_____. Metasubjective problems of constructive cognition: Forms of knowing and their psychological mechanism. *Canadian Psychological Review*, 1976, *17*, 110-125.

Pascual-Leone, J., Goodman, D., Ammon, P., & Subelman, I. Piagetian theory and neo-Piagetian analysis as psychological guides in education. In J.M. Gallagher & J. Easley (Eds.), *Knowledge and development: Vol. 2, Piaget and education.* New York: Plenum Press, 1978.

Pascual-Leone, J., & Smith, J. The encoding and decoding of symbols by children: A new experimental paradigm and a neo-Piagetian model. *Journal of Experimental Child Psychology*, 1969, *8*, 328-355.

Piaget, J. *The language and thought of the child.* New York: Harcourt Brace & Co., 1926.

Piaget, J., & Inhelder, B. *The child's conception of space.* New York: W.W. Norton & Co., 1967.

_____. *The psychology of the child.* New York: Basic Books, Inc., 1969.

Pulos, S. *M-capacity as a developmental constraint on structural learning.* Paper presented at the American Psychological Association convention, 1980.

Rosenberg, S., & Cohen, B.D. Referential processes of speakers and listeners. *Psychological Review*, 1966, *73*, 208-231.

Rosen, C., & Rosen, H. *The language of primary school children.* London: Penguin Books, 1973.

Rumelhart, D.E. Notes on a schema for stories. In D.G. Bobrow & A.M. Collins (Eds.), *Representation and understanding: Studies in cognitive science.* New York: Academic Press, 1975.

_____. Schemata: The building blocks of cognition. In R. Spiro, B. Bruce, & W. Brewer (Eds.), *Theoretical issues in reading comprehension.* Hillsdale, N.J.: Lawrence Erlbaum Associates, Publishers, 1980.

Sachs, J., & Devin, J. Young children's use of age-appropriate speech styles in social interaction and role-playing. *Journal of Child Language,* 1976, *3,* 81-98.

Scardamalia, M. How children cope with the cognitive demands of writing. In C.H. Frederiksen, M.F. Whiteman, & J.F. Dominic (Eds.), *Writing: The nature, development and teaching of written communication.* Hillsdale, N.J.: Lawrence Erlbaum Associates, Publishers, 1980.

Schank, R.C., & Abelson, R.P. *Scripts, plans, goals, and understanding.* Hillsdale, N.J.: Lawrence Erlbaum Associates, Publishers, 1977.

Shatz, M., & Gelman, R. The development of communication skills: Modifications in the speech of young children as a function of listener. *Monographs of the Society for Research in Child Development,* 1973, *38*(5, Serial No. 152).

Vygotsky, L.S. *Thought and language.* Cambridge, Mass.: M.I.T. Press, 1962.

Chapter 7

Mode of Discourse Awareness

This chapter focuses on the interaction between composition and purpose, message and intent. Mode (in the chapter title) refers to which of the four written discourse forms the individual chooses to transmit desired content. The four writing modes are narration, description, exposition, and argument. Pragmatics (discussed in the introduction to this unit) refers to writing within its social context; it involves considering an audience in composing a message as well as the effect on the receiver or recipient of the message—an effect that involves a response to the message, not just a passive reading.

The role that mode of discourse plays in the overall effect of composition is discussed first, followed by a review of several proposals that are designed to match the students' composition more effectively to successful achievement of a writing purpose.

The authors deliberately had mode awareness follow audience awareness because they felt that the cognitive decentering skills discussed in Chapter 6 had equal application in this chapter's area. The individual needs to be able to decenter in order to address audience as well as mode needs. Successful achievement of the argument mode, for example, requires that students know how to convince someone other than self of a position. To build such a proposal requires their awareness of what the other person needs to know in reference to the topic at hand, as well as how best to structure the proposal to fit the desired audience.

In other words, the audience aspect of writing takes into account what writers must *do* to address the needs of an absent group or individual. The mode aspect takes into account which mode is chosen and the writing's desired effect vs. actual effect on the audience. One represents the "sense" behind a developed sense of audience and requires decentration in writing; the other focuses on the mode to use to produce a desired effect, and the resulting success of the composition. Both approaches, however, rely on a base of decentration (Exhibit 7-1). Thus, this chapter focuses on the purpose of writing and on the writers' intended response from the reader.

THE FOUR MODES OF DISCOURSE IN WRITING

Just as speakers are aware of the needs of their social context and their speech act, so must writers be aware of the needs of their audience and chosen modes of discourse. Writers have four modes of discourse, each with its own requirements and demands. The least difficult is narration. Narration involves a simple time ordering of events into an organized plot or pattern. Writers merely relate the unfolding of events generally and in a straightforward manner. This mode requires an ability to order events logically and recount them.

The next most difficult is description, in which writers must decide what the reader needs to know in order to identify or recognize the description. As such, writers must distance themselves from their own knowledge of the topic so they can explain it clearly to others. Description involves a linguistic ability to build images and touch senses that allow the reader to "see" what the writers "see."

The third most difficult mode is exposition, which involves analysis, explanation, judgment, evidence, and other logical supports to synthesize information effectively, make intellectual sense of it, and analyze it. Exposition involves explaining to an audience the writers' own opinions or positions on a topic. Exposition requires much more of the writers because it demands the interplay of more abstract cognitive skills than either narration or description. Writers must employ many cognitive skills in order to devise their composition to effect their desired purpose.

The most complex mode of discourse is argumentation, which demands that writers convince their audience of a position. They must so structure the message as to alter the audience's position and perception or elicit sympathy from it. Crowhurst and Piche (1979) consider argument as eliciting the most complex syntax of any mode of discourse because writers use language conditionals (if/then), language resultants (therefore), and other difficult structures that are expressed in intricate form.

Just as in oral language in which speakers consider the nature of the felicity conditions of the act, the cooperative principle, and the context in which speech occurs, so should writers consider the demands and force of the mode of discourse as well as the needs of the audience to which the composition is directed.

Exhibit 7-1 Relationship between Audience and Mode Awareness in Writing

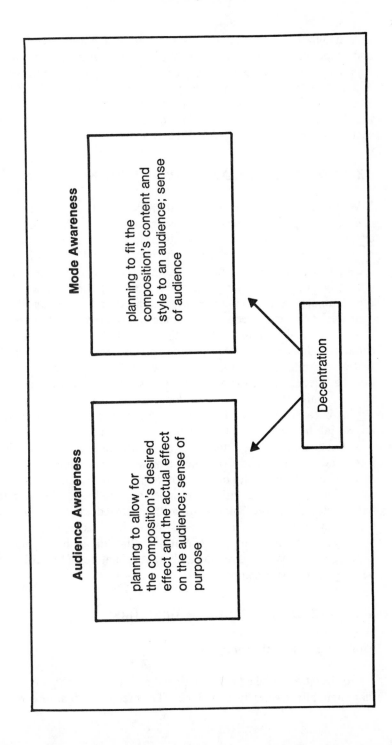

Mode Awareness

planning to fit the composition's content and style to an audience; sense of audience

Audience Awareness

planning to allow for the composition's desired effect and the actual effect on the audience; sense of purpose

Decentration

Although it has not been done yet, a comparison of the felicity conditions and cooperative principle in terms of speech and writing would provide fascinating information. Obviously, the interface is great, since the felicity conditions of a promise, for example, are similar in both speaking and writing. The study of the underlying felicity conditions of an entire composition—argumentation vs. exposition—and the building of it through its component sentences certainly would prove difficult and intriguing.

EXPRESSIVE AND TRANSACTIONAL WRITING

Writing has two other variables that are of importance here. Britton (1970) divides writing into expressive, transactional, and poetic types. He defines expressive writing as what is inner-directed to the writers, with the writers as intended audience. Expressive writing is more self-motivating, easier for the students, and gives them practice in developing language fluency. Theoretically, they develop language fluency because the demands of audience are eliminated, since the composition is directed to them and because the demands of mode are reduced by requiring primarily self-expression.

Transactional writing is at the other end of the spectrum; it involves an external audience as well as a nonself-expressive topic. In short, transactional writing is similar to exposition and narration. Britton and his followers maintain that success in expressive writing builds a base for success in transactional writing. Emig (1971) proposes that high schools focus primarily on expressive writing because of its benefits to the students. The benefits are motivational and social; however, the advantages of transactional writing are cognitive.

Transactional writing in terms of the exposition and argumentation modes forces individuals to address audience as well as the demands of the chosen mode of discourse. Such potential for cognitive development is exactly why exposition and argumentation are important modes of discourse to use in writing classes. As the Total Writing Process Model indicates, the cognitive component of audience and awareness of mode is just as important as is the language generation component. Not only that, the audience/mode component requires conscious direction and practice, not being "intuitive" as is the language generation component.

RESEARCH ON THE MODE OF DISCOURSE

Mode and Syntactic Complexity

Crowhurst and Piche (1979) designed a study to investigate the variables that might affect syntactic complexity. They recognize that research supports

Hunt's (1965) contention that T-unit lengths tend to increase with age; however, they question the norms or standards that T-unit lengths are considered to represent. They theorize that different modes of discourse demand differing levels of syntactic complexity and that writing to the intended audience requires manipulation of syntactic complexity.

To examine the variables of intended audience and mode of discourse, Crowhurst and Piche analyzed compositions by sixth and tenth graders. The students addressed compositions to a best friend and a teacher; thus, the audience variable had two levels. The students designed narrative, descriptive, and argumentative compositions; thus, the modes of discourse variable had three levels.

Crowhurst and Piche chose sixth and tenth graders because they felt that Hunt's syntactic research evidenced a growth spurt during intermediate school years. Sixth graders generally are in a stage before and tenth graders in a stage following such a spurt. Differences between the two groups are more pronounced, demonstrating the students' enormous skill increases.

The method uses three 35 mm color slides of a canoe, a classroom, and a whale. Each slide pictures as much as possible the varieties of response. Narration is defined as writing "an exciting story about the picture" (1979, p. 102), a definition omitting an audience requirement. Description is defined as describing "the picture as fully as possible" (p. 102), also omitting an audience requirement. Argumentation is defined as trying to convince the intended audience, a definition demanding audience accountability. The audience is either teacher or best friend for each of the slides, resulting in a total of six compositions. The student writes on each of the compositions over a six-week period, each writing session lasting 40 minutes.

Crowhurst and Piche (1979) report the following results. For tenth grade, compositions contrast significantly in terms of syntactic complexity when directed toward different audiences. Tenth graders increase the complexity for the teacher and reduce it for the best friend. Thus, they are able to manipulate syntax to match intended audience needs.

The sixth graders show no significant difference between audiences. Children at that level do change their language complexity orally, such as using less complex structure to speak to a baby or a pet than to an adult. This pragmatic ability, however, does not appear to translate itself into the written mode by this level. Apparently, sixth grade writers do not cognitively perceive the needs of others as demanding language manipulation or revision. The sixth graders' compositions are much less complex than the tenth graders', regardless of the audience.

In reference to mode, Crowhurst and Piche find that in tenth grade, argument correlates with greater syntactic complexity than either description or narration. In grade six, the result is the same. Grade ten argument and descriptive compositions are more complex than grade six compositions; however, the two grades' narrative compositions do not differ significantly in any measure of syntactic complexity. In other words, when narration is the target mode, the grades do not differ in terms of sentence complexity.

Language development and improvement is not essentially elicited by creative writing assignments that entail narration, according to this research. Crowhurst and Piche theorize that by its very nature, argument demands a concern for audience appraisal and needs. Therefore, students put more effort and concern into logically constructing and creating an "interrelationship of propositions which is expressed syntactically by the subordination of clauses and less than clausal elements" (1979, p. 107). In other words, argument enters the realm of condition, effect, and result—all of which tend to be expressed or correlate with similar language structures.

To express conditionality, effect, and result requires subordination, relativization, and embedding, rather than a simple proposition. Argument, then, elicits structural complexity in order to better communicate the structure of the persuasion. On the other hand, narration "places the fewest demands on writers to make use of their syntactic resources" (1979, p. 107).

This study has three implications:

1. Students not given the opportunity to use modes other than narration or description are limited seriously in language manipulability and elaboration. Merely because nonexpressive modes are harder to master is no reason to not assign them; practice in such modes develops important language skills.
2. Syntactic skills needed in description and narration are not the same as those needed in argumentation. To assume that the former build the latter is not completely true; the former do not require the structural complexity of the latter. Thus, narration cannot improve argument in terms of structure.
3. Writing assessments should be clear as to the mode that the students are using. Narrative mode scores penalize students when compared to argumentative mode scores.

Rosen's (1969) earlier research supports these findings in comparing referential and expressive writing by noting that the former display longer T-units than do expressive tasks.

Rank Ordering the Discourse Modes

Perron (1977) rank orders the differing levels of complexity associated with mode of discourse for third, fourth, and fifth graders. Overall, Perron notes that structural complexity decreases in order from argument, to exposition, to narration, and finally, to description. Interestingly, in elementary school, narration is noted to be more complex than description, an order that changes in high school. Perhaps the cognitive demands of plot development are newer, eliciting more time ordering than that of description. The time ordering appears more complex in comparison to descriptive passages, but by later grades the skills of describing require more language development while the time ordering demands of narration remain the same.

Time ordering, once mastered, is the major skill involved in narration; description, however, involves greater and greater complexity as students perceive the object from a multitude of different angles. Narration could involve such skills, but primarily follows an "and then . . . and then" format, relying on imaginative "and thens" for interest rather than on newly imagined arrangements.

The results are clear: to improve writing in a certain mode requires practice in that element. Each mode makes different demands on the writer, syntactically and cognitively. Competence in one does not imply it in another. The greater demands inherent in argument and exposition posit greater development for the writer syntactically and cognitively.

INSTRUCTION AND REMEDIATION

The next issue revolves around how best to improve writing in a given mode. Two common approaches are discussed: the "write more" school of thought and the "mark up the papers more" school.

The 'Write More' Approach

Buxton (1958) designed a study to determine the effects of writing frequency on improvement of written expression. He focuses on two points: (1) the relative effectiveness or ineffectiveness of regular or frequent writing assignments on the improvement of writing skill and (2) which of two methods coupled with increased writing will better increase skill.

The two methods represent two distinct schools of thought in reference to teaching writing. He terms the first a freedom from restraint or simply a writing method. The papers receive no error markings, no marginal marks, and no grade. Instead, at the end of the composition students receive a "generous" comment. No revision of papers is assigned. Many view such a "response" evaluation as the best method of teaching writing. Proponents feel the affirmative feedback enables the students to free their writing resources and address the compositions to a concerned and caring audience (the "generous" grader).

The second method Buxton terms revision. Papers are marked thoroughly including grades and negative comments, if necessary. Papers also are revised during 35 to 50 minutes of class time during the period in which they were returned.

Buxton used freshman students for seven months. The three groups—writing, revision, and control—had the same curriculum except that the writing and revision groups wrote 16 extra essays—about one a week. Students in the writing group were required only to write once a week; if they disliked the assigned topic, they could change to another. However, the revision group was required to write on the assigned topic and to include organized material, a thesis, and adequate development. The papers received two grades: one for content and organization and one for grammatical correctness. Students then were assigned revision work on the papers to clarify errors.

After the seven-month study, Buxton compared the groups in three measures. Before the study, the students were given the Cooperative English Test A, Mechanics of Expression, Form 2; The Cooperative English Test B_2, Effectiveness of Expression, Form 2; and an original essay. Following the experiment, students were given parallel forms of the objective tests and another essay.

Buxton (1958) finds the following results. On the objective tests, differences among the three groups are not significant. In other words, objective mechanics tests and effectiveness of expression tests do not reflect the results of increased frequency of composition. However, on the essay test, Buxton says the revision group is significantly improved over both the control and the writing groups in terms of overall compositional quality. This quality scoring is completed by raters, using a detailed score sheet. The revision group outscored the two others in diction, fluency, and variety. Interestingly, critical thinking, organization, and originality were not affected by the study. Writing plus instruction, then, affects the ability to manipulate and use language; cognitive factors are not affected directly.

Such improvements do not appear on the objective tests, suggesting a cautionary note in reference to using such instruments to measure compositional quality. Buxton's study strongly supports the value of critical grading coupled with revision; however, which variable—the revision or the grading, or both—accounts for the improvement is not clear. Nonetheless, his study demonstrates that increased frequency of writing alone is of no value, nor is an "affective" response to the composition. Rather, increased writing and critical grading plus revision account for a significant improvement.

Braddock, Lloyd-Jones, and Schoer (1963), in reviewing Buxton's study and other similar ones, point out that research has not investigated *how much* writing can be considered an increase in frequency as compared to the "typical" curriculum. Braddock et al. note that the variable "what kind of writing following what kinds of instruction for what kinds of students has also not been addressed" (p. 34). They comment that doubling poorly evaluated and poorly designed writing tasks cannot be more effective in comparison to carefully planned and evaluated, but less frequent, assignments. Thus, although practice may improve writing, the issue is more one of quality of assignment and instruction rather than of quantity of tasks.

The 'Mark Up the Papers More' Approach

The second approach involves marking and evaluating the students' papers intensely, hoping they will learn how to be more successful on their next writing effort. But intensive marking is costly in terms of teachers' time. To justify such an effort requires some support that it is achieving some gain other than the teachers' misplaced sense of martyrdom. Research does not support the effectiveness of intensive marking. Fellows (1932) and Burton and Arnold (1963) find no significant improvement in students' compositional quality following intensive teacher marking and grading.

Sherwin (1969) questions the validity of intensive marking of essays as well as the quantity approach. His review of the literature leads him to summarize:

> Motivation, selective criticism, discussion, practical experience, and revision are the important features of instruction. Intensive evaluation, like the mere multiplying of writing assignments, is costly in effort for everyone and fails to achieve positive results (p. 168).

The question now becomes: If increased writing and marking do not improve compositions, what does? The answer is simple: revision to address the needed audience and mode of discourse components. According to the Total Writing Process Model, audience and mode require conscious cognitive manipulation of the already generated language message—that is, revision. Revision is a conscious reformulation of the composition to better fit audience and mode of discourse demands. As Murray (1978) states, revision is a revisualizing.

McColley (1963) designed a multifaceted experiment that applies to revision. He sought to determine which of six instructional methods were most successful in teaching composition:

1. only writing (no instruction)
2. group discussion before writing
3. self-instruction including revision, rewriting, editing, and correcting
4. practical instruction in usage and mechanics

5. conventional theme correction
6. feedback from the instructor during the writing process

McColley used grades 8 through 12, inclusive, for one academic year. His findings lead him to state: "The activity of writing in and of itself is fruitless. The activity of tutoring, even where immediate feedback is possible, either is negative, or ineffective," or is "unfeasible" (pp. 64-65). Instead, he reports that compositions are improved significantly when compared to preexperiment essays when "functional instruction" rather than frequency of the writing task is used.

McColley maintains that "to teach composition effectively, teachers should give a weekly writing task on which they base about 2-1/2 days of practical explanation, student practice, discussion, revising, rewriting, etc." (p. 65). In other words, when students are guided to see their compositions a second time—practice in Component 2 of the Total Writing Process Model—they become better writers. "Functional instruction" essentially involves addressing audience and mode of discourse needs, yielding better organized, arranged, and developed papers. McColley also notes that proofreading errors decrease following such functional instruction.

Buxton (1958) already has demonstrated the clear superiority of revision over nonrevision in his experiment. Those who revised their work improved their compositional ability significantly in comparison with the nonreviser group. Buxton's nonrevision group wrote in an expressive manner, to use Britton's (1970) terms, whereas the revision group wrote in a transactional manner. It is interesting to speculate what effect, if any, revision would have in expressive writing because it demands so little from the writer. Revision would not need to see anything a second time.

Before revision can be successful, the students must have some competency in the assigned mode of discourse. Kirby and Liner (1980) stress that the revision process cannot be successful unless the students are practiced in a particular mode of writing. This is an important point in that too often it is assumed that practice in one mode carries over to another. For example, writing and revising descriptive compositions requires editing skills different from those for writing and revising argument. When the students attend to audience and mode of discourse demands for description, they are considering needs far different from those required by argument. The students must become familiar with the new target cognitive skills before they can refashion and see them again.

Kirby and Liner are critical of in-class writing assignments because they limit the time for revision, creating "hastily done and shoddily produced compositions" (p. 43). Instead, they feel more time on revision rather than more compositions should be stressed.

In an interview with Halpern and Mathews (1980) Shaughnessy states that when reading over a student's composition she looks for a "key." She says this key usually is "the most awful sentence but in that sentence are the seeds of the student's elaboration" (p. 34). The sentence or key is unclear, unguided, and unfocused but, with a second look, the student can expand it by removing the self until "a shape" can be seen (p. 33). Directing this shape to an audience and accounting for the mode of discourse chosen allow students to recreate and reformulate their expression effectively.

Some research has focused on how good writers differ from poor ones. Kroll (1979) postulates the existence of a discourse monitor to which good writers appeal consciously. These students can determine what works and what doesn't work. Kroll maintains that students are alerted that something is not quite right. This alarm is a conscious response to the composition that gives them cause to refashion their message. Kroll believes students can be taught to monitor or revise their compositions through interaction and immersion in the language so that "a mental approximation of the norm for standard written English" (p. 89) can be formed. This discourse monitor enables the students to match their composition against a monitor that alerts them to potential discrepancies and ambiguities.

McColley (1963) and Buxton (1958) have demonstrated the effectiveness of teaching students to address audience and mode consciously as a method to improve written expression. No systematized program exists; rather, a generalized "practice revision and editing of assignments" is all that is available. Revision is an essential component of the Total Writing Process Model; as yet, no clearly defined system of teaching revision exists. That revision can be taught and can improve written composition seems feasible. But without a more structured program or approach, the classroom teacher is left with the external structure of a method minus the content.

SUMMARY OF UNIT

Based on the ever-increasing wealth of information on pragmatics in reference to oral language, these data surely will provide fuel for the development of pragmatic writing programs. It is hoped that the in-depth discussion at the beginning of this unit provides initial motivation and orientation to the reader so that further work may be directed to pragmatic development and remediation in the written expressive language mode. The research highlighting the critical importance of revision in the writing instructional process also should lead to further study of appropriate programming to teach this element.

BIBLIOGRAPHY

Braddock, R., Lloyd-Jones, R., & Schoer, L. *Research in written composition.* Champaign, Ill.: National Council of Teachers of English, 1963.

Britton, J.N. *Language and learning.* Coral Gables, Fla.: University of Miami Press, 1970.

Burton, D.L., & Arnold, L.V. *Effects of frequency of writing and intensity of evaluation upon high school students' performance in written composition.* U.S. Office of Education, Cooperative Research Project 1523, Tallahassee: Florida State University, 1963.

Buxton, E.W. *An experiment to test the effects of writing frequency and guided practice upon students' skill in written expression.* Unpublished doctoral dissertation, Stanford University, 1958.

Crowhurst, M., & Piche, G.L. Audience and mode of discourse effects on syntactic complexity in writing at second grade levels. *Research in Teaching English,* 1979, *13*(2), 101-109.

Emig, J. *The composing process of twelfth graders.* Urbana, Ill.: National Council of Teachers of English, 1971.

Fellows, J.E. The influence of theme-reading and theme-correction on eliminating technical errors in ninth grade pupils. *University of Iowa Studies in Education,* 1932, *7,* 7-44.

Halpern, J.W., & Mathews, D. Helping inexperienced writers: An informal discussion with Mina Shaughnessy. *English Journal,* 1980, *69*(3), 32-37.

Hunt, K.W. *Grammatical structures written at 3 grade levels.* Research Report 3, Champaign, Ill.: National Council of Teachers of English, 1965.

Kirby, D.R., & Liner, T. Revision: Yes, they do it; Yes, you can teach it. *English Journal,* 1980, *69*(3), 41-45.

Kroll, B. Learning and acquisition: Two paths to writing. *English Education,* 1979, *11*(2), 83-90.

McColley, W. *Comparative effectiveness of composition skills learning activities in the secondary schools.* U.S. Office of Education, Cooperative Research Project 1528, Madison: University of Wisconsin, 1963.

Murray, D.M. Teach the motivating force of revision. *English Journal,* 1978, *67*(7), 55-60.

Perron, J.D. Written syntactic complexity and the modes of discourse. Paper presented at the annual meeting of the American Educational Research Association, 1977.

Rosen, H. *An investigation of the effects of differentiated writing assignments in English composition of a selected group of 15-16-year-old pupils.* Unpublished doctoral dissertation, University of London, 1969.

Sherwin, J.S. *Four problems in teaching English: A critique of the research.* Scranton, Pa.: International Textbook Co., 1969.

The Total Writing Process Model: Proofreading and Error Recognition

UNIT INTRODUCTION

Component 3 of the Total Writing Process Model encompasses the error recognition abilities necessary for students to match their expression to what is conventionally designated as correct. Because correct/incorrect is a convenient evaluation paradigm, this area of writing has generated countless tests to measure writing ability. It also has received substantial criticism as to the standards or conventions designated as correct. Regardless of what standards are used, effective writing at some point must attempt to match as much as necessary the designated conventions of the writing environment. Communication can break down from the recipient's point of view if certain errors are ignored; communication also can break down from the writer's point of view if "error fear" assumes large enough proportions to limit expression.

Despite the ease of test construction, it should be noted that tests that measure grammar, mechanics, punctuation, and syntax errors essentially are addressing only one component of the overall writing system—that of error recognition.

Students with problems in this area display an inability to "read" their compositions and correct errors. Because the errors are easy to note and quantify, these measures often receive the lion's share of attention. Nevertheless, effective writing does require proofreading skill, the ability to not impede or impair communicative intent by permitting mechanical, punctuation, or grammatical errors to interfere with the message.

To teach students to proofread their papers is the obvious solution. However, that requires teaching students what is acceptable and what is not. Here rests the problem. This unit reviews two approaches designed to give students the necessary background to enable them to proofread their papers for errors.

Chapter 8 presents traditional grammar theory and methodology and a review of their effectiveness in eliminating errors. Chapter 9 provides a behavioral approach, its methodology, and a review of its effectiveness.

Error recognition is but one of the components of writing effectiveness. However, it is one area that really "shows." The requirements of acceptable usage are rule governed and external to the students, requiring their acquiescence, with or without understanding of the reason. As such, error recognition seems most arbitrary, irrelevant, and forced to many students. But the issue remains that when errors interfere with communication, a problem exists. The question is not error or no error; rather, it is what kind of, and how many, errors are truly communicative impediments.

Chapter 8

Traditional Grammar Instruction

AN OBJECTIVE LANGUAGE ANALYSIS

Traditional grammar instruction is the most common method of teaching standard English usage today. It focuses on analysis of the form and the rules that make up a language's structure. Students are taught definitions and labels that they then use to decompose a sentence into given parts. They then can illustrate the relationships among the parts by diagraming. Or they can parse the sentence by naming the function or label of each word. Traditional grammar instruction assumes that study in taking a language apart enables students to develop the skills to know it well enough to put it back together in a better way. Learning how to use language by analyzing and rearranging the parts improves writing because the students learn how to manipulate it within acceptable rule-governed patterns.

Traditional grammar instruction is similar to a dissection of the language in order to gain structural knowledge of the parts. Students use this new structural knowledge to recognize correct and incorrect constructions. A traditional grammar curriculum is organized around practice in identifying the parts of speech and in discerning their misuse. Students work on numerous exercises to reinforce the target skills. Explanations of the rules are systematic and logical; the rules have reasons—or had reasons at one time. Students are to follow the prescriptions, thus displaying good or formal language choice.

Research is not clear-cut in its appraisal of traditional grammar instruction. Nevertheless, such teaching occupies a very central spot in public education, regardless of what it can or cannot deliver.

197

This chapter provides an explanation of the traditional grammar approach to teaching writing. First, the traditional grammar base is described, followed by the methodology, and a review of the major research studies, and ending with an analysis and critique of how it is taught.

THE FOCUS OF TRADITIONAL GRAMMAR

Traditional grammatical analysis focuses on the end product of a language utterance: the sentence. Traditional grammar does not concern itself with the process of sentence generation, with speaker intent, or with suprasegmental features. Rather, it begins and ends its language analysis with the sentence unit, assuming that such a basic entity encompasses all that is needed for adequate evaluation of utterances. The sentence unit is considered the basic building block, one that can be described as well as inspected. Because the sentence unit is defined not as a process but as a product, as a finished and final communicative intent, traditional grammar postulates numerous rules and regulations. For example, in the sentence "I run quickly," traditional grammar theory would consider only the following:

1. "I run quickly" is a sentence composed of parts of speech and containing a complete idea.
2. The parts of speech can be identified and described functionally as follows:
   "I" is a pronoun, replacing a noun.
   "I" functions as the subject of the sentence and therefore is in the subject case.
   "I" is first person, singular.
   "Run" is the predicate, or verb of the sentence.
   "Run" is first person, singular, indicative, and active.
   "Quickly" is a modifier of run, describing how the subject runs.
   "Quickly" functions as an adverb.
3. The sentence could be diagrammed as follows:

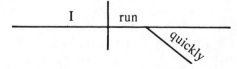

It should be noted that the analysis does not include the following:

1. What did the speaker mean? Was the speaker successful?
2. What did the listener understand the speaker to mean?
3. What intonations of inflections or bodily gestures were used?

4. How did the speaker arrive at the utterance "I run quickly"? What processes did the speaker follow to generate the sentence?

Because traditional grammar does not focus on the interactions just listed, it can be termed an objective language analysis. It assumes that the sentence contains, complete within its member parts of speech, all the information necessary for adequate analysis. Subjective investigations of suprasegmental features or of processes of generation are avoided. In short, the analysis requires only the concrete, observable sentence unit.

TRADITIONAL GRAMMAR THEORY DEVELOPMENT

The primacy of Latin as a language role model derives primarily from philosophical considerations. Latin was perceived to be the language of scholars, of science, of logic; Latin fit rules and remained constant, unchanging, and precise. The common vernacular, on the other hand, was perceived as impure, containing a multitude of idioms, pronunciations, spellings, and the like. Correctness in language was assumed to be a constant; variety and change in language were assumed to demonstrate degenerate common forms.

Medieval Latin differed from Classical Latin, necessitating the need for grammar books to teach the latter so that its literature could be studied. Grammar books were considered a means to understand and use a language. This belief still is evident today, accounting for the strong place grammar instruction continues to hold in the language arts curriculum. Even the term grammar school speaks of the importance that the subject had and still has in education.

By the eighteenth century, the precedent of learning grammar as an aid to learning a language was established firmly. The corollary, that grammar explained or systematized a language, also was accepted. The final conclusion, that grammar preserved a correct form of what language should be, also was well established.

The eighteenth century, with its penchant for orderliness and rationality, turned its energies to the systematizing of the English language. English grammars previously had been written to teach foreigners English. Such a procedure obviously followed the established mode: a grammar was used to teach a language. The rising middle class, seeking correct behavior in dress, manner, and custom, pursued correct behavior in its own language, English. For that reason grammarians turned their attention to producing an English grammar that would prescribe language usage just as books were prescribing correct dress and etiquette. Obviously, these grammarians adapted the Latin model to English.

Like its Latin model, the English grammars (1) focused on the word unit, (2) enumerated parts of speech defined in meaning as well as function terms, and (3) listed rules and regulations for correct usage. In addition, these new grammars attempted to fit English into the Latin mode, believing Latin to be the superior language. In questions of choice, the decision often went to the Latin model, not the everyday speech patterns of the citizens.

The eighteenth century grammarians felt they could "clean up" the incorrect language abounding in their land by establishing a base line of correctness. Since Latin was presumed to be the model language, the baseline for proper English usage had a distinctive Latin flavor. The teaching methodology was similar: just as Latin had been taught by rote exercises and by rule memorization often illustrated by diagramming or by parsing, so was English.

Thus, the language scholars of the eighteenth century developed an analogy between Latin and English that fit their philosophy, a philosophy that praised Latin for its stability and rule-governed structure. However, this approach did not account for the fact that English is a very dynamic and changing language, as is any language that still is spoken and in use. Rules applied better to Latin, since its spoken form no longer would undergo the magnitude of changes that affect English or any other still-spoken language. English structure also is not the same as Latin structure. Latin is an inflected language relying on inflections to transmit meanings. English, however, is a language of "word order," relying on sequence to transmit meaning. Rules that govern an inflected language do not necessarily apply to a word-ordered language.

The analogy between pure Latin and corrupt English certainly does not fit linguistically as well as it may have fit philosophically, as demonstrated by Robert Lowth's *A Short Introduction to English Grammar,* published in 1762, which went through twenty editions and was used widely. Lowth authoritatively upheld Latin as the language standard to be followed, assuming that rigidity in conformance to language principles would purify English from its then degenerate level. The popularity of his book and the many that followed demonstrate the strength of Lowth's position.

From its early inception as a grammar school, the secondary school had focused on language study. Although the study of Latin gradually was replaced with more practical subjects in America, English continued to be studied and taught as it had traditionally, following the preestablished Latin model. With the increasing growth of secondary school attendance and the possible economic and "class" improvements resulting from the opportunities of education, foreign-born parents wanted their children to speak and write correctly. Thus, the method of language study remained prescriptive and traditional. To this day, Conlin (1968) finds that the public's faith in grammar as teaching mastery of speaking and writing remains unshaken.

As a result, traditional grammar instruction maintained (and still maintains) an important place in language arts classrooms. The traditional grammar instruction is used to teach not only correct speech but also correct writing. The purpose of traditional grammar in the language arts curriculum, then, is to improve writing by focusing on prescriptive rules and regulations that supposedly yield more correct writing. A corollary is that if the students know the rules of good writing, they will be able to imitate and produce that good writing, untainted by poor usage.

In short, grammar occupies an important role in language arts education today, ironically not because of any proved efficiency but because of a long-serving tradition formulated on an intrinsically different language, Latin.

TRADITIONAL GRAMMAR CURRICULUM

Obviously the curriculum for traditional grammar instruction has remained fairly similar through the years. A widely used and representative traditional grammar text is the *Warriner's English Grammar and Composition* series (1977). The following is a brief overview of the material covered in the fifth course (eleventh grade) to illustrate curricular design.

Part One: Grammar

1. The Parts of Speech

Chapter 1 defines the eight parts of speech, using meaning categories, i.e., a noun names a person, place, or thing, as well as function categories, i.e., adjectives modify nouns. Examples then illustrate the part of speech targeted. Exercises enable students to identify the targeted part of speech from among several choices.

2. The Parts of the Sentence

Chapter 2 defines a sentence as a complete idea, containing a subject and predicate. Complements are introduced, defined, and examined.

3. The Phrase

Chapter 3 defines a phrase as a group of describer words not containing a subject or verb.

4. The Clause

Chapter 4 defines a clause as a group of words containing a subject and verb.

Chapters 3 and 4 introduce, classify, and determine the function of phrases and clauses in a sentence unit. As with the earlier chapters, the students practice identifying and classifying the parts of speech in numerous examples. The following sentence demonstrates the types of knowledge required of students using this format:

The girl in the car drove to the school.
The = article, modifier
girl = noun, subject
in = preposition
the = article, modifier
car = noun, object of preposition "in"
drove = verb
to = preposition
the = article, modifier
school = noun, object of the preposition "to"
in the car = prepositional phrase functioning as an adjective
to the school = prepositional phrase functioning as an adverb
The girl in the car drove to the school = independent clause

Part Two: Usage

In this part, the students' attention is directed to the correct and prescribed manner of using the grammatical elements learned in Part One. The students learn correct agreement and proper pronoun, verb, and modifier usage. Often correct usage appears to have no logical reason, remaining arbitrarily prescribed as correct.

For example, students have difficulty determining why "The dog smells bad" (subject-linking verb-adjective) and "The dog smells badly" (subject-active verb-adverb) are so different semantically. An extra *ly* changes the entire semantic nature of the sentence, a shift that students often find forced and arbitrary. "The dog smells bad" translates as "the dog stinks;" "the dog smells badly" translates as "the dog has difficulty using his sense of smell." When students are asked how they would communicate the two different messages encoded in these two sentences, they often reply that they would rewrite the sentences to make the meanings clear. In other words, students seem to feel that an additional *ly* is not communicatively clear enough to change "the dog stinks" into "the dog has a stuffy nose."

The distinctions required by traditional grammar often appear unreal and arbitrary, if not foolish, to students. Regardless of the amount of grammatical knowledge mastered, students recognize that when rules take precedence over meaning, rewriting looms as a communicative need. They also balk at correct/ incorrect labels that seem to have no semantic reason. For example, they may see no semantic difference distinguishing "between you and I" and "between you and me." According to traditional grammar usage rules, "between you and I" is incorrect, yet both expressions communicate the idea with no limiting interference.

Again, regardless of the grammatical knowledge mastered, many students maintain that if the point gets across clearly, with no misunderstanding, then picky grammatical rules are pointless. Both criticisms account for the difficulty in teaching the usage sections to students; the rules often are arbitrary and picky without apparent reasonable basis. The standards often are far removed from the students' own language experience. Nonetheless, traditional grammar usage remains an integral part of the text.

Part Three: Composition: Sentence Structure

This focuses on rules for writing complete sentences effectively. Students are shown errors involving fragments, subordination, coordination, reference, modifiers, and parallel structure. They learn to identify the errors, correct them, and, the teachers hope, not repeat them.

The Other Parts

Part Four focuses on the writing of compositions that use the skills just learned, Part Five on punctuation rules, Part Six on library and reference skills, Part Seven on American English and dialects, and the concluding Part Eight on an overview of college entrance examinations.

The main content of the book (Warriner et al., 1977) is contained in the first three parts, in which grammatical rules and terms are defined, explained, and illustrated. Through the exercises in the textbook, students learn to recognize and correct errors. Error-free writing is assumed to be correct writing, even good writing.

Overall, Warriner et al.'s is an excellent, well-developed, and clearly organized textbook, clear, concise, and supported with numerous reinforcing activities. Of the available traditional grammar textbooks, Warriner's certainly is one of the best. Any drawbacks derive from traditional grammar theory rather than from the makeup of the text itself.

A REVIEW OF THE RESEARCH

Harris (1963) investigated the relationship between formal grammar instruction and improved compositions, using two classes in each of five British schools for two years. The classes were termed heterogenous by the school administration, although not deliberately matched by Harris himself in terms of intelligence, socioeconomic status, or school achievement.

The experimental group spent one day a week learning formal grammar—rules, labels, and all. The control groups spent an equivalent time but used what Harris termed the "direct method." That approach concentrated on revision, writing imitation, and pattern practice. Harris compared scores before, during, and after study on a composition measurement device that he designed himself, as well as on a grammar test. The composition test contained 11 criteria designed to measure the style the students exhibited in their compositions. He theorized that grammatical success would be reflected in these categories since they were derived from grammar study. His categories were the following:

1. average length of correct simple sentence
2. omission of full stops or separation between clauses
3. words per common error
4. number of different sentence patterns used
5. number of nonsimple sentences
6. number of subordinate clauses
7. total words
8. number of correct simple sentences
9. simple sentences with two or more phrases
10. total number of correct sentences
11. adjectival phrases and clauses

Harris discovered two major points. First, one year (midtest) is too short a time and does not adequately reflect or tap the changes in student language patterns. Two years (posttest) give a more stable result of the language changes. Harris's conclusion here is extremely important: he maintains that one year is too short a term to develop stable alterations in language writing or to measure those changes accurately. Yet the majority of studies investigating theories of remediation of written language last a year at best or only one term (half a year).

Harris's (1963) second point is that his experiment demonstrates no relation between grammar test scores and composition ability. High grammar marks did not correlate with improved composition grades on an instrument Harris designed to tap grammar knowledge in a compositional setting. His 11 criteria for evaluating student composition should have demonstrated grammar ability. He calibrated the percentage of correct vs. incorrect sentences, and the percentage of complex vs. simple constructions. The first should demonstrate internalization of grammar usage rules; the second, reproduction of sentence structure knowledge—i.e., if students recognized a complex sentence, they should perhaps be able to reproduce or imitate a complex construction.

Harris concludes that "It seems safe to infer that the study of English grammatical terminology had a negligible or even a relatively harmful effect upon the correctness of children's writing in the early part of the five secondary schools" (1963, p. 83). Harris reports the disappointing results that even after a two-year program, many students in his traditional grammar class did not score better than the control group on a grammar test, with more than half of the students in one class scoring 50 percent or less. Because of a lack of correlation between grammar study and language usage improvement, Harris strongly advocates the discontinuation of traditional grammar instruction because he feels the time could be better spent on another, more effective method of language improvement.

Following an extensive review of the literature for the National Council of Teachers of English, Braddock, Lloyd-Jones, and Schoer (1963) declared that

> In view of the widespread agreement of research studies based upon many types of students and teachers, the conclusion can be stated in strong and unqualified terms: the teaching of formal grammar has a negligible, or, because it usually displaces some instruction and practice in actual composition, even a harmful effect on the improvement of writing (pp. 37-38).

The central issue remains whether grammar instruction enables students to learn how to manipulate their language appropriately and within the parameters designated as correct English. But rule-following behavior in reference to language usage involves more than rote because the students must be able to generalize the rule to similar language structures. Somehow the external rule must become part of the students' internal language monitor so that they can refer their external pattern to an internal model of correctness. The Harris study rather convincingly suggests that traditional grammar does not influence students' internal language model of language usage.

STUDENTS' INTERNAL LANGUAGE MONITOR

Traditional grammar instruction does not reveal what the student intuitively knows about language structures. DeStefano (1978) notes that conscious knowledge of rules does not correlate with ability to write because the naturalness of language is removed, leaving a learned capacity to eradicate incorrect structures. Yet this learned capacity has no meaningful relation to language, creating a difficulty for students in generalizing the rule to the language. What often happens, as many teachers will attest, is that the students learn the rule for a specific case but when presented with a similar but not identical problem, they are unable to generalize the rule to the new situation. DeStefano maintains that "knowing what (information about sentence parts, etc.) is not the same as knowing how—to write, to read" (DeStefano, 1978, p. 167).

Students already have language competence, an ability they have been using since as far back as their memory can go. Unless they use language now in a formal fashion as defined by traditional grammar prescripts, they must alter their performance to mesh better with the regulations. As a result, motivation becomes a primary factor. Many students may feel no pressing need to so alter their language performance, feeling that their communication is effective as is. Thus, one of the reasons traditional grammar prescripts are not internalized is that students may choose to not so modify their language. Even the fear (or threat) of college board tests may inspire only sporadic efforts, not consistent attention.

This point is worth pursuing. As detailed in the Total Writing Process Model explained in the Introduction to this book, traditional grammar, by addressing errors of proofreading, usage, mechanics, and punctuation, focuses on Component 3: error recognition. It does not address grammatical generation of the language utterance but rather a standard format. Traditional grammar seeks to polish the students' expression, using given parameters.

However, polishing requires a shared vocabulary system composed of correct/incorrect or better/best or formal/informal categories. Traditional grammar offers a very organized, systematized, objective language philosophy, accounting for the responses by teacher advocates who maintain that they need such a system in order to explain the reasons for good or poor language usage. Such a system also offers clearly defined parameters of language usage, in contrast to many relative, no-standards-required systems. In short, traditional grammar fills the bill in that it offers a theory or a rationale to support its extensive and thorough sanctions on correct language usage. Traditional grammar maxims also lend themselves easily to measurement and testing situations, as evidenced by achievement and college board tests.

But what do such tests really measure? Briefly this:

1. how closely the students' internal language monitor meshes with traditional grammar—a measurement of socio-economic status and background or
2. how motivated the students are to alter their internal language monitor and incorporate new sanctions—a measurement of motivation and discipline

The question arises: Would a motivated, self-disciplined student be able to learn the arbitrary prescripts of traditional grammar effectively? Following a study of the relationship between grammar knowledge and composition, O'Donnell (1963), although finding no relationship, intuitively feels that there should be a link. He believes that the nature of the study is not sensitive enough to detect the relationship. He also feels that good writing cannot happen in a void; it has to have a basis of grammatical awareness. O'Donnell's position makes sense: if students know the different sentence patterns and can recognize or identify them, surely they can use the various patterns. If they can identify pronoun cases, surely they can use them correctly.

However, the research does not support what appears on the surface to make sense. Apparently, students can recognize the specific case but do not generalize the knowledge to their own generated writing. In other words, the language they use does not seem to fit the language they practiced, or what they practiced never fit their internal language monitor, leaving the monitor essentially untouched, although in specific cases the students may remember the rule or pattern more by rote than by meaning.

A TENTATIVE RESOLUTION

The authors resolve this problem in the following manner.

First, we recognize that error recognition is an important aspect of writing, which to be effective must match as much as necessary the designated standards and conventions of the writing environment. Poor error recognition skills can limit the overall communicativeness of the message, not necessarily by blocking semantic or pragmatic transmission but by impeding syntactical decoding. When writing conventions are seriously breached, the message still may be clear but the reader must recode it in conventional forms in order to comprehend it. In other words, the reader must work to get at the meaning. We also recognize that, although conventions by nature and definition are arbitrary, when they become communicatively pointless their purpose is lost. For example, the difference between "It is I" and "It is me" has become academic and self-serving, not communicatively significant.

Second, we recognize that modifications of the traditional grammar system offer a standard for determining formal/informal language usage sanctions. Traditional grammar by its nature focuses on an analysis of the given language utterance, thereby deriving rules and regulations. We also recognize the need for such standards in writing since feedback is not immediate and since the message is context dependent. The reader needs conventions in writing that the listener easily can do without. The listener can depend on and use a variety of signals to clarify an ambiguous message; the reader cannot.

Third, we feel that when writing is viewed in its entirety as a total process, then error recognition assumes a role as a part of the whole process, not as the process itself. When students are successful in Components 1 and 2 in the Total Writing Process Model, then we feel that much of the needed error recognition and correction will have occurred already, leaving only final proofreading. When students successfully address their composition to a particular audience using a particular mode, then the writing likewise will reflect this success by not exhibiting major mechanical, punctuation, structure, or grammatical errors that would interfere with the communicative intent.

Finally, we feel that traditional grammar instruction that follows such competence in Components 1 or 2 has a much higher chance of success. Since the students' internal language monitor already is interacting with audience and discourse demands and thereby developing more accurate representations of good writing, additional usage conventions also could be interfaced more effectively as a final part of a process rather than as the whole process.

EVALUATION OF REMEDIATION

Traditional grammar instruction does not fare well under the onslaught of current research. In fact, research even suggests that traditional grammar instruction has a very serious side effect: important class time is spent on a useless method of remediation, leaving writing just as poor as before. Based on a Latin model of language structure, using Latin grammar rules for the English language appears ambiguous, particularly in definition of terms, arbitrary in usage prescriptions, and stilted in reliance on ill-fitting rules. Somewhere, somehow, traditional grammar loses the naturalness of language, usurping individuals' intuitive aptitude and grasp for communication.

But reality remains: students are judged competent for college work based on usage test scores that adhere to traditional grammar prescriptions. Rather than argue the potential merits or demerits of such evaluations, the fact remains that students need to know certain acceptable standards of written language usage. The issue remains one of how best to instruct them in error recognition so that their internal language monitor will help them evaluate their language production in terms of acceptable standards.

Error recognition of given writing samples does not necessarily involve the same skills as does generation of error-free utterances. For example:

1. Students must generate sentences similar to the ones with which they have developed familiarity in their class grammar lessons. Sample grammar sentences are notoriously simple, irrelevant, and dissimilar to student writing.

2. Students must be motivated enough to choose to proofread and revise their earlier work.
3. Students are taught that the generation of writing involves idea, composition, organization, communication, audience—a whole range of cognitive concerns. Error recognition involves different cognitive concerns such as analysis, decomposition, and discernment of error patterns. If students are not going to generate sentences similar to the ones they practiced in class, then they must be able, through proofreading, to recognize what makes the sentences correct or incorrect.

Essentially, students must match their composition to a model of good writing contained in their inner language monitor. Error recognition involves the cognitive skill of matching whereas composing involves the cognitive skill of generation. Theoretically, students should generate correct models of language, making proofreading obsolete. In reality, proofreading is necessary.

Research demonstrates fairly substantially the ineffectiveness of traditional grammar instruction in correcting production through proofreading. Results are not as clear-cut in terms of simple error recognition as on standardized tests. Such tests are similar to the instructional method used in the class as opposed to compositions that involve a variety of other demands on the students. Harris (1963) notes that although students in his experimental traditional grammar group improved their grammar test scores, they did not do better on composition. However, he reports that not all the experimental group members improved their grammar results, one group scoring less than half correct following a two-year period.

According to the Total Writing Process Model discussed in the Introduction, error recognition is distinct from generation/comprehension and audience/mode of discourse components. Traditional grammar does not improve student-developed writing in terms of structure or generation; it neither affects nor remediates problems in Components 1 or 2 of the model. Yet the research does not demonstrate that traditional grammar does much for Component 3, either; students may score better on objective grammar tests, but their compositions do not reflect the new knowledge to which they have been exposed.

The case for traditional grammar remains philosophical, as was its inception. If tests require prescriptive usage, schools will follow suit; if society values "correct" speech and writing, schools again will follow suit.

The question is: which method best remediates students' inability to proofread their papers and alter their production to fit correct/incorrect external sanctions. If the composition has not successfully ironed out these problems following an analysis of audience, purpose, and intended mode of discourse, the remaining errors most likely will be mechanical and grammatical—not essentially communicative. Somehow students need to internalize these basically noncommunicative sanctions into an inner language model and use them when needed.

Traditional grammar does not appear to be effective in such transmittal; however, no other grammar program seems to be any more so, nor do other grammars even intend to address error recognition problems. The question remains as to what method to use. As stated earlier: if the composition is communicatively clear, deficient only in arbitrary grammatical and mechanical items, apparently traditional grammar is the only method that addresses such prescriptions and rules, although admittedly in a poor fashion.

Yet the problem remains that a system that does not make sense is difficult for students to use to evaluate their sentence production, particularly when their own language patterns are very far removed from the external model. English, then, becomes like a foreign language. The students have the innate ability to acquire and use language; they just need a new symbol system in which to encode their oral or written utterances.

Nonetheless, effective writing requires some standard of conventional usage in order to ensure maximum reader comprehension as well as ease of reader decoding. Phelps-Terasaki and Phelps (1980) offer a resolution to the problem by incorporating grammar prescriptions into the overall writing process. Rather than proposing that traditional grammar instruction should remediate faulty composition, a position that most research does not support, we suggest that traditional grammar, when taught as a means of proofreading (following competency or instruction in the other prior components of the Total Writing Process Model), can be more successful in enabling students to broaden their internal language monitor to include such external sanctions as are needed to communicate within formal bounds.

We caution that grammar prescriptions that have lost common support such as certain pronoun case forms still may be difficult to teach—should anyone even desire to so do. ("It is me" is more common than "It is I" though incorrect.) However, when traditional grammar is viewed as an aid to proofreading as the conclusion of the compositional process, rather than as a substitute for it, we feel that the proofreading results will be more successful for both students and teachers.

BIBLIOGRAPHY

Braddock, R., Lloyd-Jones, R., & Schoer, L. *Research in written composition.* Champaign, Ill.: National Council of Teachers of English, 1963.

Conlin, D.A. *A modern approach to teaching English.* New York: American Book Co., 1968.

DeStefano, J.S. *Language and the language arts.* Boston: Little, Brown and Co., 1978.

Harris, R.J. An experimental inquiry into the functions and value of formal grammar in the teaching of English, with special reference to the teaching of correct written English to children aged 12-14. In R. Braddock, *Research in written composition.* Champaign, Ill.: National Council of Teachers of English, 1963.

Lowth, R. *A short introduction to English grammar,* 1762, as found in David A. Conlin, *A modern approach to teaching English.* New York: American Book Co., 1968.

O'Donnell, R.C. *The correlation of awareness of structural relationships in English ability and written compositions.* U.S. Office of Education: Cooperative Research Project 1524. Mount Olive, N.C.: Mount Olive College Press, 1963.

Phelps-Terasaki, D., & Phelps, T. *Teaching written expression: The Phelps sentence guide program.* Novato, Calif.: Academic Therapy Publications, 1980.

Warriner, J. E., Mersand, J., & Griffith, F. *Warriner's English grammar and composition.* New York: Harcourt Brace Jovanovich, 1977.

Chapter 9

A Behavioral Approach

Donald E. P. Smith (1976) has built a four-volume framework devoted to reading and writing. Termed a technology by Smith himself, the overall format is behavioral: task analysis, stimulus-response (S-R) learning conditions, and the like. His analysis of the components involved in writing is a comprehensive and useful product. His discussion of the nature of a learning target and the requirements of S-R relationships is useful for the development of individual instructional strategies.

Smith's system seems particularly appropriate to the mastery of usage, punctuation, and mechanics. The STARS (Standard Achievement Recording System) (1977) profile yields a survey of what students can or cannot do, leading directly to remediation. But the exact nature of the remediation is up to each teacher.

This chapter discusses his theoretical position, instructional methodology, task analysis of writing, and overall program merit.

THEORETICAL BACKGROUND

The basis of Smith's (1976) approach derives from identification of the learning target, defined as what is learned—the product or percept of learning. The individual's percepts develop on the basis of experience and interaction with the environment. For language learning tasks to be successful, they must be both theoretically and behaviorally sound. In other words, the task must reflect the constraints of both the language and learning systems.

A task that does not lead to understanding of the language is just as pointless as one that is too difficult for students to perform. As a result, Smith labels his work "an engineering handbook, concerned with the technology of effective discrimination programing" (p. 5).

In keeping with this engineering framework, Smith calibrates the requirements of reading or writing by counting the number of necessary steps and tasks needed. For example, he reports that on one occasion when counting the number of responses that comprised a reading act, beginning with letter discrimination and concluding with sentence comprehension, he measured 18,000 steps. While this admittedly is a rather unwieldy number, the approach is clear. He defines the learning target, then decomposes it into the number of steps or tasks that comprise it. The benefits of such a task analysis are clear: the students' performance can be evaluated thoroughly, yielding a profile of which tasks they perform successfully or unsuccessfully. Instructional attention then focuses on specific deficiencies, individual for each student.

The merits of Smith's approach are obvious. Without a task analysis, the components of the learning target remain visceral, vague, and poorly articulated. For example, current research demonstrates the dearth of literature identifying just what reading is or does while still offering suggestions for improving writing. Unless the task is broken into clear component parts, the overall conception of the product loses a comprehensive framework. Another merit involves the naturalness of diagnosis and remediation. Rather then deciding students cannot read or write, a task analysis program allows the instructor to determine what steps they cannot perform; remediation begins exactly where the students stand and builds naturally upon what they can do. Strengths are not ignored; the students are not coded as nonreaders, below grade level, or whatever. Instead, they have an ability profile.

The one major disadvantage to such an engineering approach is theoretical, not instructional. Multifaceted tasks such as writing do not lend themselves easily to a completely objective analysis. At best, such an analysis offers valuable information as to the nature of writing; at worst, it may strip writing of its multidimensionality. The value of Smith's work is that he never loses track of the overall product by narrow focus on its component parts.

INSTRUCTIONAL FRAMEWORK

Smith defines writing as "the production of visual symbols designed to produce differential verbal responses in a reader (including the writer as reader). The production is itself under the control of either a visual stimulus (copying) or an auditory stimulus (dictation or autodictation)" (1976, p. 24). Several points derive from this definition:

1. His writing paradigm is essentially behavioral in that it is objective, analytic, and devoid of subjective and cognitive dimensions.
2. His writing paradigm also is behavioral in its stimulus-response framework.
3. He perceives writing as following oral dictation, a position quite opposite to that theorized by cognitive psychologists who generally define written language as coming directly from inner language or thought units; writing shapes or codes these thought units in a fashion cognitively different from that of oral language.

Smith, instead, defines writing as a cross-modality process in which it "entails an aural input and a visual output" or, more simply, in which individuals dictate to themselves (1976, p. 45). They *say,* then they *hear* what they say, then they *draw* what they said. Just as reading involves see-say cross-modalities, so does writing involve say-hear-draw cross-modalities.

Smith differentiates between single-modality and cross-modality systems. Vision and audition are the two sensory modalities. In a visual single-modality system, the visual input leads to visual output, or the students see the word and *draw* it. In an auditory single-modality system, the aural input leads to aural output, or the students *hear* the word, then say it. Input, seeing, and hearing involve recognition whereas output, drawing, and saying involve recognition.

Reading is a cross-modality system because the see-say circuit derives from both the visual (see) and the aural (say) modalities. Writing (say-hear-draw) also is a cross-modality process involving both the aural (say, hear) and visual (draw) modalities. Writing is more complex in that it involves three circuits, reading only two. Input/recognition and output/reproduction also apply to cross-modality processes. In reading, learners see or recognize the stimulus, then say or reproduce it. In writing, learners say or reproduce, hear or recognize, and draw or reproduce.

Methodology

This recognition/reproduction continuum is the basis for task instruction in Smith's (1976) framework. Following a detailed breakdown of the component parts of learning targets into steps or tasks, he analyses each task individually. He determines methods to teach learners to recognize the targeted task, reproduce it, then substitute it for another targeted task. He defines this as discrimination learning.

Smith says the goal of the teacher is to so construct an environment that the students' behavior is under stimulus control of the learning task, not the countless other stimuli abounding in the classroom. The learning task will elicit new responses (recognition, reproduction, and substitution) that are the goals of instruction. These discriminative responses are under the control of a stimulus. Two points apply here: first, the response is discriminative. It occurs only following a certain stimulus. The child's response "cat" to a picture of a cat discriminates that recognition from one of a dog. Second, the stimulus controls behavior. The stimulus picture of a cat controls the resultant response and elects the word "cat," not "dog."

Once a learning target is identified, it can be analyzed for instructional strategies to teach the necessary stimulus and response patterns. Smith maintains that recognition of a stimulus precedes reproduction of response. As a result, he constructs strategies that start with recognition.

The Learning Target

Smith (1976) begins developing an instructional strategy for a learning target by determining the force of the target. Foil refers to what the target is *not*. A foil is a close distractor of the target item designed to force the student to discern finer and finer discriminations. Forced choice situations allow the learners to choose the target. Next, he narrows identification to the parts of the target, and finally, he focuses on the spatial or temporal relationships of those parts. Thus, to identify a target the instructor moves from what it is not to what it is composed of and ends with the relationship and arrangement of its parts.

This analysis is worth a second look. Often in devising instructional strategies, the nature of the target is not explained clearly to the learners; instead, a general explanation is given, followed immediately by exercises testing application of the new knowledge. Application of new knowledge no doubt is more successful when students "own" the new concept.

Recognition

Smith defines recognition as a response following a particular stimulus. If children can discriminate stimuli adequately, they will make correct responses. However, if they have difficulty discriminating stimuli, they will not recognize or identify the stimuli or make the correct response. In writing, if children do not recognize a complete sentence, they will not comprehend the need for an end mark or period.

Reproduction

Smith defines a reproduction as a response that "produces a previously learned stimulus" (1976, p. 33). The learners compare the response produced to one recognized previously. For example, they compare their use of an apostrophe to what they earlier recognized as correct. Success is when the two match. Often, school instructional tasks ignore the importance of recognition and move immediately to reproduction, a mistake in that the students have no chance to develop a model upon which to evaluate their productions.

Recognition involves identifying the target from a foil; reproduction involves discriminating incorrect variants of the target. Smith enumerates recognition and reproduction tasks as concerning content such as "sentence forms, punctuation, paragraph forms, and the order of sentences in paragraphs" (p. 35). He essentially is listing usage and structure (sentence forms), punctuation, mechanics (paragraph forms), and sentence order, all aspects of Component 3 of the Total Writing Process Model as explained in the Introduction.

Substitution

Substitution occurs when the learners can recognize equivalence or association between past and new stimuli. Substitution follows recognition and reproduction responses. This increases the students' storehouse of learning responses by allowing for new ones coming from associations and generalizations.

Instructional Strategy

Smith has developed a framework for the instructor to use in devising a particular curricular method. First, the instructor identifies the specific target task that comprises the overall learning objective. Next, the instructor devises recognition experiences, using foils of the method. Third, the instructor designs reproduction experiences using variations of the model. Association exercises also are used. Finally, the instructor measures task performance, using (usually) 80 percent accuracy or better as an indication of successful performance. The instructor then moves on to the next task.

A WRITING TASK ANALYSIS

Smith, Smith, and Brink (1977) have designed a Language Arts Competency Profile: STARS (Standard Achievement Recording System) that breaks language competency into five categories: letters, words, sentences, paragraphs, and books. The entire profile is a massive undertaking—195 pages, with two tests per page. The sheer comprehensiveness of the profile is impressive. The section on sentences and paragraphs is reviewed next.

Sentence Competency

Smith et al. divide sentence knowledge into three parts:

1. Perceptual skills involve oral reading, spaces between words, sentence memory, and dictation.
2. Grammatical skills involve capitalization, punctuation, and transformations.
3. Referential skills involve directions, questions, sentence meaning, and figurative language.

Smith et al. define perception as an initial step followed by structure or grammar and ending with meaning or referential skills. Each skill has a recognition and reproduction component. The Smith et al. factors (1977) are outlined in Exhibit 9-1.

Summary of Sentence Competency

Just as each skill has a recognition/reproduction factor, so are responses grouped hierarchically. For example, perception of what writing looks like from memory or from dictation involves the basic level of identification. A grammatical response, involving more than identification of graphic relationships, focuses on structural knowledge, language fluency, and language facility. A referential response builds on language grammatical manipulation, and concerns deriving meaning from sentences.

At no point does this task analysis of sentencing focus on the process of generation or elaboration of language; rather, it measures the objective or observable characteristics of writing. Although referential responses measure the target, it is reading comprehension that is assessed, not understanding of one's own generated communication as gauged by a match to inner language intent. As such, Smith et al.'s breakdown of the sentence task into specific target skills addresses Component 3, error recognition, of the Total Writing Process Model.

Correct capitalization, punctuation, and usage involve error recognition and acceptable reproduction. Following evaluation on the Smith et al. profile, the instructor can identify immediately which errors the students have difficulty recognizing or correcting. Remediation can begin at the specific problem level for each individual student as the instructor designs recognition/reproduction tasks necessary to teach the deficient skill.

Paragraph Competency

Smith et al. define a paragraph as a related group of sentences. They consider four components of paragraphing knowledge: form, content, equiv-

Exhibit 9-1   Outline of Skill Factors

Perceptual

1. Perceptual: Oral Reading
   Contains three tests requiring reading aloud, each test more difficult in terms of length and content.
2. Perceptual: Spaces between Words
   Contains one test requiring knowledge of sentence form.
3. Perceptual: Sentence Memory
   Contains two tests requiring recall, the second one using longer recall units.
4. Perceptual: Dictation
   Contains six tests requiring dictation ability, each test involving longer dictation units.

Grammatical

1. Grammatical: Capitalization
   Contains 10 tests, each measuring different capitalization rules such as Place Names, Direct Quotations, or Titles.
2. Grammatical: Punctuation
   Contains 21 tests, each measuring a specific punctuation skill such as Color, Period, or Comma: Appositives.
3. Grammatical: Transformations
   Contains 17 tests, each measuring a specific transformation such as Singular Subject, Plural Subject, Negation, Pronouns, Verb Tenses, Auxiliaries, Passive, Links, and Word Order.

Referential

1. Referential: Directions
   Contains two tests measuring following direction ability.
2. Referential: Questions
   Contains six tests, each devoted to one WH word: who, what, where, when, why, and how.
3. Referential: Sentence Meaning
   Test 1 matches the relationship of a sentence to an external, such as a picture. Test 2 matches the students' ability to recognize the internal sensibleness of a sentence. Test 3 measures the ability to pick out order of sentences in a larger unit such as a paragraph.
4. Referential: Figurative Language
   Contains four tests measuring use of idioms and similes.

alents, and impact. Form refers to the graphic patterns of paragraphing, similar to the perceptual area of sentences. Content is the meaning dimension of the paragraph, similar to the referential responses of sentencing. Equivalents and impact are the intent and effect of the paragraph as a communicative whole, not similar to any individual sentence response. Exhibit 9-2 is a survey of the parts comprising paragraphing knowledge (1977).

Summary of Paragraph Ability

As with sentence knowledge, paragraphing ability also is hierarchical, with each level containing recognition/reproduction aspects. The graphic pattern level precedes the literal meaning level; which in turn precedes recognition of more abstract meanings such as focus, point of view, and mood.

The Smith et al. (1977) task analysis of paragraphing competency corresponds to Component 2 aspects of the Total Writing Process Model. The Content unit of their STARS profile considers organizational skills; the Equivalents unit involves logic and reasoning skills; and the Impact unit covers discourse requirements. Audience is measured indirectly through a concern with intent of discourse.

However, Smith et al.'s test is, by its nature, objective and unambiguous, avoiding complexities, interpretations, shades of meaning, and other abstract considerations. For example, the section measuring a happy/sad mood description is concrete, basic, and literal. The Smith et al. profile is an introductory instrument, not a sophisticated measure of finely developed abilities. In its proper perspective, the profile is an amazing instrument of technology. As behaviorists, Smith et al. focus on the objective, measurable components of writing and reading, omitting consideration of underlying cognitive factors.

SMITH'S REMEDIATION PROGRAM EVALUATED

Smith et al. (1977) do not address the issue of generation or elaboration of language, preferring to measure what is observable. In recognizing this position and theoretical framework, the therapist or instructor can use the program effectively to remediate observable writing problems, primarily of error recognition. But the program is not designed to interface with cognitive factors.

Recognition tasks that compare target and foil or reproduction tasks that compare variants of the target do not lend themselves easily to sophisticated cognitive factors. But in reference to error recognition factors, Smith et al.'s framework is easily followed. Research has not evaluated the efficacy of the program in reference to writing remediation, an oversight that should be rectified. Behavioral programs that focus on specific skills have been quite

Exhibit 9-2 The Components of Paragraph Knowledge

Form

1. Form convention
   Contains two tests requiring knowledge of indented form.
2. Grammatical patterns
   Contains four tests requiring knowledge of parallel and consistent tense, number, and structure.
3. Phonological patterns
   Contains five tests requiring knowledge of rhyme, alliteration, and rhythm.

Content

1. Universe of discourse
   Contains two tests requiring recognition of topic and genre.
2. Topic
   Contains five tests requiring ability to recognize the topic of given paragraphs.
3. Plot
   Contains eight tests requiring ability to construct various kinds of plots.
4. Referential links
   Contains two tests requiring ability to use pronouns, conjunctions, and other links.
5. Relational links
   Contains six tests requiring knowledge of links such as "therefore," "of course," "later," and the like.
6. Information
   Contains nine tests requiring ability to produce and respond to literal questioning.

Equivalents

1. Summarization
   Contains five tests requiring knowledge of summary statements.
2. Induction
   Contains six tests requiring ability to use inference, similarity, difference, and reasons.
3. Deduction
   Contains three tests requiring ability to draw conclusions.

Exhibit 9-2   continued

Impact

1. Focus
   Contains five tests requiring knowledge of setting, topic, action, time, and motive.
2. Point of view
   Contains two tests requiring recognition of point of view and author's bias.
3. Mood
   Contains three tests recognizing mood such as happy/sad, mysterious/adventurous, or humorous/serious.

---

successful in the past; although recognizing the limitations of a behavioral approach in reference to the cognitive dimensions of writing, this program seems valid in teaching concrete error recognition skills.

BIBLIOGRAPHY

Smith, D.E.P. *A technology of reading and writing: Vol. I; Learning to read and write: A Task Analysis.* New York: Academic Press, 1976.

Smith, J., Smith, D.E.P., & Brink, J.R. *A technology of reading and writing: Vol. II; Criterion-referenced tests for reading and writing.* New York: Academic Press, 1977.

The Total Writing Process: Motivational Remediation

UNIT INTRODUCTION

The Total Writing Process Model does not consider motivation as a separate component in writing; rather, it presumes motivation to be a given. Recognizing the potential rashness of this statement, the authors wish to clarify the difference between motivation and motivational remediation.

Motivation is the initial action of getting students involved in the writing task itself or in any of the component remediation programs. The students then can benefit more directly from the remediation program because they are involved and concerned. Motivational remediation, on the other hand, assumes that the act of motivating is remediating in and of itself. This assumption posits writing disability as a student-engineered choice. If applicable, the program no doubt will be successful; however, too often students do not write or do not do it well because they cannot write. Wanting to write remediates intent, not ability.

This unit focuses on specific curricular lesson plans, creative writing, and the Bay Area Writing Project and its affiliates. The unit describes and evaluates motivational programs that intend to remediate student writing without using systematized programs or plans for skill deficiencies.

Chapter 10

Motivational Remediation

Motivational writing remediation is based on an assumption that the key to writing ability is a positive attitude on the part of the students. As a result, attention and care are devoted to devise curricula that are inventive, relevant, and exciting—in short, motivational. Several publications, primarily the *English Journal,* offer countless new methods designed to "turn kids on" to writing. Often at the base of such programs are the following points:

1. Writing in and of itself is a nonreinforcing project for most students. They generally do not enjoy writing and often dread the task. They perceive it not only as dull but as wasteful of time and effort, yielding very unaffirming results. They often prefer to communicate ideas orally, feeling more comfortable in discussion than in writing sessions (the lesser of two evils, perhaps).
2. Students generally do not write well, perhaps accounting for their aversion to the task. Television, magazines, and newspapers all paint in great detail the sad state of writing in the public schools, resulting in the students' bearing failure tags not only in class but outside as well. Standardized test scores reflect the decline in students' usage abilities; colleges decry compositional inadequacies. In the classroom, teachers daily cope with inadequate or undeveloped students' written expressions, not to mention their dislike of the task. In other words, students are bombarded with the problem of written language inadequacy.
3. Many teachers report success in improving written language expression when their students are motivated and choose to produce. Hence, a large body of literature has developed detailing past successful measures

that in the future may increase students' ability at least to choose to participate in writing. Improved participation obviously affects the final composition and is bound to produce better essays than when the students barely tried.

4. The various methods proposed for increasing student interest focus on highly motivated, committed, and conscientious teachers whose enthusiasm and concern inspire students to engage in the activities.

5. Curricular activities that are highly original and of great interest to students can capture their attention and performance. Such activities, although well-thought out but loosely organized beforehand, often are unstructured in presentation in that the teacher follows the direction of emerging student interest. Group work often is used as a means of fostering peer interaction as well as peer commitment to the process.

6. Such writing activities more often than not are not marked for errors, containing instead reinforcing comments by the teacher.

7. The result is improved student attitudes that overcome previous failures as well as help to lessen the constant barrage of "why Johnny can't write" that surrounds the pupils. Students begin to feel that Johnny *can* write.

8. Students essentially feel successful, teachers are happy, and all profit; however, since much of the work is nongraded, the motivational result can affect attitude. It remains to be seen whether the method improves written language.

This chapter focuses first on the basic philosophy behind motivational remediation, then on different curricular interpretations including creative writing and the Bay Area Writing Project, and concludes with an evaluation of the merits of the motivational method. However, an important distinction needs to be made at this point. Initial motivation is needed for any remediation program. When motivational activities are ends in themselves, and not means to introduce other remediation programs, then they assume themselves to be the remediating factor. This chapter concerns programs that focus on remediation essentially through motivation alone, not motivation coupled with a systematic remediation program, since systematic programs are covered elsewhere in this work.

PHILOSOPHY OF MOTIVATIONAL REMEDIATION

The philosophical basis of motivational remediation is simply this: once freed from external limitations and restraints, students' natural language ability will flow. Exterior restraints derive from a variety of sources, all of which cause students to choose to not write up to their potential or capability.

Exterior restraints originate under three headings: those in the curriculum, from the method, or from the instructor.

Curriculum Restraints

The first point of criticism is that students may elect to perform poorly on writing tasks that they conceive of as boring, irrelevant, or monotonous. Many assignments are accompanied by students' anguished groans, suggesting their basic dislike for writing. If they also judge the task itself as useless or wasteful, they may opt not to perform well. Motivational remediation assumes that students, when challenged by appropriate curricular material, will *choose* to perform well.

Curricular motivation focuses on remediating writing disability by improving students' attitudes rather than their skill. Students are considered language disabled because of an external element (the curriculum) and not because of an internal skill or ability deficiency. Great attention, therefore, is devoted to devising interesting new curricula, lessons, and plans that will elicit increased student attention and thereby attract better responses as well.

Methodological Restraints

A second area of criticism concerns the methods used to teach writing. Traditional methods of write-rewrite are judged as turn-offs, leading to the use of new instructional instruments, primarily audiovisual or aural-oral-visual. These new methods attempt to bridge the gap between television and the traditional classroom. In spanning that gap, teachers hope these new methods will stimulate the students to produce the required assignments. For example, students experience activities such as watching well-made open-ended films, after which they are assigned to write possible endings. Another method is to place student writing on transparencies for intraclass evaluation. Or teams of teachers may alternate class instruction, maintaining a high level of preparation for each one's assigned topic (like a media blitz).

A methodological focus remediates writing problems by attempting to improve student attitudes through exciting methods of instruction. Once the attitudes are improved, motivational remediation assumes that the writing performance also will make progress.

Teacher Restraints

The third area of criticism concerns the role of the teachers, primarily in terms of their evaluation of student writing. The argument here is that extensive teacher criticism fosters a negative environment that inhibits written expression. Writing becomes a drudge, an unsuccessful exercise, a task associated with failure. To inspire pupils to write, teacher evaluation is redefined to become a personal and positive communication between student as initiator and instructor as responder. The quality of written expression is secondary to the intent of changing the students' attitudes about using writing as a means of expression.

Once these limiting constraints are removed, students should be able to write naturally, freed from boring curriculum and methodology or error-conscious evaluation. Motivating lessons, techniques, and grading processes can create an environment in which they will elect to participate, produce, and write.

Once these three restraints are eliminated, students can tap into their natural reservoir of writing ability. Thus, the factors of curriculum, method, and the role of the teacher are manipulated in each form of motivational remediation. The types of motivational remediation programs or approaches are explained next.

SPECIALIZED LESSON FORMATS

A number of professionals have devised or adapted curriculum components to provide for increased student motivation and participation. A number of representative approaches are described here to highlight the scope and utility of such procedures.

Letter-Writing Unit

Hagemann (1980) proposes a letter-writing unit that focuses not on the letter but on the reply. She notes that the usual curricular methods to teach letter writing rely on the traditional, proper form of required opening, closing, address position, and punctuation. She feels that somewhere the excitement of letter writing is lost, replaced by a stilted and nonmotivating form in which students are to write letters for "tap wrenches, pin vises, and one-year subscriptions to *American Technology*" (p. 38).

Hagemann proposes a self-motivating and exciting curriculum designed to reinforce and encourage students in letter writing. The hope is that the students will choose to write because they want to communicate, not because they have to meet a curriculum unit objective. Hagemann proposes that students write away for free items. As a corollary, they must read and follow the instructions necessary to receive their free articles. She points out that students receive nothing if they omit a required self-addressed stamped envelope. The unit is designed to conclude with a show-and-tell speech in which students display their items and demonstrate their utility, or lack thereof.

She includes a fairly comprehensive collection of resources for free materials, including sample topics.

Hagemann's article is a good example of motivational remediation in writing. Substitution of a more exciting or rewarding curriculum for a staid and stultifying course accomplishes the primary objective: writing involvement. She does not stress "fixing" writing; rather she fosters an environment in which writing is an enjoyable activity.

A Multitext Approach

Egan (1979) proposes a multitext approach in the language arts curriculum. Her approach is to plan, for example, a unit on the short story. She then records ideas under three headings: projects, writing assignments, and comprehension questions. She notes that students marvel at the inclusion of their own insights and ideas in the designed curriculum. Egan thus creates a sharing system in which all students can contribute to the ideas from which projects, writing assignments, and comprehension questions will come.

At first the class members work together on the same text. They practice reading aloud their written responses to the writing assignments or comprehension questions. Egan maintains that the students become "eager to learn ways to improve their writing style" following oral presentation and peer response (p. 34).

The evaluation, coming from peers rather than from the teacher, has a less stinging effect. However, a very trusting classroom attitude and environment is a must for such sharing to take place. Students next are arranged in individual groups, structured as before but now utilizing nonclassroom sets of stories. For the group work to progress, a classroom attitude of responsibility must be in evidence.

Each group is responsible for the assigned story. Since no others will read it, the group feels a responsibility to instruct the class thoroughly about the story; otherwise the others will miss something. All work is written within the group and then presented orally to the class. Clarity is essential since the rest of the class will not be familiar with all the stories. Because the students have the support of the group as well as the responsibility of the assignment, Egan maintains that they enjoy the writing tasks, wish to perform, and do so successfully. They feel the assignment is important and they relate to the group method of instruction.

Egan's system is another good example of motivational remediation. A more reinforcing method is used to replace the traditional "we all do it this way right now" system. Her goal is to achieve student involvement in the writing task. If the necessary classroom climate can be fostered, then this involvement probably will increase as outlined.

A Brainstorming Period

Schwartz (1979) proposes eight to ten minutes of lively talk before the writing assignment in order to excite and motivate the students to want to write. She maintains that such brainstorming reduces prewriting tension by generating ideas, images, words, and ultimately confidence in the students' ability to perform well. Brainstorming "leads to richer expression" (p. 42). She discusses a Kenneth Koch film in which he was teaching a poetry writing class. The students were so eager to communicate their ideas in oral discussion that when Koch said "Start writing," all of the students, without groans, began to communicate in writing.

Schwartz suggests that open-ended questions and nonconventional responses keep the discussion fresh and exciting. Brainstorming and class discussion obviously are effective motivators. However, it must be kept in mind that the best class discussion possible cannot help language disabled writers develop the linguistic skills necessary to express adequately in written form the ideas they discussed so effectively orally.

'Constantpace' Remediation

Bernstein (1977) proposes another motivational remediation program that also is based on revamping traditional curricular standards. She believes classroom instruction is one-sided; the concern for an orderly and logical expository paper outweighs the concern for smoothness and ease of style. She notes that teachers become innocent pawns by blindly following syllabuses and textbooks that stress arbitrary conventions such as an introduction, a topic sentence, a clincher, and a "proved" thesis (p. 50). Such restrictive form eliminates new ideas or approaches and permits only "utter single-mindedness" (p. 50). Bernstein feels conventions undermine good writing more than they help generate it. As a result, students focus on rules, not writing, leading to an "awkward and unnatural style" that "lacks a smooth flow" (p. 51).

To correct the stifling nature of an inflexible curriculum and method, Bernstein proposes a "constantpace" instructional remediation. Using the analogy of a car, she counsels students to strive for a balanced, smoothly flowing, constant pace. She believes this will be fresh, new, and self-motivating for the students. Bernstein concludes that "uneven tempo is the ultimate source of all errors (e.g., dullness, choppiness, repetition)" but once "brought to the student's attention" the problem can be overcome easily, resulting in "a dramatic improvement in writing quality" (p. 51).

Bernstein offers a program based on the term "constantpace," a term she defines abstractly by way of analogy. Her article illustrates the other side of motivational remediation: the elixer of health program. A revamping of a standard curriculum goal (the essay), plus an encouraging "do your own style," establishes writing as an enjoyable activity because the students now have success. The students just needed to be told to find a pace (have teachers ever counseled students *not* to find a pace?), and writing then flows smoothly.

Schwartz (1979) offers a reduction of prewriting tension through brainstorming, a realistic goal. Egan (1979) suggests peer evaluation of group writing to develop interest and commitment in the act of writing while removing individual deficiencies and substituting group strengths, also a realistic goal. Hagemann (1980) proposes replies to letters as encouraging more letter writing, again a realistic goal. However, Bernstein (1977) suggests that style, a highly abstract and complex element, can be improved by stressing pace, another highly abstract term: a less realistic goal because it is difficult to conceive of an instruction method that would concretely demonstrate poor pace to a disabled writer.

Bernstein's (1977) article points up the difficulty with much motivational remediation literature: often the authors of the various articles substitute personal success, derived no doubt from the specialness and charisma of the instructor's own personality and teaching ability, her assumption that the method (minus the teacher) can be packaged. The package is not theoretically consistent, offering more than it can deliver realistically in terms of the average student.

EVALUATION OF SPECIFIC LESSONS

Motivation cannot be assumed to aid anything but intent to write or the climate of the writing environment itself. When students write poorly because of choice, motivational techniques are more than adequate. When they write poorly because of difficulty with written language, motivational approaches only add fuel to fire: telling students they can write if they want to is no help to those who realize they can try all they want but still cannot perform adequately.

REMEDIATION THROUGH CREATIVE WRITING

The Development of Writing Ability

Britton (1970) defines expressive writing as what is produced from the individuals' own experiences, feelings, and perceptions. Writers "express" or communicate their own world to an audience; essentially, they share themselves with an audience. Because expressive writing has such a strong social or emotional coloring—sharing self—evaluation becomes difficult. The issue revolves around how teachers can justly downgrade students' feelings about such topics as life, love, or death despite the poor form of the expression. The students are sharing their souls; any criticism would be painful even if valid from an instructional viewpoint. Instead, teachers react to the content and context of the students' responses, giving affirmation for the deed of sharing and expressing feelings. Teachers do not tend to respond to the syntax of expressive writing because they might squelch students' offerings. Much of what is termed "creative writing" in the schools today is similar to the Britton et al. category of expressive writing.

Britton differentiates poetic writing from expressive writing, defining the former as communication using a variety of different linguistic patterns, such as rhyme or meter. The linguistic patterns create the form into which the students arrange content. For example, if the assigned form is a sonnet, the students must use that pattern and adapt it to their choice of material. Poetic writing requires language facility in order to manipulate the given patterns. Not all students can play with language easily enough to write, for example, in free verse.

Expressive writing puts no demands or requirements on student expressions; all the pupils must do is express their ideas on a given topic in whatever manner of writing they can. They are secure in their knowledge that sharing does not involve critical evaluation; thus, they are more likely to enjoy sharing their feelings, opening up to the act of communication through written language.

Creative or expressive writing has a two-fold goal:

1. to give the students opportunities to express their views or opinions about the world, minus the suppression that grading may entail
2. to give the students opportunities to practice using language and developing a resultant feel for it in a written form

Both goals seek to create a positive environment in which the students will feel free enough to express themselves and feel successful in doing so. To meet both goals, teachers attempt to assign topics that are of importance and interesting to the students since they write more freely and more often, with more enthusiasm, when the subject is one they can relate to or care about.

The first objective concerns the students' social world, the second their language world. In theory the writing goal or objective postulates that if the students encounter success in writing on topics of personal interest, then they will attempt to write on other, less personal, topics with a greater degree of assurance. Creative writing often assumes that locked within each student is the ability to communicate reactions and thoughts about the world. For whatever reason, the students either do not choose to share or express these communications in the classroom or are not asked to do so in the right instructional procedure.

Need for a Positive Environment

Creative writing theory hopes to give students a positive environment in which to (1) learn to share expressions utilizing both written and oral language, and (2) learn to express perceptions and thoughts that usually are not required or not elicited in school. Given the affirming and positive environment needed to foster creative writing, several results occur.

First, a writing benefit results in that the students practice using written language. Since they write about topics that interest them rather than those that are merely academic or schoolish, they are not limited by lack of knowledge or information on the subjects. Instead, they have total control of the topics. The subjects essentially are the students' feelings—and they have no dearth of those or of thoughts or ideas. Thus, they are not limited by poor academic achievement or other external topic demands and can focus directly on the writing itself. The topic stimulates the students and gives them practice in using written language.

Another beneficial result is that writing loses its earlier negative aura, which is replaced with an interest in having the opportunity to really express their feelings. Creative writing assignments range in length from the short paragraph to the extended essay. For example, current common creative writing tasks are to ask the students to describe favorite colors and why they like them, or why a friend is like a favorite color. These are short, fairly unstructured tasks requiring little preparation or time to administer but generating great interest.

However, creative writing tasks have one shortcoming: not all students are inventive, witty, clever, and imaginative to the degree that instructors admire and openly praise. Sometimes the nature of the task requires more invention than some students can handle. In such cases, the task merely reinforces students' feelings of inadequacy as they notice that other pupils seem to have no lack of ideas that bring praise from the teacher.

The Writing of Children's Stories

Wiseman (1979) has developed a curriculum on writing children's stories, illustrating the best of an extended creative writing task. Using high schoolers, she begins by asking them to try to remember how it felt to be between ages 5 to 8. All students can share memories and feelings of that time; none are limited by previous academic performance. She then relates her favorite children's story and asks the students to discover why it "works." Students are asked what they remember about their favorite childhood stories. Answers usually invoke responses that a good story is one in which they can identify with the characters, or with a happy ending, or with words that sound good or rhyme. Wiseman spends the rest of the first week teaching figurative language appropriate for kindergarteners as illustrated in various children's books.

During the second week, students are asked to find a favorite story and read it to the class orally. In the third week, they are asked to read the same story to a kindergarten class while carefully observing the youngsters' responses—what excites and interests them. In the fourth week, the elementary school children visit the high school and read their own creative stories to the older students. Wiseman then requests the high schoolers to write stories for the elementary children. At this point, Wiseman notes, the high schoolers learn how difficult it is to write; at all times they must remember their audience and what bored or excited the children. The fifth week is spent in revision, followed in the sixth week with the students' reading their own creations to the kindergarteners and other elementary school children.

Wiseman notes that the high schoolers feel motivated and excited about the project and seem comfortable in producing work; her students choose to write because the task is "a fun approach to writing" (p. 49). She has developed an excellent example of a creative writing unit that enables students to write about nonacademic topics.

However, two problems emerge from her instructional method. First, a six-week unit in a high school involves an enormous block of time; a unit that could justify such a commitment should yield fairly substantial results. Second, not all students can think of a creative story, much less communicate it in writing and perform or read it before children.

Creative writing is effective and liberating for students who have such a bent, but not all high schoolers have possible children's stories in their head or heart, waiting to be tapped. When writing involves topics such as "describe how you would feel if you were a cloud," students can let their imaginations go. However, more structured tasks such as stories, plays, and dramatic monologues are more complex and may be too demanding, rather than liberating, for other than the few who are the most inventive.

Extensive vs. Reflexive Modes

Emig (1971) takes another task: she distinguishes between the extensive and reflexive modes. She defines extensive as conveying ideas or feelings back out to an external audience. Extensive writing is very reportorial; it may not involve the students directly through commitment but indirectly through assignments from the instructor. She defines reflexive writing, on the other hand, as reflecting back to the students as audience. Reflexive writing directly involves the students as they are addressing themselves.

Emig notes that reflexive writing involves more student commitment and seems to elicit more prewriting. However, prewriting and reformulation of reflexive writing may be far different from that required for extensive writing. She finds that reflexive writing topics involve more student prewriting and editing, inspiring the qualities needed for good writing. Yet since the audience is self, what polishing occurs still seeks to clarify a topic aimed for the writer alone; if students attempt to explain to an outsider, the reformulation task is much more taxing.

Writing aimed at outsiders requires cognitive skills more complex than when addressing self. The language needed to communicate intent must be manipulated and arrayed to suit an audience, perhaps an unknown one. The students know what they think and feel; for the most part they are manipulating language but not intent and ideas. They may polish their reflexive writing more than their extensive writing; the former is not only a much less difficult task but usually is nongraded. The question becomes a matter of what this polishing ultimately does and what purpose it serves: how has 't improved the writing?

Emig proposes that more high school tasks be reflexive; otherwise, she fears, students will be prevented from truly learning to write. She believes that the best contemporary writing is reflexive and that extensive work turns the process into mechanical steps.

In response to this contention, it should be pointed out that not all good writing is reflexive. Much of what can be considered good writing is extensive and directed outside of the self. Extensive writing also does not have to be mechanical and rule-bound. Reflexive or creative or expressive writing has its place but not at the expense of other modes that strengthen and develop new and equally valid cognitive skills.

Many educators have heeded Emig's call and advocate a return to more reflexive writing in the classroom and a lessening of formal tasks such as expositional essays or research papers. These educators point out that, if given creative writing tasks, students are more motivated and tend to perform better. The theory seems to be that success in reflexive tasks will help develop students' language skills so that eventually they will be able to write extensively. The key is that the instructor, upon determining that extensive writing is unsuccessful, can remediate by turning to reflexive writing tasks.

Problems at the College Level

In evaluating the kinds of writing required in college, Gere (1977) notes that the majority of assignments are extensive in nature: essays, research papers, critical essays, laboratory write-ups, essay examinations, and the like. The purpose of these tasks is to communicate an analysis or an idea to the instructor. Gere maintains that college professors may decry the poor state of written expression but until they "become more informed about the essence of composition" the problem will remain (p. 64). Gere proposes that college assignments be expressive and reflexive as well as analytical, enabling students to "draw upon the full power of their language" (p. 64). When college writing "elicits response as well as assessment," then Gere feels that the "laments" over poor performance will cease (p. 64).

For this reason, Gere suggests that high schools should stress expressive and reflexive writing so that students will develop their language abilities fully and be able to produce expository tasks in college. If reflexive tasks are not stressed, then students will not know the "value of language for its own sake, the delight of showing and exploring ideas . . . the effect writing can have on their own lives" (p. 64).

Gere makes a strong case for increasing creative writing in high school to develop self-knowledge as well as to play with language in fairly unstructured settings. However, creative writing tasks remediate intent to write by creating a desire to write, thus freeing students from external restrictions such as curriculum, method, or teacher evaluation that may inhibit their involvement. Creative writing does not remediate a linguistic or cognitive restriction or an inability to manipulate modes of discourse. Wanting and being motivated to write are not the same as being able to do so. Creative writing has an important and useful place in the language arts curriculum, but certainly not at the expense of other writing tasks. In Chapter 6, on Audience Awareness, the cognitive demands and nature of creative writing are contrasted with the cognitive demands inherent in expository writing. The differing modes require discrete and unique skills that necessitate individual practice. Analytical expository skills do not develop from practice in self-expression skills; rather, they develop following practice with analytical expository assignments.

EVALUATION OF CREATIVE WRITING: PLUS AND MINUS

Creative writing is an excellent motivator, fostering a supportive and sharing classroom climate in which emotional and personal growth can occur and in which students can elect to perform to the best of their capabilities, unrestricted by stifling curriculum, methods, or evaluation procedures. But should they have difficulty generating written language or addressing their composition to audience and discourse demands, more than creative writing is needed. Should they have difficulty recognizing errors, again, more than creative writing is required.

THE BAY AREA WRITING PROJECT (BAWP)

The most promising and currently the most developed system of motivational remediation is the Bay Area Writing Project (BAWP). Launched in 1974 at California's Berkeley campus, the BAWP has expanded to more than 50 locations throughout the country. Created in response to the apparent decline in quality of writing produced by many freshmen, the program has had a profound effect on education. Each new location modifies the original program to better fit the needs and requirements of the locale. Generally, the project is housed at a university during a summer session.

Gonder (1979), in reviewing the program, reports that the original BAWP has three basic assumptions that underlie most member programs as well:

1. The writing problem is defined as belonging to no one segment or field of education, such as English, but is a problem shared by all.
2. Many successful methods of improving writing have been developed by teachers. The BAWP offers them a forum to share these methods as well as to understand and evaluate why other programs or techniques did not succeed. Since teachers often are unaware of current research, the Bay Area Writing Project also offers updates plus an opportunity to discuss and evaluate the literature.
3. The Bay Area Writing Project is not committed to any one way of teaching writing; rather, it strives to introduce teachers to a variety of ideas and methods, allowing them to choose the ones with which they feel most comfortable. J. Gray in the *Carnegie Quarterly* comments that "Each teacher needs to find his or her own best approach" since the BAWP preaches no formulas or methods (1979, p. 4). The program is practical, focusing on success rather than theory.

The hallmark of a Bay Area Writing Project or affiliate is that the teachers themselves are expected to write during the program and submit their work for peer editing and evaluation. Teachers write two to three times a week—a high proportion of time, given the span of a summer session. The hope is that they gain insight into how it feels to be a writer undergoing criticism. More importantly, though, many teachers begin to enjoy the act of writing and discover a naturalness and value in the art itself. When this happens, teachers carry their enthusiasm over into their classrooms, motivating students not only with the new ideas and techniques they have learned but also with their own personal commitment to the value of writing. BAWP graduates are lavish with testimonials praising the changes the program has made in their instructional abilities. Gray in the *Carnegie Quarterly* reports teachers' positive comments reflecting "conversion from demoralized drudge to self-confident professional" are more the rule than the exception (p. 4).

Most projects attempt to construct classes that contain teachers from all grade levels as well as from all instructional fields. This enables teachers to share common problems and recognize that they are not alone in facing many writing situations. More importantly, they can develop a theory of writing that takes into account more than just their own specialized area or field. They are exposed to the process and philosophy of the process across all levels and ages, acquiring a more comprehensive view of the nature of the writing or composing acts.

Each teacher is expected to present at least one successful instructional idea. From such presentations come a wealth of new techniques for the other class members to adopt, adapt, or reject. Gonder (1979) reports that the new ideas and methods generally are not a "bag of gimmicks but a carefully-coordinated sequence that builds writing skills" (p. 34).

Although the new locations modify the original BAWP model, they retain the general format and structure. The primary objective of the BAWP and its derivatives is to train a cadre of committed teachers, termed consultants, who will lead inservice programs in their schools and communities. Potentially, the knowledge and techniques that a few teachers acquire in the summer session can be transmitted to the many through such inservice programming. This never-ending staff development, reaching wider and wider numbers of teachers, has been the BAWP's most important development. The inservice programs are practical, useful, and of immediate aid to teachers, in contrast to the usual inservice programs that often can be dull, pointless, and irrelevant.

The BAWP relies on the classroom teacher, rather than on the college professional, as an expert in writing matters. This has given the program more credibility and practicality than other college programs usually achieve. Some colleges have even hired teachers who have no background other than public school as instructors in the program. As a result, techniques and theories are grounded in reality; participating teachers know that the techniques have worked somewhere at some time—that is, the techniques are not tainted by the ivory tower unreality of some college educational departments.

An editorial in *English Education* (1979) credits the BAWP with introducing a new professionalism in inservice programs and teacher instruction. The project views teachers as professionals with as much to offer as college professors, not as graduate students soaking up a professor's wisdom. This focus on teachers as experts and professionals in their own fields has stirred them to new enthusiasm and commitment to writing instruction.

HOUSTON-HARRIS COUNTY WRITING PROJECT

The Houston-Harris County Writing Project, designed by Z. Verner and
M. B. Bauer (1980) is a representative offshoot of the BAWP. This program
focuses on five factors:

1. inservice education on writing
2. practical rather than theoretical bases for teaching writing
3. development of materials needed to implement the proposed instruction
4. motivational techniques
5. materials and concepts that address the entire composing process from
   prewriting to rewriting.

The program has three major outcomes that derive from those five factors:

1. Teachers gain knowledge in writing instruction from studying research
   and recounting successful classroom experiences.
2. Teachers become master teachers of composition as a result of taking
   the project. In so doing, each designs at least two instructional packets
   of activities designed to achieve key educational objectives. These packets are shared with the other members. Upon completion of the course,
   all of the teachers possess a large variety of completely formulated
   instructional techniques.
3. Teachers become teacher/consultants by developing and presenting a
   writing inservice program. The program must have the following:

   a. rationale
   b. content
   c. activity
   d. assessment procedures
   e. bibliography

The activities already have been field tested in the classroom and judged
successful; therefore, the inservice program is based on proved methods, not
on theoretical "maybe's". The inservice program then is given in class as a
trial run. Following evaluation, it is refined and ready for a presentation to
a school district inservice session.

Upon completion of the summer session, the teachers also are asked to
enroll in a fall university class workshop in which they function as instructors
for the new crop of potential teacher/consultants.

EVALUATION OF BAWP

In summary, the BAWP has become a powerful tool for motivating teachers and in turn stimulating students. The program is well thought out and uses the best possible resource available: the classroom teacher. It offers countless successful methods and techniques; opportunities for sharing, supporting, and learning; familiarity with current research; and a continuing and ever-increasing professional cadre of teacher/consultants leading practical, field-tested, and relevant inservice workshops.

Scriven (1979) attempted to evaluate the success of BAWP on student writing. However, given that teachers do not have the same students following the summer workshop as they had prior to it, before-and-after checks became impossible. As a result, Scriven was unable to determine any experimental statistics. Nevertheless, testimonials as to the project's effectiveness are numerous. Yet such improved writing abilities could have resulted from many factors other than the BAWP. Without an experimental study, the encouraging reports remain just that: encouraging reports.

The Bay Area Writing Program is an excellent example of motivational remediation. It devises new curriculum programs, creates new techniques, and elicits strong and enthusiastic teacher commitment. For example, Gonder (1979) reports that teacher/consultants interface writing and social studies by asking students to rewrite a poem about Paul Revere from the standpoint of the horse. Or in a science class, students are asked to pretend that they are an animal cell talking to a plant cell, or to describe how it feels to be a biceps muscle. Verner and Bauer in the Houston project (1980) use the newspaper as an effective model to encourage editorial writing or other responses. They also devise writing tasks based on conversations between famous couples. All of these assignments are designed to elicit student response and performance by removing previous negative sanctions involved with the use of written language.

The Bay Area Writing Project also offers techniques for motivating expository writing, although the main focus seems to be more expressive in intent. The BAWP is successful in that the teacher leaves with new ideas from the workshop that already have been proved in classrooms. The ideas come complete with handouts, activities, and explanations. BAWP's focus on practicality of new techniques by formulating them into packets ready for use underscores how classroom-oriented the program is.

But BAWP, as with other motivational remediation programs, requires one cautionary comment. Intent, climate, and technique all may add up to a desire to write, but students who are disabled linguistically, or have poor audience awareness, or limited conceptions of writing mode demands may require a more structured remediation program, rather than several general lesson plans that are clever, fun, and exciting. The BAWP is not really a remediation program derived from a conceptual theory and analysis of writing disability.

Although expressive creative writing has much to offer, and new and effective teaching techniques such as stories about animal cells can be instructive, writing has other linguistic dimensions. The BAWP allows teachers to choose the techniques they are most comfortable with; that is, it believes there is no one right way to teach writing, making it a motivational approach but one with close ties to the nature of the process itself. The BAWP focuses on units of instruction rather than an overall systematic approach of language as, for example, Mykelbust (Chapter 3) does.

The limitations of a motivational program should not obscure its many benefits. The BAWP illustrates a remarkable writing program.

EVALUATION OF MOTIVATIONAL REMEDIATION

Whether short or week-long individual lesson plans are used, when the major focus of the writing task is expressive or reflexive and when it is placed in a highly inventive and exciting framework under an enthusiastic teacher, the outcome is a motivational approach. As such, the approach attempts to free students from restricting and limiting classroom curriculum, methods, or evaluative procedures, hoping to thereby tap their language resources—resources that were not in evidence earlier because the pupils were not involved in the task.

The approach stresses expressive writing (often termed creative writing), hoping to engender the students' commitment by turning the process into a sharing, growing experience that is not limited by academic knowledge or lack thereof. (Creative writing that is similar to Britton's term—poetic writing—by using a set linguistic framework attempts to do more than permit students to express themselves. That framework gives them practice in manipulating a linguistic given.) Motivational techniques address students' intent to write and to perform to the best of their capability as well as the development of a supportive group climate.

However, motivational remediation is not a systematic program to remedy specific or general language deficiencies other than a choice to not write because of boredom, for example. As stated earlier, desire to write is not the same as ability to write. Coupling motivational techniques in a systematic remediation program offers the best of both; using motivational techniques as a substitute for a systematic remediation program is a poor compromise.

BIBLIOGRAPHY

Bernstein, B.E. Remedial therapy for the lost art of writing. *English Journal,* 1977, *66*(9), 49-51.

Britton, J.N. *Language and learning.* Coral Gables, Fla.: University of Miami Press, 1970.

Egan, M., & O'Shea, C. In search of motivation. *English Journal,* 1979, *68*(2), 33-35.

Emig, J. *The composing process of twelfth graders.* Urbana, Ill.: National Council of Teachers of English, 1971.

Gere, A. Writing and WRITING. *English Journal,* 1977, *66*(8), 60-64.

Gonder, P.O. Updating the Bay Area Writing Project. *American Education,* April 1979, *15,* 33-38.

Gray, J. Teaching and learning: The art of composition: The Bay Area Writing Project. *Carnegie Quarterly,* 1979, *27*(2), 4-7.

Hagemann, M.C. Taking the wrench out of letter writing. *English Journal,* 1980, *69*(3), 38-40.

Schwartz, M. Talking your way into writing. *English Journal,* 1979, *68*(7), 42-44.

Scriven, M., as quoted in Teaching and learning: The art of composition: The Bay Area Writing Project. *Carnegie Quarterly* (article by James Gray), 1979, *27*(2), 4-7.

Verner, Z., & Bauer, M.B. *Proposal to establish the Houston-Harris County Writing Project,* University of Houston, 1979-1980.

Wiseman, N. A unit on writing children's stories. *English Journal,* 1979, *68*(5), 47-49.

The writing projects: Toward a new professionalism. *English Education,* 1979, *10*(3), 131-133.

Chapter 11

Survey of Written Language Evaluative Measures

WRITTEN EXPRESSIVE LANGUAGE ASSESSMENT

Before teachers or clinicians can ascertain the appropriate remediation program or approach to use to correct student writing errors, they need to determine exactly what the pupils' strengths and weaknesses are. Currently, there is no single test that evaluates writing from its generation to its final proofreading requirement; that is, the entire system as illustrated in the Total Writing Process Model (see Introduction). Instead, tests are designed to evaluate certain specific target or skill areas. For classroom teachers or clinicians to use and choose tests effectively, they must be aware of the purpose, procedure, results, and possible interpretation of the available instruments. More importantly, they need to know which component of the Total Writing Process Model the test is measuring.

As always in reference to tests, professionals should be aware that they are only as good as the persons using them. Bearing this in mind, professionals should recognize that written language by its very nature is a very complex process, not easily quantified nor reduced to a single task analysis. Aside from the issues of test reliability and validity, examiner reliability, and selection of an instrument appropriate to the examiner's needs, the baseline issue remains: any language measurement evaluates performance only on a given day, not the students' "true" ability.

The variables that interfere with obtaining true writing ability scores include the following:

- Test directions often must be read to be understood, and a reading disability may interfere with performance on a test involving a spontaneous writing sample. On an objective test, reading disability inter- feres with efficient completion of the questions and assumes critical importance in terms of obtaining a valid score.

- Student performance varies from day to day, based on uncontrollable influences such as fatigue, anxiety, or emotional state.

- The personal feelings, fatigue, or emotional state of the examiner may interfere with the score on an essay test.

- An examiner may not understand fully what an essay test's results actually denote. Evaluation of an essay test is an acquired skill, not a given that comes with a teaching certificate.

- The development of less biased ways of evaluating essay tests and ques- tions has demonstrated the need for a systemized approach as well as a knowledgeable examiner.

- Care should be taken in an essay test that the examiner controls the topic and mode of discourse to ensure that the students as a whole are judged fairly and uniformly.

Research has directed attention to the critical matter of how best to judge student compositions reliably. Kincaid (1953) investigated the reliability of using one sample of a student's work to judge writing competency. This study focused on four groups of college freshmen who wrote on three topics, some- times under the situational pressure of an examination and at other times in a free, relaxed atmosphere. Some of the topics were similar among the four groups and some were dissimilar. The compositions were evaluated and ranked by raters.

Kincaid reports that judged variations in the quality of writing affected primarily the upper ability group. For example, of the 50 students whose grades on the compositions varied by two or more letters, 43 are in the upper ability segment. In other words, poor writers produce consistently poor com- positions, good writers a wide range of grades. Kincaid concludes that a single paper cannot demonstrate adequately what a student knows unless the in- dividual is in the lower level.

Kincaid also says that for poor writers, the mode of discourse—whether argument or exposition—is responsible for significant variation in the quality of output. The subject matter—life as a freshman in a college environment— remains constant but what the poor writers are asked to do with the topic is important. When asked to write in one mode rather than another (for ex- ample, persuasion instead of description), the poor writers have difficulty in transforming the familiar material into the required structure. In other words, poor writers lack the skills to convince or argue as effectively as to describe.

Poor writers, then, are penalized by a nonuniform mode of discourse on an essay examination. Good writers can compose adequately in many modes; poor writers cannot. In short, poor writers require a systematic, nonvariable mode or they will compare unfavorably to those who can switch modes easily.

As to test or nontest pressure situations, the results do not demonstrate any significant difference; in short, the testing situation does not affect the students' writing quality adversely. An interesting point is that Kincaid differentiates between group and individual results, noting that the average quality of a group of students is not affected by number of writing assignments or by their mode. However, the quality of individuals' written composition varies; it is affected by day-to-day factors in the good writer group and by the mode assigned in the poor writer group.

OBJECTIVE TESTS VS. WRITING SAMPLES

A final issue is the choice of whether to use an objective test or a writing sample. The controversy between these two types of examinations in terms of the evaluation of student output has not yielded any clear-cut resolution. Objective tests, primarily of multiple-choice design, are quick to administer and, most importantly, quicker to grade. They also are the delight of statisticians, who can formulate item analysis, various reliability procedures, and norms and rankings with the results. The topic or mode bias in influencing the outcome is minimized; a topic bias, for example, favors a student in one school who may be much more familiar with a certain subject or mode of discourse than a student in another school, thereby potentially scoring higher.

But objective tests have a serious drawback: validity. They do not directly measure what they directly evaluate: writing. The examination results are used to infer competence, yet the test never elicits nor measures actual writing. Instead, they measure such factors as punctuation, capitalization, mechanics, grammar, or sentence structure. Moreover, objective tests cannot as yet measure the whole composition. Such compositional abilities as unity, coherence, organization, development, focus, support, logic, and clarity do not lend themselves to objective testing. In fact, tests do not tap the very act of writing—generating sentences that are formulated into paragraphs and essays by means of compositional abilities. As illustrated by the Total Writing Process Model, objective tests at best measure Component 3; at their worst, they measure nothing.

Defenders of objective testing dispute criticism by maintaining two points: (1) actual writing tests are highly unreliable, and (2) objective tests can give a fairly reliable prediction of success in compositions. According to Braddock, Lloyd-Jones, and Schoer (1963), objective test defenders "seem to overlook or regard as suspicious the high reliabilities obtained by some investigators"

(p. 41). In reference to evaluating composition, Kincaid (1953) obtained rater reliabilities from .77 to .91 in evaluating compositions. Braddock et al. conclude that high reliability ratings are possible; they even offer suggestions in their book for obtaining such results.

As to the second advantage, Braddock et al. counter that a correlation between colleges that focus on grammatical and mechanical skills and a test that measures these skills should be evident. But common sense balks at correlating a test that measures grammatical and mechanical skills with the larger dimensions of composition. Colleges themselves emphasize various aspects of composition instruction, causing a difficulty in determining the standards by which essays should be examined. Objective tests are not open to emphasis or interpretation and only appear to resolve the issue. Upon closer examination, however, the apparent reliability of such tests cannot account for their obvious invalidity as instruments to measure the act of writing in all its component areas.

The dilemma remains, however: actual writing samples are prohibitive in terms of time required to rate them reliably. Raters have to be trained; many papers need to be read more than once. The best resolution is offered by Braddock et al. (1963):

- Objective tests should be used as general indicators of success for large groups if needed, coupled with reclassification by teachers upon receipt of first writing samples. In such cases, they function as achievement tests designed to measure instructional success in observable areas such as mechanics, capitalization, punctuation, grammar, and sentence structure.

- Actual writing samples are essential and necessary in diagnosing individuals' areas of ability and disability. Only actual writing samples give evidence of writing ability beyond Component 3 of the Total Writing Process Model.

The authors have chosen several representative tests illustrating objective and writing sample measurement techniques. The objective example is the Sequential Tests of Educational Progress (STEP). The four tests selected that use writing samples or sentence combining (although some of these also include objective items in addition to the writing sample) are the Picture Story Language Test, Test of Adolescent Language, Test of Written Language, and three instruments based on T-units. Each test is described in terms of purpose, method, and information derived that can be used to assess written expression ability. Each test also is analyzed as to its effectiveness for a professional in relation to the following requirements:

- The examiner, most importantly, should be able to understand what the results of the test mean. If it is based on a complicated marking, grading, and evaluating procedure, then its use as an indicator of written language ability is limited by the knowledge required of the examiner for appropriate use.

- The test should yield results within a framework that allows the examiner to determine exactly what the students can and cannot do. The score should have a meaningful relationship to the students' performance. A score that simply implies poor ability in syntax does not provide clear remedial goals for instruction.

These two requirements are developed into a grid at the end of this unit after each test has been described individually, followed by an analysis of each test according to these two established criteria.

Also at the conclusion of this unit, each test is be placed on a grid designed to reflect abilities included in each component of the Total Writing Process Model. The authors evaluate and explain the ways in which the test measures various aspects of writing.

SEQUENTIAL TESTS OF EDUCATIONAL PROGRESS:
English Expression, Mechanics of Writing, Writing, and Essay Tests
Educational Testing Service
Addison-Wesley Publishing Co.

Although a number of objective writing examinations are available on the market, the Sequential Tests of Educational Progress (STEP) is one of the most widely used and is a good representative example of such instruments. Many research studies have relied on it. The other tests described in this unit consist, all or in part, of spontaneous writing samples.

The English Expression Test is composed of two parts: Correctness of Expression and Effectiveness of Expression. Correctness of Expression consists of 40 items and requires the student to read a sentence and decide whether an underlined portion is grammatically incorrect or acceptable. The judgments focus on usage of verb forms, pronouns, adjective/adverb structures, sentence structure, diction, and idiom.

Effectiveness of Expression requires the student to read four alternatives and select the one that best states all or part of a sentence. The focus of the test is on sentence structure, diction, and idiom. At the grade 4-9 level, the test consists of 20 items; at the grade 10-14 level, 25 items.

The Mechanics of Writing Test also consists of two parts, one on spelling and one on punctuation and capitalization. The spelling test consists of 45 items arranged in lists of three words each. The child must decide whether the list does or does not include a·misspelled word. No information is given as to how the items were selected or classified.

The punctuation 'and capitalization test consists of 45 items and focuses on four error categories: capitalization, apostrophe, comma, and a miscellaneous group that includes the semicolon, period, hyphen, question mark, and quotation marks. The student's task is to read a sentence, analyze the underlined part, and decide whether it is correct or in error.

The STEP Writing Test consists of five parts: organization, conventions, critical thinking, effectiveness, and appropriateness. The student must choose which items best illustrate the target writing skill.

The STEP Essay Test consists of two parts: quality of thought and style. The student must choose the item that best illustrates the target writing skill.

The norms of this test are based on a large and representative sample of students; the standardization took place during fall and spring periods. Raw scores on the test yield converted scores, percentiles, and national stanines. The test can be used with regular education students at grade levels from 4 to 14 or the examiner can use a level lower than the student's grade placement if a learning problem is suspected.

The Kuder-Richardson 20 tests of internal consistency yield high correlation coefficients. Validity measures also are adequate, although content validity is not well explained in terms of the item selection process.

DEVELOPMENT AND DISORDERS
OF WRITTEN LANGUAGE:
Picture Story Language Test

Helmer R. Myklebust
New York: Grune & Stratton, Inc., 1965.

Myklebust's Picture Story Language Test (PSLT) assesses the ability of children (approximately second grade and up) or adults to express themselves in writing. It is designed to interface with Myklebust's philosophy of language. A language hierarchy is proposed (Myklebust, 1967) that regards written expression as the highest form of language. A disorder of written expressive language can be the result of a breakdown anywhere in the hierarchy—from inner language on up to higher levels—or from a breakdown purely in the written expressive mode. In Chapter 3 of this text, describing Myklebust's approach to written language, the various disorders are analyzed in detail, accompanied by a discussion of the performance of normal and a variety of handicapped children on the Picture Story Language Test. These group results should be referred to again after reading this chapter.

Myklebust (1965) states that the purpose of the test is to "develop a scale for quantifying one's facility with the written word and thereby provide a measure of this type of verbal behavior in a given individual" (p. 70). He notes that his instrument does not attempt to measure such factors as creative writing or mechanical handwriting skills; rather, it is strictly for analyzing communicative ability in writing for purposes of research into developmental acquisition issues and for use in a differential diagnosis. The test is designed for use with both children and adults. Although norms have been compiled for normal children only, research with a variety of groups of handicapped pupils has resulted in group trends that can be used for comparison purposes.

Basically, the test uses one picture (a photograph) and the students are to write a story about it. A single picture is used so that the test procedure can be standardized. There is no time limit for taking the test and the picture is available for the students to study throughout the test, i.e., a memory component is not involved.

Myklebust explains that, at first, his intent was to use a different picture for every story written by a student; however, research showed that results were not changed from a reliability standpoint whether the same picture or different ones were used in subsequent testings. The single picture was chosen because it was active and interesting to the entire range of ages in the normative group. The picture also had a definite figure against a background and was large enough for 8 to 10 persons to view simultaneously.

The test is administered in an appropriate environment—quiet, no distraction, appropriate furnishings and materials—and the children are given pencil and paper on which to write. (Young children are given a primary pencil and lined paper, if necessary.) The examiner asks the students to look carefully at the picture, allows 20 seconds of visual scanning, and then asks them to write a story about it. The students can look at the picture as much as is needed. The examiner cannot answer questions or provide story prompting, being allowed only to tell the children to write whatever seems to be appropriate. Although there is no time limit for the test, Myklebust says most pupils finish in 20 to 30 minutes.

Three Scoring Scales

The test is scored according to three scales: productivity, syntax, and abstract-concrete meaning. The productivity scale refers to the total number of words, sentences, and words per sentence used in the students' writing sample. While not saying directly that the more words and sentences used the more effective the communication, Myklebust does note that a minimum level of words and sentences probably exists, below which communication is less effective. The scoring for the productivity scale has three aspects:

1. Total words: Every recognizable word the students use is counted, including misspellings or those used in error. One exception is the use of a list of words within a sentence. Only three words in such a list are counted, unless the items are related and are critical to the whole sentence meaning, in which case a maximum of four words are counted. Titles are not included in the count. Students receive one point for each word.
2. Total sentences: The total sentences in the sample are counted. Poor syntax is disregarded at this point; however, at times, deviant punctuation, run-on sentences, or overuse of conjunctions such as "and" may make the counting difficult. In such cases, the meaning or intent is analyzed carefully and the examiner must decide at what point to erect sentence barriers.
3. Total words per sentence: This score is found by dividing the total words by the total sentences.

The syntax scale assesses the grammatical aspects of the writing sample, focusing on word usage, word endings (morphology), and punctuation. Syntax is scored by carefully reading the students' story and determining what they appeared to want to say. This "ideal" story is compared with the actual example, and the accuracy of the following points is assessed:

1. Word usage (not meaning or style, but correctness): This aspect is evaluated in terms of:
   a. additions of inappropriate words: "A boy he played."
   b. omissions of necessary words: "A boy driving the car."
   c. substitutions of inappropriate words: "Me and her went to school."
2. Word order: Any error in word order within a sentence is counted.
3. Word endings: Errors in morphology are evaluated in terms of:
   a. additions of word endings: "He did played."
   b. omissions of word endings: "He was sleep in bed."
   c. substitutions of word endings: "She waked him up."
4. Punctuation: Errors are evaluated in terms of:
   a. additions of elements of punctuation: "She went, and saw the girl."
   b. omissions of elements of punctuation: "She saw a bird tree fish flower girl."
   c. substitutions of elements of punctuation: "She laughed cried and ran home."

One penalty point is given to errors in word usage and one-third of a penalty point to those of morphology and punctuation. This weighted scoring system was devised because word usage is more critical to meaning, and hence to the communicative effectiveness of writing, than is punctuation and morphology. The syntax score is a ratio between the total words that should have been written (the ideal story) minus the total number of errors in the ideal story over the total number of words that should have been written. That is, the numerator is the total of what should have been said minus the errors, and the denominator is the total of what should have been said had there been no errors. Put another way, the ratio is as follows:

$$\frac{\text{total words per sentence} + \text{total omissions} - \text{total errors}}{\text{total words per sentence} + \text{total omissions}}$$

The result is multiplied by 100 to yield the syntax score.

The abstract-concrete scale attempts to measure the use of abstract ideas in the students' story. This scale consists of five levels, with a steadily increasing point system corresponding to each increment in level.

Level I: Meaningless Language—The story has meaningless words or words with no reference to the picture.
No point is given.

Level II: Concrete-Descriptive Writing
1 point—use of a list of uncategorized objects in the picture or use of sterotypical sentences.
2 points—use of categorized word lists.
3 points—use of subject-verb constructs indicating action.
4 points—use of a one-verb construct paired with a categorized list of objects.
5 points—use of two or more verb constructs with categorized objects.
6 points—use of verb constructs, object categories, and adjectives.

Level III: Concrete-Imaginative Writing
7 points—use of the central character in the picture as a subject, with a predicate relating to the character's actions.
8 points—use of a description of what the central character is doing and feeling.
9 points—anthropomorphizing the dolls in the picture, with the underlying relationship of the dolls apparent (mother doll, father doll, etc.).
10 points—use of action in reference to the dolls, either individual or group.

11 points—use of action and interaction among the doll figures.
12 points—use of two or more interactions among the dolls, indicating beginning narrative writing.

Level IV: Abstract-Descriptive Writing
13 points—use of a series of two or more sequential events revolving around the central character.
14 points—use of a sequence of events revolving around the central character, but including the other characters (the dolls).
15 points—use of plot and setting, but not the total scene.
16 points—use of the total scene in the picture, with the story unit organized and structured in relation to the scene.
17 points—use of characters other than those appearing in the picture.

Level V: Abstract-Imaginative Writing
18 points—use of a plot, that is, clear cause and effect planning in terms of the narrative of the characters.
19 points—use of imaginary events in the future tense, these events anchored to the story in the picture.
20 points—use of future, imaginary events not so closely anchored to the story directly observable in the picture.
21 points—use of motivation behind characters' actions.
22 points—use of a complex plot without inconsistencies.
23 points—use of highly abstract ideas.
24 points—use of allegory.
25 points—use of allegory and explanation of moral values pertaining to the story.

As can be perceived, Myklebust has broken down the meaning aspect of writing into a hierarchical scale of 25 features. In his book (1965), he provides numerous examples of each feature. This overview presents the basic core of the Picture Story Language Test. The corresponding 1965 book must be studied in depth before the test is used.

Interpretation of the Test

Test interpretation involves three components: mean age score, percentile equivalents, and stanine equivalents. The mean age score has midpoints calculated by interpolation, since the norm group consists of children and adolescents in alternate ages from 7 to 17. The three interpretive components are used to evaluate student scores on each of the three scales—productivity, syntax, and abstract-concrete meaning. The scales are compared with each other, as well as individually, to identify trends and contribute to the overall profile of abilities.

The validity of the Picture Story Language Test has been studied in two ways. It should be remembered that the authors could find almost nothing with which to compare test performance; that is, other than some data on words per sentence in writers at various ages, no other test was available for comparison purposes.

The predictive validity of the test was evaluated in reference only to words per sentence, an area that had been researched previously. The result was a high validity between the Picture Story Language Test and the other measures.

The face validity of the test was evaluated by assessing the growth in writing ability of normal children as reflected in their scores. There was clear progress in Picture Story Language Test scores as age increased, indicating that the validity was good. This validity also was attested to by the fact that handicapped children performed significantly poorer than the normal ones showing that the test did reflect lower scores where there was a diagnosed language disorder.

Test-retest reliability was difficult to engineer through standard methods. If done after a six-month interval, maturational changes could be expected to distort data to some degree; therefore, a test-retest analysis was done with an intertest interval of a few days. The result was significant at the 1 percent level of confidence.

Odd-even reliability measures were also used for the syntax and words per sentence components. Again, the result was significant at the 1 percent level of confidence.

The test was shown to be reliable in terms of results with children who had diagnosed language disorders before a certain period of therapy and at a later date. Progress was noted in that the second administration of the test usually showed an increased score.

Finally, interscorer reliability was assessed between persons at the Ph.D. level who were trained in the test scoring system and graduate students who were not so trained. The results showed no significant difference in the ability of the two groups to administer and score the test.

Before concluding the description of this test, the norm group and its trends in test performance should be described. The sample consisted of the following:

- 307 children from a metropolitan area, representing a wide range of socioeconomic and ethnic groups
- 178 children from a suburban area, representing an upper middle class socioeconomic group, and
- 262 children from a rural setting

All the children were in one midwestern state. The number of females and males was approximately equal and none of the children were mentally retarded, physically handicapped, learning disabled, emotionally disturbed, or sensory impaired. Since it was not known whether there would be a clear growth at one-year age levels, the subjects were tested at two-year levels: 7, 9, 11, 13, 15, and 17.

The results of the norm group in terms of the total words used indicated that there was a slow, steady growth over the years, with a plateau at around 13, then a continued increase. For total sentences, there was a plateau at around 11 after which there was no growth. The words per sentence results showed continuous growth up to 17 and, since there was no leveling off, these results seem to indicate that this aspect continues to develop beyond that age. That is, there are more words per sentence but not more sentences after the 11-year age level, and the words per sentence continue to increase even after 17.

The results in reference to syntax showed rapid growth from 7 to 9 years, less rapid growth from 9 to 11, a plateau from 11 to 13 years, and a little more growth after the age of 13. So, by around the fourth grade, normal, average children will have achieved the majority of their proficiency in reference to adult abilities. Myklebust notes that this finding makes sense in view of the fact that after about age 11, syntax is developed and the total sentences score plateaus. At this point, maturity for complex sentences has been reached and only the words in sentences will continue to grow.

In terms of the abstract-concrete scale, results indicated that there was dramatic growth from 7 to 9 years of age, with females advancing steadily until 15 and males until 17.

In reference to sex difference, the females exceeded the males in growth rate, overall equality of the sexes not being reached until about age 17.

TEST OF ADOLESCENT LANGUAGE

Donald D. Hammill, Virginia L. Brown,
Stephen C. Larsen, & J. Lee Wiederholt.
Austin, Texas: PRO-ED, 1980.

The Test of Adolescent Language (TOAL) actually is a battery of subtests screening language skills, both oral and written, in adolescents between the ages of 11 and 18 years, five months. The authors recommend the test be given only to students of the correct age who can understand the directions, have the capacity to attempt to perform the tasks, and can demonstrate some reading and/or speaking proficiency in English.

The test is designed to provide a language instrument specifically for adolescents. The authors point out that numerous instruments exist for use in language assessment of young children but that very few are available for adolescents. A critical need exists for a standardized test that evaluates the range of language modes in oral and written form and with emphasis on both semantic and syntactic elements. The Test of Adolescent Language is such an instrument.

The authors describe a number of benefits in the use of this test, among them that it:

- identifies adolescents who may have language difficulties and who should be referred for in-depth testing and, if indicated, remediation

- eliminates the need to decide subjectively when a student has an actual problem as well as to estimate the severity without a standardized yardstick of measurement

- allows for screening in receptive and expressive oral and written language in semantics and syntax

- requires an average total test time of about an hour and forty-five minutes

- allows six of the eight subtests to be administered in groups, a significant timesaver

- provides an overview of abilities and disabilities in the various language modes, in reference to both semantic and syntactic factors; possible disabilities then can be investigated further and therapy provided if indicated

- establishes a system for professionals to use to monitor progress in language remediation

- provides a research tool for investigating language development and disorders at the adolescent level

The Test of Adolescent Language consists of eight subtests: Listening/Vocabulary, Listening/Grammar, Speaking/Vocabulary, Speaking/Grammar, Reading/Vocabulary, Reading/Grammar, Writing/Vocabulary, and Writing/Grammar. Only the two writing subtests are pertinent here and are described.

The test environment should be quiet and free of distraction. There are no time limits, although the authors state that the usual range is 10 to 25 minutes for the Writing/Vocabulary subtest and 15 to 35 minutes for the Writing/Grammar subtest. The examiner provides the students with all test materials.

In giving instructions, the authors caution the examiner to be certain that the students understand the directions and stay busy and on-task.

The Writing/Vocabulary subtest requires the children to read a series of words, then write a sentence using them correctly. The authors choose this particular task because they note that adolescents often can use a word but not define it precisely. Using the target word in a sentence also has proved to have more reliability than writing the word's definition.

The students are given one demonstration item, then proceed on with the 24 test items. There is a basal of five correct items and a ceiling of three errors out of five consecutive items. Sample words include "solitary," "liable," and "elusive."

The students get one point for each correct item. Misspelled words, dialect, and stylistic errors are not counted against their response. Only the meaning and word use in the sentence are judged. Vague sentences are given the point; only grammatical errors receive no score.

The Writing/Grammar subtest requires students to complete a sentence combining task. This procedure was chosen by the authors because of its wide use. When given a series of simple sentences, the students must combine them into a single, complex sentence without distorting the informative content. They must be able to imbed, conjoin, and perform other grammatical combining techniques. A sample item is as follows:

We went to the party.
It was on Sunday.

The students are urged to combine the sentences and compose the complex structure mentally, then write the sentence on paper. They get one point for every correct complex sentence. The basal is five correct items in a row and the ceiling is three errors in five consecutive items. The student is not penalized for errors in spelling, punctuation, or capitalization. Syntactic errors, of course, are not given points.

The raw scores for both of these subtests can be converted into scaled scores. The Test of Adolescent Language also uses an Adolescent Language Quotient that is a composite score for the eight subtests, as well as composite scores for various subtest groupings. The Writing/Vocabulary and Writing/Grammar subtests combine to form a writing composite score.

The authors stress that a low score does not necessarily mean a language disorder; rather, such factors as fatigue, motivation, or misunderstanding of directions must be investigated to ensure that other variables did not contribute to poor performance. The authors also state that since language is a broad area and the subtests focus on only certain aspects of functioning, remediation should not be tailored strictly to tasks similar to the tests themselves. Instead, if for example a written expression problem is identified, therapy should include a wide variety of writing activities.

The Test of Adolescent Language was standardized on 2,723 students from a wide array of urban, suburban, and rural areas in the United States and Canada. The students ranged in age from 11 to 18 and none were handicapped.

Reliability studies showed high levels of internal consistency for the subtests and the composite scores, high test-retest consistency, and high coefficients for interexaminer reliability in scoring the subtests.

The studies yielded good content validity, based on the item analysis and the choice of types of language tasks, i.e., expressive and receptive oral and written language in semantic and syntactic dimensions. Although there were not many tests with which to compare the Test of Adolescent Language results, the four that were used indicated good criterion-related and construct validity.

THE TEST OF WRITTEN LANGUAGE

By Donald D. Hammill & Stephen C. Larsen
Austin, Texas: PRO-ED, 1978.

The authors of this test state in the manual that their written language assessment was developed for two reasons: (1) to provide a well-designed and normal instrument for evaluating writing, since few such instruments exist, and (2) to provide an alternative to the Picture Story Language Test (Myklebust, 1965) since its "serious problems involving reliability and validity limit the confidence one can have in its results" (1978, p. 9).

The purposes of the Test of Written Language (TOWL) include identification of students who may be in need of remediation, delineation of writing strengths and weaknesses that will contribute to a profile of ability, assessment of remedial progress if a student already is enrolled in therapy, and utilization as a tool for research into pupils' writing abilities. The test evaluates students' proficiency in penmanship and the ability to:

1. produce an appropriate quantity of written language for communicative purposes
2. adhere in writing to conventional rules of punctuation, spelling, and capitalization
3. use appropriate syntactic, morphological, and semantic structures
4. write well-developed, logical, and ordered compositions.

This test includes both objective testing measures, similar to standard achievement testing format, and a spontaneous writing sample. The sample is written by the children after they study three sequence pictures relating to a space story. The objective subtests consist of spelling, style, and word usage; the spontaneous writing sample is used to evaluate handwriting, clarity and coherency, vocabulary, and productivity or quantity of sentences. The seven subtests evaluate the following skills:

1. *Vocabulary:* A list of 25 words is selected at random from the students' spontaneous writing samples. These words are given values according to a scale based on their frequency in basal readers, workbooks, newspapers, and other sources. The students' raw score is equal to the sum of the word values for the 25 words.

2. *Thematic Maturity:* Twenty criteria are used to judge the clarity, order, and cohesion of the students' spontaneous writing sample—for example, whether or not the pupils express a moral or philosophic theme.

3. *Thought Units:* The number of complete sentences, containing a subject and a verb and having the capacity to stand alone, is tallied. This criterion eliminates subordinate clauses and sentence fragments.

4. *Handwriting:* The students' penmanship is estimated by comparison with graded samples.

5. *Spelling:* This subtest consists of 25 words selected on the basis of discriminatory ability from the Test of Written Spelling (Larsen & Hammill, 1976). The original test's items were selected from among the more popular basal spelling series used in the country. The students are required to write the words from dictation.

6. *Word Usage:* This subtest evaluates grammatical ability through the use of a cloze technique. The students read a sentence from which an element is missing and supply the absent factor. For example, "The hungry dogs have _____ all the food" is used to elicit the past perfect tense for the verb "eat."

7. *Style:* On this subtest, the students read and correct a series of sentences that were written without punctuation or capitalization.

The Test of Written Language is designed to be used with children from third to eighth grade level, can be given individually or in groups, and requires approximately 40 minutes for administration. The scores for each subtest are converted into Scaled Scores and Grade Equivalents. The Vocabulary, Thematic Maturity, Spelling, Word Usage, and Style subtests are grouped to equal a Scaled Score that represents the Written Language Quotient.

This test was standardized on 1,700 randomly selected children from nine states. Internal consistency for the three objective subtests, Style, Spelling, and Word Usage, was good, as were stability and interscorer reliability. A criterion-related validity measure involving the test of Written Language, Picture Story Language Test, and independent teacher ratings of the spontaneous writing sample resulted in overall good validity. Good results also were obtained in terms of the test's ability to differentiate among ages and of intercorrelations among its subtests.

DIXON-HUNT-CHRISTENSEN INDEXES OF SYNTACTIC MATURITY

Edward Dixon
Arlington, Va.: Computer Microfilm
International Corporation.

This test is designed to assess growth in written syntactic ability and has its foundations in the research of Hunt (1965) and Christensen (1967). These researchers studied the analysis of writing through the use of T-units, or transformational units. Dixon used such a T-unit analysis approach in his dissertation (1970) to assess the usefulness of this method in evaluation of syntactic maturity. The dissertation study subjects were public school students and college seniors in the Chicago area. The test used was the original version of the Dixon-Hunt-Christensen Indexes of Syntactic Maturity.

The validity of the test was not measured statistically, but was assumed to be good based on the supportive research by Hunt and Christensen. Reliability also was not calculated. The performances by the students were used as norms and illustrated as means for grades 4, 8, 12, and 16 based on the following indexes:

1. mean length of T-unit
2. number of words in free modifiers, final position only
3. number of instances of free modifiers, final position only
4. number of words in coordinations within T-units
5. number of instances of coordinations within T-units
6. total number of words in free modifiers, all positions in words
7. total number of instances of free modifiers, all positions in words

This test is appropriate for use with persons from primary to adult ages.

HUNT-MELLON FACTORS OF SYNTACTIC FLUENCY

John Mellon
1969.

The purpose of this test is to evaluate growth in written syntax. It is useful for assessment with students from primary to adult levels. It analyzes a written composition in reference to 12 factors:

1. mean T-unit length
2. ratio of subordination to coordination
3. nominal clauses per 100 T-units
4. nominal phrases per 100 T-units
5. relative clauses per 100 T-units
6. relative phrases per 100 T-units
7. relative words per 100 T-units
8. embedded kernel sentences per 100 T-units
9. cluster frequency
10. mean size of cluster
11. frequency of embedding
12. mean maximum depth level

As in Dixon's (1970) test, the validity for the Mellon instrument stems from Hunt's (1965) research. Reliability was not calculated.

SYNTACTIC MATURITY TEST

Roy O'Donnell & Kellogg W. Hunt
(1970)

The purpose of this instrument (SMT) is to use the T-unit analysis approach to assess the written syntactic ability of students from grade four to adult level. The norm group consisted of students in grades 4, 6, 8, 10, and 12, plus adept adults. The students' task is to read a paragraph that uses simple, direct sentences, then rewrite it by combining and imbedding the sentences. The result should be a paragraph of greater syntactic complexity but with the same basic informational content.

The test is scored by counting the mean T-unit length in the rewritten paragraph. The validity of this instrument has not been calculated statistically but is assumed based on the data in the literature regarding syntactic maturity deriving from increased use of T-units. Reliability of the test was not calculated.

The T-unit index has engendered considerable controversy (see Chapter 5: Sentence Combining). The major criticisms concern the following points:

- The test norms have been questioned seriously because the norming procedure involved small numbers of rather similar populations.

- The norms reflect only one mode of discourse, not accounting for the syntactical differences originating from the unique demands of different modes of discourse.

- Sentence complexity is not always more mature writing semantically than is sentence simplicity.

- The difficulty of the scoring system is a problem because raters require a significant mastery of grammar.

EVALUATION OF THE TEST INSTRUMENTS

As explained in the Introduction, the Total Writing Process Model holds that writing derives from three basic components. The chart in Exhibit 11-1 is a grid based on that model. Each of the tests discussed in this chapter is plotted on the grid according to which aspects of writing they address and measure.

Component 1—generation, comprehension, and elaboration of language—is measured by students' ability to generate a complete sentence, to elaborate a simple sentence, to exhibit basic grammatical ability such as correct word order and syntax, and to generate adequate vocabulary.

Component 2—attention to audience and mode of discourse demands—is measured by the students' ability to formulate clear, organized, logical compositions that demonstrate unity, focus, and effective style, all of which are necessary items to communicate successfully with an audience given the chosen mode of discourse.

Component 3—error recognition—is measured by the students' ability to implement correct and standard usage, punctuation, mechanics, capitalization, and sentence structure. Theoretically, if students' competence always matched their performance, there would be no need for error recognition because they always would generate acceptable language. However, performance errors interfere with languaging and need to be caught and corrected. If all students had the same environmental background, regional and dialec-

Exhibit 11-1   Evaluation of Tests in Relation to Total Writing Process Model

		STEP	PSLT	TOAL	TOWL	T-UNITS
COMPONENT 1 Elaboration and generation of language	Specific sentences		X			
	Elaborated sentences (develop concepts)		X			
	Grammar knowledge (word order, syntax)		X	X	X	
	Sentence complexity		X	X		X
	Complete sentencing (no fragments)		X		X	
	Creative use of language choice		X		X	
COMPONENT 2 Attention to audience and mode of discourse demands	Style, appropriateness	X				
	Organization, order	X	X		X	
	Logical explanation, critical thinking, use of details and development	X				
	Focus, effectiveness, emphasis	X				
	Unity	X			X	
	Coherence	X				
	Successful communicative intent to audience					
	Successful use of different modes of discourse (argument, exposition, description, narration)		X			
COMPONENT 3 Error recognition	Grammar usage (standard and appropriate)	X				
	Punctuation	X	X		X	
	Mechanics	X				
	Capitalization	X			X	
	Sentence structure	X				

Source: Key: STEP = Sequential Tests of Educational Progress; PSLT = Picture Story Language Test; TOAL = Test of Adolescent Language; TOWL = Test of Written Language.

tical differences would be at a minimum, eliminating the appropriate/inappropriate label on some speech and writing patterns. Error recognition is not the same as generating grammatically and communicatively adequate sentences; error recognition refers to fitting the generated language expression into certain arbitrary standards and conventions.

The grid in Exhibit 11-2 illustrates the areas tapped by the STEP, PSLT, TOAL, TOWL, and T-unit measurements. As yet, no test addresses the entire range of the Total Writing Process Model. If the full spectrum of writing process is not tested, then obviously the concomitant therapy program will be limited to only aspects of the whole. However, given the need for efficient evaluative measures, clinicians and teachers can make better use of a measurement instrument if they at least know how it interfaces with the total writing process. The fact remains that a well-developed, easily scored and administered, comprehensive writing test still is needed.

Perhaps the best analysis of student writing would be a series of compositions, scored subjectively on the basis of the Total Writing Process Model. Four conditions must be met: (1) more than one writing sample should be used, (2) the samples should be of appropriate length, (3) the samples should derive from assignments addressing different audience and mode of discourse factors, and (4) efforts should be made to maintain rater reliability. The major limitation, of course, is time—for both students and teacher evaluation.

EVALUATION OF TEST USEFULNESS

A usable test also should meet two requirements. It should yield:

1. clear explanation of the scoring procedure so that it is time efficient and not overly complicated in construction, scoring, or administration demands
2. meaningful results that lead directly to lesson planning by giving direction as to further testing or diagnostic therapy

Each of the tests discussed in this chapter also is evaluated in Exhibit 10-2 based upon the two requirements noted above.

This chapter has presented an overview of the tests available and in use in evaluating written expression. In so doing, the authors have formulated a grid based on the Total Writing Process Model developed in the Introduction upon which to evaluate the scope and design of the individual tests. The authors also have evaluated each test in terms of its practicality, usefulness, and ease of administration and scoring. Recognizing the superiority of samples as an index of student writing performance, the authors have noted the impracticality of using such samples in terms of time and evaluation, although realizing the lack of a comprehensive alternative on the market as of now.

Exhibit 11-2 Evaluation of Test Usefulness

	Clear, efficient, and noncomplicated scoring and administration factors.	Meaningful results that lead directly to therapy or lesson planning or further testing.
STEP	Yes	Yes; however, this test yields a very limited perspective of writing.
PSLT	Yes, except for the abstract/concrete scale, which is highly subjective and vague.	Yes; however, some of the components seem inappropriate for classroom instructional therapy as, for example, remediating allegory usage.
TOAL	Yes	Yes; however, this testing yields a very limited perspective of writing.
TOWL	Yes	Yes, but some aspects of Thematic Maturity seem inappropriate for classroom instruction as, for example, remediating humor usage or moral usage.
T-UNIT TESTS	Yes, but scoring the test requires substantial grammatical knowledge.	Yes, but results do not indicate which aspects of deficient "complexity" upon which to base individual remediation.

Source: Key: STEP = Sequential Tests of Educational Progress; PSLT = Picture Story Language Test; TOAL = Test of Adolescent Language; TOWL = Test of Written Language.

BIBLIOGRAPHY

Braddock, R., Lloyd-Jones, R., & Schoer, L. *Research in written composition.* Champaign, Ill.: National Council of Teachers of English, 1963.

Buxton, E.W. *An experiment to test the effects of writing frequency and guided practice upon students' skill in written expression.* Unpublished dissertation, Stanford University, 1958.

Christensen, F. *Notes toward a new rhetoric.* New York: Harper & Row Publishers, Inc., 1967.

Dixon, E. *Dixon-Hunt-Christensen indexes of syntactic maturity.* Arlington, Va.: Computer Microfilm International Corporation, 1970. (ERIC Document Reproduction Service No. ED 091 748).

Educational Testing Service. *STEP.* Addison-Wesley Publishing Co.

Fagan, W.T., Cooper, C.R., & Jensen, J.M. *Measures for research and evaluation in the English language arts.* Urbana, Ill.: National Council of Teachers of English, 1975.

Hammill, D.D., & Larsen, S.C. *The test of written language.* Austin, Texas: PRO-ED, 1978.

Hammill, D.D., Brown, V.L., Larsen, S.C., & Wiederholt, J.L. *Test of adolescent language.* Austin, Texas: PRO-ED, 1980.

Hunt, K.W. *Grammatical structures written at three grade levels.* Research Report 3, Champaign, Ill.: National Council of Teachers of English, 1965.

Johnson, D., & Myklebust, H.R. *Learning disabilities: Educational principles and practices.* New York: Grune & Stratton, Inc., 1967.

Kincaid, J.L. *Some factors affecting variation in the quality of students' writing.* Unpublished doctoral dissertation, Michigan State University, 1953.

Larsen, S.C., & Hammill, D.D. *Test of written spelling.* Austin, Texas: PRO-ED, 1976.

Mellon, J. *Hunt-Mellon factors of syntactic fluency,* 1969. (ERIC Document Reproduction Service No. ED 091 758), pp. 199-200.

Myklebust, H.R. *Development and disorders of written language,* Vol. I. New York: Grune & Stratton, Inc., 1965.

O'Donnell, R., & Hunt, K.W. *Syntactic maturity test,* 1970. (ERIC Document—No Number).

Sequential tests of educational progress: English. Princeton, N.J.: Cooperative Tests and Services, Educational Testing Service, 1972, pp. 191-192.

Conclusion

The scope of this book has been to survey the available programs and approaches in remediating written expressive language problems. In so doing, the authors have established a framework within which to analyze and evaluate the various methods. This framework, designated the Total Writing Process Model and explained in the Introduction, effectively illustrates the components and interrelationships of the parts that comprise written expression.

Unit I reviewed five programs that addressed problems and disabilities illustrated in Component 1 of the Total Writing Process Model. That component concerns the basic generation and elaboration factor that correlates with the writing act. As such, Component 1 focuses on the in-process skills needed for effective sentencing. Remediation programs and approaches in this area attempt to facilitate the generation, elaboration, and, it is hoped, the internalization of basic syntactical structures in English.

Of the methods reviewed, the Fitzgerald Key program, the Sentences and Other Systems program, and the Myklebust approach do not offer writing curricula per se. The Fitzgerald Key and Sentences and Other Systems programs are total language curricula, of which writing is but one component of the whole. The Myklebust approach never was designed to be a curriculum; rather, it consists of a perspective as well as evaluative and remedial suggestions. As such, the professional must provide much adaptation, modification, and creative generation to use these methods as purely writing programs.

Only the Phelps Sentence Guide program and the sentence combining approach represent complete writing curricula and thus allow for individualizing instruction without requiring major adaptations, modifications, and additions. A successful program to remediate deficits in Component 1 must have as its goal the ultimate internalization of language structure as presented by the program. Research studies therefore should demonstrate a certain stability resulting from the students' language performance. A problem with research in this area is that the studies are longitudinal and lengthy by definition, since improvements in basic language generation do not occur rapidly. Thus, there are few studies of this nature available other than those demonstrating the effectiveness of the program within a limited time span.

Unit II focused on the students' ability to cognitively encounter written messages by tailoring them to an audience, as well as meeting the demands of their mode of discourse. This pragmatic attention to the results and effects of the intended message is dependent upon the capability to decenter self from audience. Writing to self requires little manipulation of composition variables such as unity, coherence, emphasis, logic, arrangement, and organization. This area of the writing process has received attention by researchers in the psychological field but very little in terms of the development of a systemized, structured remedial program. Rather, instruction has centered on specific lesson plans coupled with practice in composition and editing.

Given a facilitating teacher and environment, effective procedures can be developed and used; however, the lack of a comprehensive framework limits the effectiveness of a new or inexperienced teacher. Admittedly, this area, because of the strong influence on it by psychological processes, does not lend itself to easy systematizing and structure, but the abundance of haphazard "programs" in existence illustrates the need for more thorough methodology that encompasses more than just the daily or weekly lesson plan. This unit evaluated role playing, editing, and rewriting approaches, which demonstrated the need for instruction in each of these areas, but no structured format for so doing.

Unit III analyzed the proofreading skills necessary to make written expression effective for its intended audience. Essentially, the students need to be able to reread their compositions and catch inappropriate errors in grammar, punctuation, capitalization, mechanics, and sentence structure. As this area is primarily what has been tested by standardized and college board examinations and since it is objective and easy to evaluate, it has received the primary research focus.

Unfortunately, many define good writing as having essentially this aspect: an error-free message, perhaps minus other compositional qualities. Therefore, the last decade has witnessed an increasing demand for classes that teach such error-free writing. Grammar instruction, traditional or linguistic, has received an increased emphasis in classroom curricula but the results have been disappointing. The students may proofread somewhat better than before and catch certain target errors, but they do not produce essentially better quality compositions or error-free compositions.

In fact, in Buxton's (1958) study, after two years, his traditional grammar students still missed approximately 50 percent of their test questions. Thus, this area, because of the public attention focused upon it, has assumed critical importance. Interestingly, cognitive attention to audience as illustrated in Component 2 of the Total Writing Process Model seems to enable students to proofread better than does grammar instruction.

Unit IV discussed motivational methods to increase student participation in classroom writing activities. Offering no system or methodology derived from the nature of writing, it assumed that intent could produce result. Having almost a social rather than a linguistic frame, many of the methods sought to affirm the students as individuals rather than to remediate their writing errors. When coupled with a more systematic approach or program, motivational instruction certainly is of critical importance—but not as an end in itself. The Bay Area Writing Project attempts to bridge the gap between theory and intent but in a very loosely fashioned manner that is open to multiple interpretations.

Unit V provided an overview of several current tests that address the Total Writing Process to provide the professional with an awareness of what instrument type to use to judge or evaluate student performance adequately. The authors noted that no test measures all three components; however, the Test of Written Language comes the closest to covering the entire writing process.

The T-unit tests suffer from serious validity questions related to norming and the objective tests from serious questions about measurement. The value of spontaneous writing samples is mitigated by the prohibitive cost in time and effort on the part of the examiner. However, these tests do offer the most adequate content for effective evaluation, although there is no systematic or comprehensive methodology to standardize their use. In fact, standardized measures of writing samples may not be a reasonable goal. Nonetheless, effective testing requires some system of comparison in relation to rating criteria and examiner reliability.

The authors hope that this text has furnished readers with a helpful overview and framework with which to survey written language and all its facets. The area deserves more attention and much more research as it impacts significantly on the lives and careers of many young people.

Index

Note: Italicized page numbers include references to tables and figures.

About the Authors

TRISHA PHELPS-GUNN has taught both ninth and eleventh grade English at Clear Lake High School, Houston. She has helped develop literature, composition, and grammar curricula for the district. She coauthored *Teaching Written Expression: The Phelps Sentence Guide Program*, has worked on experimental projects field testing that program, and has spoken at national conventions on the topic of written expression. She is working on a doctorate at the University of Houston in the field of educational psychology.

DR. DIANA PHELPS-TERASAKI is a member of the adjunct faculty of the University of Houston Communication Disorders Department and has a speech-language pathology private practice in Victoria, Texas. She has coauthored two books, has had numerous journal articles published, and has spoken at state and national professional meetings. She coauthored the grant that originated the University of Houston Interdisciplinary Clinic and coordinated the clinic for two years before assuming her present roles. Dr. Phelps-Terasaki obtained her bachelor's and master's degrees in speech-language pathology and audiology and her doctorate in reading and language, all at the University of Houston.

DR. BARBARA FOORMAN is a member of the Educational Psychology Department of the University of Houston. She recently completed a cross-cultural investigation of young children's communication performance in Japan, Mexico, and the United States. She has a Ph.D. from the University of California, Berkeley, an M.A.T. from Harvard University, and a B.A. from Stanford University.